THE SPANISH STORY OF

THE ARMADA

AND OTHER ESSAYS

AMS PRESS
NEW YORK

THE SPANISH STORY OF

THE ARMADA

AND OTHER ESSAYS

BY

JAMES ANTHONY FROUDE

ἐγὼ δὲ ἴδιος ἐν κοινῷ σταλείς
μῆτίν τε γαρύων παλαιγόνων
πόλεμόν τ᾽ ἐν ἡρωΐαις ἀρεταῖσιν
οὐ ψεύσομ᾽ ἀμφὶ Κορίνθῳ

Pindar, *Olymp.* Carm. XIII.

NEW YORK
CHARLES SCRIBNER'S SONS
1892

Library of Congress Cataloging in Publication Data

Froude, James Anthony, 1818-1894.
    The Spanish story of the Armada.

    1. Armada, 1588. 2. Pérez, Antonio, d. 1611.
3. Teresa, Saint, 1515-1582. 4. Templars.
5. Norway--Description and travel. I. Title.
D7.F88 1972   940.2'3   71-144613
ISBN 0-404-02628-1

Reprinted from the edition of 1892, New York
First AMS edition published in 1972
Manufactured in the United States of America

International Standard Book Number: 0-404-02628-1

AMS PRESS INC.
NEW YORK, N.Y.   10003

PREFACE

AFTER completing my "History of England" from the fall of Wolsey to the defeat of the Spanish Armada, I had intended to pursue the story of the sixteenth century, and to write the lives of Charles the Fifth and Philip the Second. To them had fallen the task of confronting the storm which had broken over the rest of Europe. The opening of the Archives of Spain, Paris, and Vienna had for the first time made it possible to see the position in which they found themselves, to understand their characters and to weigh impartially their conduct in a situation so extraordinary. My own partial researches had already shown me that the prevailing opinions about these two princes required wide correction, and I thought that I could not better employ the remainder of my life than on an inquiry so profoundly interesting. To regard the Emperor, to regard Philip, merely as reactionary bigots, is as unjust as it is uninstructive. They had to deal with a world in arms, with a condition in which society was disintegrated by a universal spiritual revolt, of which the outcome was still utterly uncertain, and at such a crisis the wisest statesmen must have necessarily been divided on the conduct which duty required of them.

The labor of investigation would have been very great, and the years which I could have devoted to it would at most have been none too many for so ambitious an enterprise. I was obliged by circumstances to lay my purpose aside until it was too late to begin ; and it will fall to others, perhaps better qualified than myself, to execute what, if successfully performed, will be the best service that can now be rendered to modern history. Of my own attempts nothing has come, or now can come, save a few separate studies, such as the story of Queen Catherine's Divorce as related by Charles the Fifth's ambassadors, with the slight essays which form half this present volume, and have been already published in different periodicals.

The Divorce of Catherine has been brought out in a separate form as a supplement to my "History of England." The essays I reproduce because they were carefully written, and I hope may have some interest to historical students. The defeat of the Armada transferred the Empire of the Sea from Spain to England, and the Spanish account of it cannot be read without curiosity and even sympathy. The "Relacion" of Antonio Perez has, for three centuries, been the chief authority for the private character of Philip the Second. Philip was once titular King of England. I have thought it worth while to examine the character of his accuser. The "Life of Saint Teresa" exhibits the spiritual enthusiasm of the Spanish nation in its noblest form.

The subjects which occupy the remainder of the volume have no connection with the sixteenth century. Others, however, besides myself will have observed, at least with curiosity, the majestic figures which lie on the floor of the Antechapel in the Temple Church, and will have asked themselves who and what these men could have been when they lived on earth in flesh and blood. The publication of the "Procès des Templiers" by M. Michelet provides an answer to the question.

Sir George Lewis said that life would be very tolerable if it was not for its amusements. Life, however, without any amusements would be tedious, and books given wholly to serious matters are tedious also. Authors, like school-boys, require holidays, and the sketches of the Norway Fjords are the records of two summer excursions into those delightful regions, as a guest in the yacht of a friend. Our graver writings are the reflections of our studies. Some taste of the flavor of our enjoyments may be preserved in the diaries of our idleness.

CONTENTS

THE SPANISH STORY OF THE ARMADA

I.

THE fate of the great expedition sent by Philip the
Second to restore the Papal authority in England has
been related often in prose and verse. It is the most
dramatic incident in our national history, and the materials for a faithful account of it in the contemporary
narratives are unusually excellent. The English nature
on that occasion was seen at its very best. The days
had not yet come of inflated self-praise ; and the spirit
which produces actions of real merit is usually simple
in the description of such actions. Good wine needs no
bush ; the finest jewels need least a gaudy setting ; and
as the newspaper correspondent was not yet born, and
the men who did the fighting wrote also the reports
the same fine and modest temper is equally seen in
both.

Necessarily, however, Englishmen could only tell
what they themselves had seen, and the other side of the
story has been left untold. The Spanish historians have
never attempted to minimize the magnitude of their disaster but they have left the official records to sleep in the
shades of their public offices, and what the Spanish
commanders might have themselves to say of their defeat and its causes has been left hitherto unprinted. I
discovered, myself, at Simancas the narrative of the Ac-
countant-General of the Fleet, Don Pedro Coco Calderon,

and made use of it in my own history. But Don Pedro's account showed only how much more remained to be discovered, of which I myself could find no record either in print or MS.

The defect has now been supplied by the industry and patriotism of an officer in the present Spanish Navy, who has brought together a collection of letters and documents bearing on the subject which are signally curious and interesting.* Captain Fernandez Duro deserves grateful thanks and recognition, as enabling us for the first time really to understand what took place. But more than that, he reproduces the spirit and genius of the time ; he enables us to see, face to face, the De Valdez, the Recaldes, the Oquendos, the De Leyvas, who had hitherto been only names to us. The "Iliad" would lose half its interest if we knew only Agamemnon and Achilles, and knew nothing of Priam and Hector. The five days' battle in the English Channel in August, 1588, was fought out between men, on both sides, of a signally gallant and noble nature ; and when the asperities of theology shall have mellowed down at last, Spanish and English authorities together will furnish materials for a great epic poem.

Until that happy and still far-distant time shall arrive, we must appropriate and take up into the story Captain Duro's contribution. With innocent necromancy he calls the dead out of their graves, and makes them play their drama over again. With his assistance we will turn to the city of Lisbon on April 25 of the *Annus Mirabilis.* The preparations were then all but completed for the invasion of England and the overthrow of the Protestant heresy. From all parts of Catholic Europe the prayers of the faithful had ascended for more than a year in a

* *La Armada Invencible.* Por el Capitan Fernandez Duro.

stream of passionate entreaty that God would arise and make His power known. Masses had been said day after day on fifty thousand altars; and devout monks and nuns had bruised their knees in midnight watches on the chapel pavements. The event so long hoped for was to come at last. On that day the consecrated standard was to be presented in state to the Commander-in-Chief of the Expedition. Catholics had collected from every corner of the world; Spanish and Italian, French and Irish, English and German, owning a common nationality in the Church. The Portuguese alone of Catholic nations looked on in indifference. Portugal had been recently annexed by force to Spain. The wound was still bleeding, and even religion failed to unite the nobles and people in common cause with their conquerors. But Lisbon had ceased to be a Portuguese city. Philip dealt with it as he pleased, and the Church of Portugal, at least, on this occasion, was at Philip's disposition.

There was something of real piety in what was going on; and there was much of the artificial emotion which bore the same relation to piety which the enthusiasm of the Knight of La Mancha bore to true chivalry. Philip himself in certain aspects of his character was not unlike Don Quixote. He believed that he was divinely commissioned to extirpate the dragons and monsters of heresy. As the adventure with the enchanted horse had been specially reserved for Don Quixote, so the "Enterprise of England," in the inflated language of the time, was said to have been reserved for Philip; and as analogies are apt to complete themselves, the short, good-humored, and entirely incapable Medina Sidonia, who had been selected for Commander-in-Chief, had a certain resemblance to Sancho. The Duke of Medina had no ambition for such adventures ; he would have greatly preferred staying at home, and only consented to take the command out of a certain dog-like obedience to his master. The representatives of the imaginary powers had been called in to bring him to accept the danger- ous responsibility. A pious hermit told him that he had been instructed by the Almighty to promise him victory. The Prioress of the Annunciata, Maria de la Visitacion, who had received the five wounds and was punished after- ward as a detected impostor, had seen Santiago and two angels smiting Drake and his unbelieving comrades, and she assured the Duke of glory in both worlds if he went. The Duke's experience of English Admirals had been, so far, not glorious to him at all. He had been in command at Cadiz a year before when the English fleet sailed up the harbor, burnt eighteen large ships, and went off unfought with, taking six more away with them. All Spain had cried shame and had called the Duke a coward, but Philip had refused to be displeased, and had deliberately chosen him for an undertaking far more arduous than the defence of a provincial port. On this April 25 he was to receive his commission, with the standard under which he was to go into ac- tion, and the Catholic Church was to celebrate the oc- casion with its imposing splendors and imperious sol- emnities.

The Armada lay in the Tagus waiting the completion of the ceremony. It was the most powerful armament which had ever been collected in modern Europe, a hun- dred and thirty ships—great galleons from a thousand to thirteen hundred tons ; galliasses rowed by three hun- dred slaves, carrying fifty guns ; galleys almost as for- midable, and other vessels, the best appointed which Spain and Italy could produce. They carried nine thousand seamen, seasoned mariners who had served in all parts of the world, and seventeen thousand soldiers, who were to join the Prince of Parma and assist in the conquest of England. Besides them were some hundreds of nobles and gentlemen who, with their servants and retinues, had volunteered for the new crusade, gallant, high-spirited youths, quite ready to fight with Satan himself in the cause of Spain and Holy Church. In them all was a fine profession of enthusiasm—qualified, indeed, among the seamen by a demand for wages in advance, and a tendency to desert when they received them. But a regiment of priests, dispersed through the various squadrons, kept alive in most the sense that they were going on the most glorious expedition ever undertaken by man.

The standard which was to be presented itself indicated the sacred character of the war. Into the Royal Arms of Spain there had been introduced as supporters on one side Christ on the Cross, on the other the Virgin mother; and on the scroll below was written : "Exsurge Deus et vindica causam tuam," "Arise, O Lord, and avenge thy cause." "Philip, by the grace of God King of Castille, of Leon, of Aragon, the two Sicilies, Jerusalem, Portugal, Navarre, Granada, Toledo, Valencia, Gallicia, Majorca, Sardinia, Cordova, Corsica, Murcia, Jaen, Algaves, Algesiras, Gibraltar, the Canary Islands, the East and West Indies, the Isles and Continents of the Ocean ; Archduke of Austria, Duke of Burgundy, of Brabant and Milan, Count of Hapsburgh, Count of Flanders, Tirol, and Barcelona ; Lord of Biscay and Molina," etc.; the monarch, in short, whose name was swathed in these innumerable titles, had determined to commit the sacred banner to his well-beloved Don Alonzo de Guzman, surnamed El Bueno, or the Good, and under its folds to sweep the ocean clear of the piratical squadrons of the English Queen. The scene was the great metropolitan church of Lisbon, the Iglesia Major. It was six o'clock in the morning; streets and squares were lined with troops who had been landed from the ships. The King was represented by his nephew, the Cardinal Archduke, who was Viceroy of Portugal. The Viceroy rode out of the Palace with the Duke on his right hand, followed by the gentlemen adventurers of the expedition in their splendid dresses. At the church they were received by the Archbishop. The standard was placed on the altar. Mass was sung. The Viceroy then led the Duke up the altar steps, lifted a fold of the standard and placed it in his hands, while, as the signal was passed outside, the ships in the river and the troops in the streets fired a salute—" una pequeña salva," a small one, for powder was scarce and there was none to waste. The scene was not impressive; and the effect was frittered away in a complexity of details. The Archbishop took the Holy Sacrament and passed out of the church, followed by a stream of monks and secular clergy. The Archduke and the newly-made Admiral went after them, the standard being borne by the Duke's cousin, Don Luis of Cordova, who was to accompany him to England. In this order they crossed the great square to the Dominican Convent, where the scene in the Iglesia Major was repeated. The Dominicans received the procession at the door. The standard was again laid on the altar, this time by the Duke of Medina himself, as if to signify the consecration of his own person to the service of the beings whose forms were embroidered upon it. The religious part of the transaction finished, they returned to the Palace, and stood on the marble stairs while the troops fired a second volley. The

men were then marched to their boats, with an eye on
them to see that none deserted, and His Royal Highness
and the Captain General of the Ocean, as the Duke was
now entitled, went in to breakfast.

The presentation had wanted dignity and perhaps
seriousness. There was no spontaneous enthusiasm.
The Portuguese aristocracy were pointedly absent, and
the effect was rather of some artificial display got up by
the clergy and the Government. And yet the expedition
of which this scene was the preliminary had for sixty
years been the dream of Catholic piety, and the discharge
at last of a duty with which the Spanish nation appeared
to be peculiarly charged. The Reformation in England
had commenced with the divorce of a Spanish Princess.
Half the English nation had been on Catherine's side
and had invited Philip's father to send troops to help
them to maintain her. As the quarrel deepened, and
England became the stronghold of heresy, the English
Catholics, the Popes, the clergy universally had entreated
Charles, and Philip after him, to strike at the heart of
the mischief and take a step which, if successful, would
end the Protestant rebellion and give peace to Europe.
The great Emperor and Philip, too, had listened reluct-
antly. Rulers responsible for the administration of
kingdoms do not willingly encourage subjects in rebellion, even under the plea of religion. The divorce of
Catherine had been an affront to Charles the Fifth and
to Spain, yet it was not held to be a sufficient ground
for war, and Philip had resisted for a quarter of a century
the supplications of the suffering saints to deliver them
from the tyranny of Elizabeth. It was an age of revolt
against established authority. New ideas, new obligations of duty were shaking mankind. Obedience to God
was held as superior to obedience to man ; while each

man was forming for himself his own conception of
what God required of him.   The intellect of Europe was
outgrowing its creed.   Part of the world had discovered
that doctrines and practices which had lasted for fifteen
hundred years were false and idolatrous.   The other
and larger part called the dissentients rebels and children of the Devil, and set to work to burn and kill
them.   At such times kings and princes have enough to
do to maintain order in their own dominions, and even
when they are of opposite sides have a common interest
in maintaining the principle of authority.   Nor when
the Pope himself spoke on the Catholic side were
Catholic princes completely obedient.   For the Pope's
pretentions to deprive kings and dispose of kingdoms
were only believed in by the clergy.   No secular sovereign
in Europe admitted a right which reduced him to the
position of a Pope's vassal.   Philip held that he sufficiently discharged his own duties in repressing heresy
among his own subjects without interfering with his
neighbors.   Elizabeth was as little inclined to help
Dutch and French and Scotch Calvinists.   Yet the
power of princes, even in the sixteenth century, was
limited, and it rested after all on the goodwill of their
own people.   Common sympathies bound Catholics to
Catholics and Protestants to Protestants, and every
country in Europe became a caldron of intrigue and
conspiracy.   Catholics disclaimed allegiance to Protestant sovereigns, Protestants in Catholic countries
looked to their fellow-religionists elsewhere to save
them from stake and sword, and thus between all parties,
in one form or another, there were perpetual collisions,
which the forbearance of statesmen alone prevented
from breaking out into universal war.

Complete forbearance was not possible.   Community

of creed was a real bond which could not be ignored, nor in the general uncertainty could princes afford to reject absolutely and entirely the overtures made to them by each other's subjects. When they could not assist they were obliged to humor and encourage. Charles the Fifth refused to go to war to enforce the sentence of Rome upon Henry the Eighth, but he allowed his ambassadors to thank and stimulate Catherine's English friends. Philip was honestly unwilling to draw the sword against his sister-in-law, Elizabeth; but he was the secular head of Catholic Christendom, bound to the maintenance of the faith. He had been titular King of England, and to him the English Catholics naturally looked as their protector. He had to permit his De Quadras and his Mendozas to intrigue with disaffection, to organize rebellion, and, if other means failed, to encourage the Queen's assassination. To kill dangerous or mischievous individuals was held permissible as an alternative for war, or as a means of ending disturbance. It was approved of even by Sir Thomas More in his "Utopia." William the Silent was murdered in the Catholic interest. Henri Quatre was murdered in the Catholic interest, and any one who would do the same to the English Jezebel would be counted to have done good service. Elizabeth had to defend herself with such resources as she possessed. She could not afford to demand open satisfaction; but she could send secret help to the Prince of Orange; she could allow her privateers to seize Spanish treasures on the high seas or plunder Philip's West Indian cities. She could execute the traitorous priests who were found teaching rebellion in England. Philip in return could let the Inquisition burn English sailors as heretics when they could catch them. And thus the two nations had drifted on, still nominally at peace, and each unwilling to declare open war; but peace each year had become more difficult to preserve, and Philip was driven on by the necessities of things to some open and decided action. The fate of the Reformation in Europe turned on the event of a conflict between Spain and England. Were England conquered and recovered to the Papacy, it was believed universally that first the Low Countries and then Germany would be obliged to submit.

Several times a Catholic invasion of England had been distinctly contemplated. The Duke of Alva was to have tried it. Don John of Austria was to have tried it. The Duke of Guise was to have tried it. The nearest and latest occasion had been after the Conquest of Portugal and the great defeat of the French at the Azores in 1583. The Spanish navy was then in splendid condition, excited by a brilliant victory, and led by an officer of real distinction, Alonzo de Bazan, Marques de Santa Cruz. A few English privateers had been in the defeated fleet at the battle of Terceira; and Santa Cruz, with the other naval commanders, was eager to follow up his success and avenge the insults which had been offered for so many years to the Spanish flag by the English corsairs. France, like all Northern Europe, was torn into factions. The Valois princes were Liberal and anti-Spanish. The House of Guise was fanatically Catholic, and too powerful for the Crown to control. Santa Cruz was a diplomatist as well as a seaman. He had his correspondents in England. In Guise he had a friend and confederate. The plan of action had been secretly arranged. One of the many plots was formed for the murder of Elizabeth. Santa Cruz and the Spanish navy were to hold the channel. Guise was to cross under their protection and land an army in Sussex. The Catholics were to rise, set free

Mary Stuart, and make her Queen. This was the scheme. The fleet was ready. Guise was ready ; and only Philip's permission was waited for. Santa Cruz was a rough old sailor, turned of seventy, who meant what he said, and spoke his mind plainly. Like his countrymen generally, he was tired of seeing his master for ever halting on his leaden foot (*pié de plomo*) ; and on August 9, 1583, while still at the Azores, he wrote to stimulate him to follow up his success by a still more splendid achievement. Philip was now master of the Portuguese Empire. He (Santa Cruz) was prepared, if allowed, to add England to his dominions. The Low Countries would then surrender, and the Jezebel who had wrought so much evil in the world would meet her deserts.

Now was the time. The troops were ready, the fleet was in high condition. Philip talked of expense and difficulty. If difficulty was an objection, the bold admiral said that nothing grand could ever be achieved ; and for money, great princes could find money if they wished. The King should have faith in God, whose work he would be doing ; and if he was himself permitted to try, he promised that he would have as good success as in his other enterprises.

Charles the Fifth, among his other legacies to his son, had left him instructions to distrust France and to preserve the English alliance. The passionate Catholics had assured Philip over and over again that the way to keep England was to restore the faith. But plot after plot had failed, Elizabeth was still sovereign, and Catholic conspiracies so far had only brought their leaders to the scaffold. Mary Stuart was a true believer, but she was herself half a Frenchwoman, and Guise's father had defeated Philip's father at Metz, and Guise and Mary masters of France and England both was a perilous pos-

sibility. Philip did not assent ; he did not refuse. He
thanked Santa Cruz for his zeal, but said that he must
still wait a little and watch. His waiting did not serve
to clear his way.   Elizabeth discovered what had
been designed for her, and as a return Sir Francis
Drake sacked St. Domingo and Carthagena.   More than
that, she had sent open help to his insurgent provinces,
and had taken charge, with the consent of the Hollanders, of Flushing and Brill.   Santa Cruz could not
but admire the daring of Drake and the genius of the
English Queen.   They were acting while his own master
was asleep.   He tried again to rouse him.   The Queen,
he said, had made herself a name in the world.   She
had enriched her own subjects out of Spanish spoil.   In
a single month they had taken a million and a half of
ducats.   Defensive war was always a failure.   Once
more the opportunity was his own.   France was
paralyzed, and Elizabeth, though strong abroad, was
weak at home, through the disaffection of the Catholics.
To delay longer would be to see England grow into a
power which he would be unable to deal with.   Spain
would decline, and would lose in mere money more than
four times the cost of war.*

This time Philip listened more seriously.   Before, he
had been invited to act with the Duke of Guise, and
Guise was to have the spoils.   Now, at any rate, the lead
in the campaign was to be his own.   He bade Santa
Cruz send him a plan of operations and a calculation in
detail of the ships and stores which would be required.
He made him Lord High Admiral, commissioned him to
collect squadrons at Cadiz and Lisbon, take them to sea,
and act against the English as he saw occasion.   Santa
Cruz would probably have been allowed his way to do

* Santa Cruz to Philip the Second, January 13, 1586.

what he pleased in the following year but for a new complication, which threw Philip again into perplexity. The object of any enterprise led by Santa Cruz would have been the execution of the Bull of Pope Pius, the dethronement of Elizabeth, and the transference of the crown to Mary Stuart, who, if placed on the throne by Spanish arms alone, might be relied on to be true to Spanish interests. Wearied out with Mary's perpetual plots, Elizabeth, when Santa Cruz's preparations were far advanced, sent her to the scaffold, and the blow of the axe which ended her disconcerted every arrangement which had been made. There was no longer a Catholic successor in England to whom the crown could go on Elizabeth's deposition, and it was useless to send an army to conquer the country till some purpose could be formed for disposing of it afterward. Philip had been called King of England once. He was of the blood of the House of Lancaster. He thought, naturally, that if he was to do the work, to him the prize should belong. Unfortunately, the rest of the world claimed a voice in the matter. France would certainly be hostile. The English Catholics were divided. The Pope himself, when consulted, refused his assent. As Pope Sextus the Fifth, he was bound to desire the reduction of a rebellious island ; as an Italian prince, he had no wish to see another wealthy kingdom added to the enormous empire of Spain. Mary Stuart's son was natural heir. He was a Protestant, but gratitude might convert him. At any rate, Philip was not to take Elizabeth's place. Sextus was to have given a million crowns to the cost of the armament ; he did not directly withdraw his promise, but he haggled with the Spanish Ambassador at the Holy See. He affected to doubt the possibility of Philip's success, and even his personal sincerity. He declined to advance a ducat till a Spanish army was actually on English soil. The Prince of Parma, who was to cross from Flanders and conduct the campaign in England itself, was diffident, if not unwilling ; and Philip had to feel that even the successful occupation of London might prove the beginning of greater troubles. He had been driven forward himself against his inclination. The chief movers in the enterprise, those who had fed the fire of religious animosity through Europe, and prevented a rational arrangement between the Spanish and English nations, were the Society of Jesus, those members of it especially who had been bred at Oxford in the Anglican Church, and hated it with the frenzy of renegades. From them came the endless conspiracies which Spain was forced to countenance, and the consequent severities of the English Government, which they shrieked in Philip's ears ; and Philip, half a bigot and half a cautious statesman, wavered between two policies till fate decided for him. Both on Philip's part and on Elizabeth's part there was a desire for peace if peace could be had. Philip was weary of the long struggle in the Low Countries, which threatened to be endless if Elizabeth supported it. Elizabeth herself wished to be left in quiet, relieved of the necessity of supporting insurgent Protestants and hanging traitorous priests. An arrangement was possible, based on principles of general toleration.

The Pope was right in not wholly trusting Philip. The Spanish King was willing to agree that England should remain Protestant if England wished it, provided the Catholics were allowed the free exercise of their own religion, and provided Elizabeth would call in her privateers, surrender to him the towns which she held in Holland, and abandon her alliance with the Dutch

States. Elizabeth was perfectly ready to tolerate Catholic worship if the Catholics would cease their plots
against her and Spain would cease to encourage them.
It was true that Flushing and Brill had been trusted to
her charge by the States, and that if she withdrew her
garrison she was bound in honor to replace them in
the States' hands. But she regarded the revolt of the
Low Countries as only justified by the atrocities of the
Blood Council and the Inquisition. If she could secure
for the Dutch Confederation the same toleration which
she was willing herself to concede to the English Catholics, she might feel her honor to be acquitted sufficiently, and might properly surrender to Philip towns
which really were his own. Here only, so far as the two
sovereigns were concerned, the difficulty lay. Philip
held himself bound by duty to allow no liberty of religion among his own subjects. On the other hand, if
peace was made the Spanish garrisons were to be withdrawn from the Low Countries ; the Executive Government would be left in the hands of the States themselves,
who could be as tolerant practically as they pleased. On
these terms it was certain that a general pacification was
within reach. The Prince of Parma strongly advised it.
Philip himself wished for it. Half Elizabeth's Council
recommended it, and she herself wished for it. Unless
Catholics and Protestants intended to fight till one or
the other was exterminated, they must come to some
such terms at last ; and if at last, why not at once ?
With this purpose a conference was being held at Ostend
between Elizabeth's and Parma's commissioners. The
terms were rational. The principal parties, it is now
possible to see—even Philip himself—were sincere about
it. How long the terms of such a peace would have
lasted, with the theological furnace at such a heat, may

be fairly questioned. Bigotry and freedom of thought had two centuries of battle still before them till it could be seen which was to prevail. But an arrangement might then have been come to at Ostend, in the winter of 1587 8, which would have lasted Philip's and Elizabeth's lifetime, could either party have trusted the other. In both countries there was a fighting party and a peace party. In England it was said that the negotiations were a fraud, designed only to induce Elizabeth to relax her preparations for defence. In Spain it was urged that the larger and more menacing the force which could be collected, the more inclined Elizabeth would be to listen to reason ; while Elizabeth had to show on her part that frightened she was not, and that if Philip preferred war she had no objection. The bolder her bearing, the more likely she would be to secure fair terms for the Hollanders.

The preparations of Cadiz and Lisbon were no secret. All Europe was talking of the enormous armament which Spain was preparing, and which Santa Cruz was to convoy to the English Channel. Both the Tagus and Cadiz Harbor were reported to be crowded with ships, though as yet unprovided with crews for them. With some misgivings, but in one of her bolder moments, the Queen in the Spring of 1587 allowed Drake to take a flying squadron with him down the Spanish coast. She hung about his neck a second in command to limit his movements ; but Drake took his own way, leaving his vice-admiral to go home and complain. He sailed into Cadiz Harbor, burnt eighteen galleons which were lying there, and, remaining leisurely till he had finished his work, sailed away, intending to repeat the operation at Lisbon. It might have been done with the same ease. The English squadron lay at the mouth of the river

within sight of Santa Cruz, and the great admiral had to
sit still and fume, unable to go out and meet him *por
falta de gente*—for want of sailors to man his galleons.
Drake might have gone in and burnt them all, and would
have done it had not Elizabeth felt that he had accomplished enough and that the negotiations would be broken
off if he worked more destruction. He had singed the
King's beard, as he called it; and the King, though
patient of affronts was moved to a passing emotion. Seamen and soldiers were hurried down to the Tagus.
Orders were sent to the Admiral to put to sea at once
and chase the English off the shore. But Philip, too,
on his side was afraid of Santa Cruz's too great au-
dacity. He, too, did not wish for a collision which
might make peace impossible. Another order followed.
The fleet was to stay where it was and to continue its
preparations. It was to wait till the next spring, when
the enterprise should be undertaken in earnest if the
peace conference at Ostend should fail in finding a conclusion.

Thus the winter drove through. Peace perhaps was
not really possible, however sincerely the high contract-
ing parties might themselves desire it. Public opinion
in Spain would have compelled Philip to leave the con-
queror of Terceira in command of the expedition. Santa
Cruz would have sailed in March for the English Channel, supported by officers whom he had himself trained;
and, although the Armada might still have failed, history
would have had another tale to tell of its exploits and
its fate. But a visible coldness had grown up between
the King and the Admiral. Philip, like many men of
small minds raised into great positions, had supreme
confidence in his own powers of management. He
chose to regulate everything, to the diet and daily hab-

its of every sailor and soldier on board. He intended to direct and limit the action of the Armada even when out and gone to its work. He had settled perhaps in his own mind that, since he could not himself be King of England, the happiest result for him would be to leave Elizabeth where she was, reduced to the condition of his vassal, which she would become if she consented to his terms ; and with the presence of an overpowering fleet in the Channel, a moderate but not too excessive use of force, an avoidance of extreme and violent measures, which would make the strife internecine and make an arrangement hopeless, he conceived that he could bring Elizabeth to her knees. For such a purpose Santa Cruz was not the most promising instrument; he required some one of more malleable material who would obey his own instructions, and would not be led either by his own ambition or the enthusiasm and daring of his officers into desperate adventures. It was probably, therefore, rather to his relief than regret that in February, when the Armada was almost ready to sail, the old Admiral died at Lisbon. Santa Cruz was seventy-three years old. He had seen fifty years of service. Spanish tradition, mourning at the fatal consequence, said afterward that he had been broken-hearted at the King's hesitation. Anxiety for the honor of his country might have worn out a younger man. He came to his end, and with him went the only chance of a successful issue of the expedition. He was proud of his country, which he saw that Philip was degrading. The invasion of England had been his dream for years, and he had correspondents of his own in England and Ireland. He was the ablest seaman that Spain possessed, and had studied long the problems with which he would have had to deal. Doubtless he had left men behind among those who had served under him who could have taken his place, and have done almost as well. But Philip had determined that, since the experiment was to be made, he would himself control it from his room in the Escurial, and in his choice of Santa Cruz's successor he showed that naval capacity and patriotic enthusiasm were the last qualities for which he was looking.

Don Alonzo de Guzman, Duke of Medina Sidonia, was the richest peer in Spain. He was now thirty-eight years old and his experience as a public man was limited to his failure to defend Cadiz against Drake. He was a short, broad shouldered, olive-complexioned man, said to be a good rider ; but, if his wife was to be believed, he was of all men in Spain the least fitted to be trusted with the conduct of any critical undertaking. The Duchess, Doña Aña de Mendoza, was the daughter of Philip's Minister, Ruy Gomez, and of the celebrated Princess of Eboli, whom later scandal called Philip's mistress, and whose attractions were supposed to have influenced Philip in favor of her son-in-law. Royal scandals are dreary subjects. When they are once uttered the stain is indelible, for everyone likes to believe them. The only contemporary witness for the amours of Philip and the Princess of Eboli is Antonio Perez, who, by his own confession, was a scoundrel who deserved the gallows. Something is known at last of the history of the lady. If there was a woman in Spain whom Philip detested, it was the wife of Ruy Gomez. If there was a man whom the Princess despised, it was the watery-blooded King. An intrigue between a wild-cat of the mountain and a narrow-minded, conscientious sheep-dog would be about as probable as a love-affair between Philip and the Princess of Eboli ; and at the time of her son-in-law's appointment she was locked up in a castle in defiant disgrace. The Duke had been married to her daughter when he was twenty-two and his bride was eleven, and Doña Aña, after sixteen years' experience of him, had observed to her friends that he was well enough in his own house among persons who did not know what he was; but that if he was employed on business of State the world would discover to its cost his real character. That such a man should have been chosen to succeed Alonzo de Bazan astonished everyone. A commander of Gold, it was said, was taking the place of a commander of Iron. The choice was known to Santa Cruz while he still breathed, and did not comfort him in his departure.

The most astonished of all, when he learnt the honor which was intended for him, was the Duke himself, and he drew a picture of his own incapacity as simple as Sancho's when appointed to govern his island.

"My health is bad," he wrote to Philip's secretary, "and from my small experience of the water I know that I am always sea-sick. I have no money which I can spare. I owe a million ducats, and I have not a real to spend on my outfit. The expedition is on such a scale and the object is of such high importance that the person at the head of it ought to understand navigation and sea-fighting, and I know nothing of either. I have not one of those essential qualifications. I have no acquaintances among the officers who are to serve under me. Santa Cruz had information about the state of things in England; I have none. Were I competent otherwise, I should have to act in the dark by the opinion of others, and I cannot tell to whom I may trust. The Adelantado of Castile would do better than I. Our Lord would help him, for he is a good Christian and has fought in naval battles. If you send me, depend upon it, I shall have a bad account to render of my trust." *

The Duchess, perhaps, guided her husband's hand when he wrote so faithful an account of himself. But his vanity was flattered. Philip persisted that he must go. He and only he would answer the purpose in view, so he allowed himself to be persuaded.

" Since your Majesty still desires it, after my confession of incompetence," he wrote to Philip, "I will try to deserve your confidence. As I shall be doing God's work, I may hope that He will help me."

Philip gratefully replied : " You are sacrificing yourself for God's service and mine. I am so anxious, that if I was less occupied at home I would accompany the fleet myself, and I should be certain that all would go well. Take heart; you have now an opportunity of showing the extraordinary qualities which God, the author of all good, has been pleased to bestow upon you. Happen what may, I charge myself with the care of your children. If you fail, you fail ; but the cause being the cause of God, you will not fail."

Thus the Duke was to command the Armada and to sail at the earliest possible moment, for the Commissioners were sitting at Ostend, and his presence in the Channel was of pressing consequence. Santa Cruz besides had fixed on the end of March as the latest date for the departure, on account of the north winds which later in the season blow down the coast of Portugal. The Duke at the time of his nomination was at his house at San Lucar. He was directed to repair at once to Lisbon, where his commission would reach him. An experienced but cautious Admiral, Don Diego Flores De

* Medina Sidonia to Secretary Idiaquez, Feb. 16, 1588. Duro, vol. i. 414.

Valdez, was assigned to him as nautical adviser, and
Philip proceeded to inflict upon him a series of instructions and advice as wise and foolish as those with which
Don Quixote furnished his squire. Every day brought
fresh letters as suggestions rose in what Philip called
his mind. Nothing was too trifling for his notice, nothing was to be left to the Duke's discretion which could
possibly be provided for. In a secret despatch to the
Prince of Parma, the King revealed alike his expectations and his wishes. He trusted that the appearance of
the Armada and some moderate victory over the English
fleet would force Elizabeth to an agreement. If the
Catholic religion could be tolerated in England, and
if Flushing and Brill were given up to him, he said
that he was prepared to be satisfied. To Medina
Sidonia he reported, as his latest advice from England,
that the Queen was inclining to the treaty, but was dis-
suaded by Leicester and Walsingham, and he gave him
a list of the English forces which he might expect to
meet, which was tolerably accurate and far inferior to
his own.

So far Philip wrote like a responsible and sensible
prince, but the smallest thing and the largest seemed to
occupy him equally. He directed the Duke to provide
himself with competent Channel pilots, as if this was a
point which might be overlooked. He laid down regulations for the health of the crews, he fixed himself the
allowances of biscuit and wine, salt fish and bacon.
Beyond all he charged the Duke to attend to their
morals. They were in the service of the Lord, and the
Lord must not be offended by the faults of his instruments. The clergy throughout Spain were praying for
them and would continue to pray, but soldiers and
sailors must do their part and live like Christians. They

must not swear; they must not gamble, which led to swearing. If they used low language God would be displeased. Every man before he embarked must confess and commend himself to the Lord. Especially and pre-eminently, loose women must be kept away, and if any member of the expedition fell into the *pecado nefando* he must be chastised to the example of the rest. This was well enough, also, but from morals the King went next to naval details, of which he could know nothing. He had heard, he said, that the gentlemen adventurers wanted state-rooms and private berths. It would encumber the ships, and the Duke was not to allow it. As the Duke was ignorant of navigation, the King held himself competent to instruct. He was to make straight for the English Channel, advance to the North Foreland, and put himself in communication with Parma. If foul weather came and the ships were scattered, they were to collect again, first at Finisterre, and then at the Scilly Isles. In the Channel he must keep on the English side, because the water was deeper there. Elizabeth's fleet, Philip understood, was divided, part being under Drake at Plymouth, and part in the Straits of Dover. If the Duke fell in with Drake he was to take no notice of him unless he was attacked, and was to keep on his course. If he found the two squadrons united, he would still be in superior force and might join battle, being careful to keep to windward.

There were limits even to Philip's confidence in his ability to guide. He admitted that he could not direct the Duke specifically how to form the ships for an engagement. Time and opportunity would have to determine. "Only," he said, "omit no advantage and so handle the fleet that one part shall support another. The enemy will try to fight at a distance with his guns.

You will endeavor to close. You will observe that their practice is to shoot low into the hulls rather than into the rigging. You will find how to deal with this. Keep your vessels together, allow none to stray or go in advance. Do not let them hurry in pursuit of prizes after a victory. This fault has often caused disaster both on sea and land. Conquer first, and then you will have spoil enough. The Council of War will order the distribution of it. What I am now saying implies that a battle will have to be fought; but if the enemy can be got rid of without an action, so much the better. The effect will be produced without loss to yourself. Should the Prince be able to cross, you will remain with the Armada at the mouth of the Thames, lending such assistance as you can. Consult with the Prince, and land none of your forces without his approval. Remember that your only business is to fight at sea. Differences between leaders are injurious, and always to be avoided. I am confident that you will co-operate cordially with the Prince as my service demands; but I must charge you to follow these injunctions of mine strictly according to the exact words. I have similarly directed the Prince on his own conduct, and if you two acting together can succeed in your undertaking, there will be honor to spare for both of you. You will remain at the Thames's mouth till the work is done. You may then, if the Prince approves, take in hand Ireland, in which case you will leave your Spanish troops with him and exchange them for Germans and Italians. You will be careful in what you spend. You know how costly the Armada has been to me. You will also see that I am not cheated in the muster rolls, and that the provisions are sound and sufficient. You will watch the conduct of the officers and keep them attentive to their duties.

This is all which occurs to me at present. I must leave the rest to your own care and prudence, and for any further advices which I may have to send you." *

Much of all this was no doubt reasonable and true. But Generals chosen to conduct great enterprises do not require to be taught the elements of their duties. That Philip thought it necessary to write all these details was characteristic both of himself and of the Duke. But it was characteristic of Philip also, that he had not made up his mind what the fleet was after all to do, or what he himself wished it to do. The first set of instructions was followed by a second, addressed both to the Duke and the Prince of Parma. The original purpose was that the fleet should make its way to the North Foreland. Parma was to use its presence in the channel, to cross at once with the army, advance to London and take possession of the Government, where, in conjunction with Cardinal Allen and the Catholic Nobles, he was to restore the authority of the Roman Church. This, however, implied that the English squadrons should have been first destroyed, or driven off the sea into their harbors. It was possible, as Philip foresaw, that the victory at sea might be less complete. He assumed that the English would be overmatched, but they were bold and skilful, and, even if defeated, might be left in a condition to be troublesome. The passage of the army might in that case be dangerous ; and Parma was left on his own responsibility to resume the negotiations at Ostend. Medina Sidonia was to gain and fortify the Isle of Wight, and the presence of the Armada in the Solent was to be used as an instrument to extort favorable terms from Elizabeth's Government. It would be no longer possible

* Philip the Second to the Duke of Medina Sidonia, April 1. Duro, vol. ii. pp. 5-13.

to demand the restoration of Catholicism in England, but the free exercise of the Catholic religion was to be insisted on. As the first point, and for the sake of the toleration of the Catholics, Philip would be willing to abandon his claim to compensation for the plundering expeditions of Francis Drake. The next condition was to be the restoration to the King of the towns which Elizabeth held in the Low Countries. It was possible that, before consenting, the Queen would demand the same liberty of religion for the Protestants of the Low Countries which she was required to grant to her own Catholics. To this, however, Parma was in no case to consent. The English might argue that the Huguenots were tolerated under the Edicts in France. Parma was to answer that the example was not to the point, that the King, at any rate, would not give way. The Isle of Wight would be in his own hands. The fleet would be safe in the Solent. Other fortresses could be seized along the coast, and Elizabeth would be forced to consent to a peace, under which she would be virtually reduced into the position of Philip's vassal.

Accidents, however, might happen, and the Prince of Parma also was perplexed with minute conditional instructions.

Disaster it is evident that Philip did not anticipate. Something less than complete success he probably did anticipate, and on the whole might prefer it. Satisfied with having provided for all contingencies, he was now only anxious to see the Armada on its way. The nuns and hermits, meanwhile, had removed the alarms of Medina Sidonia, had convinced him that God could not neglect a business in which He was so peculiarly concerned, and that, in the fine language of theological knight-errantry, the service which he was to execute had been specially reserved by Providence for the King to achieve.*

Such thoughts and such experiences were doubtless indications of a high-wrought frame of mind ; but men may dwell too exclusively on the conviction that God is on their side, and perhaps forget that God will not be found there if they neglect to do their own parts. While the priests were praying and the King and the Duke were calculating on the Divine assistance, they were omitting, all of them, the most obvious precautions by which moderate success could be looked for. Santa Cruz had reported that the fleet was almost ready to sail. The stores of provisions had been laid in while he was still alive, and the water-casks had been filled. But after his death there was no responsible person left in Lisbon to see to anything. Great naval expeditions were nothing new in Spain. The West Indies and Mexico and Peru had not been conquered by men in their sleep ; and what ships and ships' crews required for dangerous voyages was as well understood at Lisbon and Cadiz as in any harbor in the world. But the Armada was surrounded by a halo of devout imagination which seemed to paralyze all ordinary sense. It was to have sailed in March, but, even to the inexperienced eye of Medina Sidonia when he arrived at his command, the inadequacy of the preparations was too obvious. The casks of salt meat were found to be putrefying ; the water in the tanks had not been renewed, and had stood for weeks, growing foul and poisonous under the hot Lisbon sun. Spare rope, spare spars, spare anchors—all were deficient. The powder-supply was short. The

* " Y que lo tiene guardado á V. Md. para que por su mano y con su gran zelo y christiandad, se reduzca aquel Regno al gremio y obediencia de su Iglesia." Medina Sidonia to Philip, April 11.

balls were short. The contractors had cheated as au-
daciously as if they had been mere heretics, and the
soldiers and mariners so little liked the look of things
that they were deserting in hundreds, while the muster-
masters drew pay for the full numbers and kept it.   Instead of sailing in March, as he had been ordered, the
Duke was obliged to send to Madrid a long list of in-
dispensable necessaries, without which he could not
sail at all.   Nothing had been attended to save the state
of the men's souls, about which the King had been so
peculiarly anxious.   They at any rate had been sent to
confession, had received each his ticket certifying that
he had been absolved, and had duly commended himself to the Lord.   The loose women had been sent away,
the cards and dice prohibited, the moral instructions
punctually complied with.   All the rest had been left
to chance and villainy.   The short powder-supply was
irremediable.   The Duke purchased a few casks from
merchant ships, but no more was to be had.   For the
rest, the King wrote letters, and the Duke, according to
his own account, worked like a slave, and the worst de-
fects were concealed if not supplied.   Not, however, till
the end of April were the conditions advanced sufficiently for the presentation of the standard, and even then
the squadron from Andalusia had not arrived.

All was finished at last, or at any rate seemed so.   The
six squadrons were assembled under their respective
commanders.   Men and officers were on board, and
sailing orders, addressed to every member of the expedition, were sent round, in the Duke's name, to the
several ships, which, remembering the fate to which all
these men were being consigned by their crusading enthusiasm, we cannot read without emotion.

"From highest to lowest you are to understand the

object of our expedition, which is to recover countries
to the Church now oppressed by the enemies of the
true faith. I therefore beseech you to remember your
calling, so that God may be with us in what we do. I
charge you, one and all, to abstain from profane oaths
dishonoring to the names of our Lord, our Lady, and
the Saints. All personal quarrels are to be suspended
while the expedition lasts, and for a month after it is
completed. Neglect of this will be held as treason.
Each morning at sunrise the ship boys, according to
custom, shall sing 'Good Morrow' at the foot of the
mainmast,* and at sunset the 'Ave Maria.' Since bad
weather may interrupt the communications, the watch-
word is laid down for each day in the week: Sunday,
Jesus; the days succeeding, the Holy Ghost, the Holy
Trinity, Santiago, the Angels, All Saints, and our Lady.
At sea, every evening, each ship shall pass with a salute
under the lee of the Commander-in-Chief, and shall follow at night the light which he will carry in his stern."

So, as it were, singing its own dirge, the doomed
Armada went upon its way, to encounter the arms and
the genius of the new era, unequally matched with un-
believers. On May 14 it dropped down the river to
Belem, and lay there waiting for a wind. A brief account may here be given of its composition and its chief
leaders. The fleet consisted of a hundred and thirty
ships. Seven of them were over a thousand tons and
sixty-seven over five hundred. They carried two thousand five hundred guns, chiefly small, however—four,
six, and nine pounders. Spanish seamen understood
little of gunnery. Their art in their sea-battles was to
close and grapple and trust to their strength and cour-

---

* "Los pajes segun es costumbre daran los buenos dias al pié del
mástil major."

age in hand-to-hand fighting. Large for the time as
the galleons were, they were still overcrowded. Soldiers, sailors, officers, volunteers, priests, surgeons, galley-slaves, amounted, according to the returns, to nearly
thirty thousand men. The soldiers were the finest in
Europe; the seamen old trained hands, who had learned
their trade under Santa Cruz. They were divided into
six squadrons, each with its Vice-Admiral and Capitana,
or flag-ship. The Duke carried his standard in the San
Martin, of the squadron of Portugal, the finest vessel in
the service, and, as the Spaniards thought, in the world.
The other five, of Biscay, Castile, Andalusia, Guypuscoa,
and the Levant, were led by distinguished officers. There
was but one commander in the fleet entirely ignorant of
his duties, though he, unfortunately, was Commander-in-
Chief.

As the names of these officers recur frequently in the
account of what followed, some description may be given
of each.

The Vice-Admiral of the Biscay squadron was Juan
Martinez de Recalde, a native of Bilbao, an old, battered
sea-warrior, who had fought and served in all parts of
the ocean. He knew Ireland; he knew the Channel; he
had been in the great battle at Terceira, and in the
opinion of the service was second only to Santa Cruz.
His flag-ship was Santa Aña, a galleon of eight hundred
tons; he sailed himself in the Gran Grin, of eleven hundred; so far fortunate, if anyone in the expedition could
be called fortunate, for the Santa Aña was disabled in a
storm at the mouth of the Channel.

The leaders of the squadrons of Castile and Andalusia
were two cousins, Don Pedro and Don Diego de Valdez.
Don Diego, whom Philip had chosen for the Duke's
mentor, was famous as a naval architect, had been on

exploring expeditions, and had made a certain reputation
for himself. He was a jealous, suspicious, cautious kind
of man, and Philip had a high opinion of him. Don
Pedro was another of the heroes of Terceira, a rough,
bold seaman, scarred in a hundred actions with English
corsairs, and between the two kinsmen there was neither
resemblance nor affection. Don Pedro's misfortune in the
Channel, which will soon be heard of, brought him more
honor than Don Diego earned by his timidity. He lived
long after, and was for eight years Governor of Cuba,
where the Castle of the Moro at Havannah still stands as
his monument. Two other officers deserve peculiar mention : Miguel de Oquendo, who sailed in the Señora de
la Rosa, of Guypuscoa, and Alonzo de Leyva, who had
a ship of his own, the Rata Coronada. Oquendo's career
had been singularly distinguished. He had been the
terror of the Turks in the Mediterranean. At Terceira,
at a critical point in the action, he had rescued Santa
Cruz when four French vessels were alongside of him.
He had himself captured the French Admiral's flag-ship,
carrying her by boarding, and sending his own flag to
her masthead above the smoke of the battle. He was an
excellent seaman besides, and managed his ship, as was
said, as easily as a horse. Alonzo de Leyva held no
special command beyond his own vessel ; but he had
been named by Philip to succeed Medina Sidonia in case
of misadventure. With him, and under his special
charge, were most of the high-born adventurous youths
who had volunteered for the crusade. Neither he nor they
were ever to see Spain again, but Spanish history ought
not to forget him, and ought not to forget Oquendo.

Of priests and friars there were a hundred and eighty ;
of surgeons, doctors, and their assistants, in the entire
fleet, not more than eighty-five. The numbers might have

been reversed with advantage. Among the adventurers
one only may be noted particularly, the poet Lope de
Vega, then smarting from disappointment in a love-affair,
and seeking new excitement.

Meanwhile, the winds were unpropitious. For fourteen days the fleet lay at anchor at the mouth of the
Tagus unable to get away. They weighed at last on
May 28, and stood out to sea ; but a northerly breeze
drove them to leeward, and they could make no progress,
while almost instantly on their sailing the state of the
stores was brought to light. The water had been
on board for four months ! the casks were leaking, and
what was left of it was unfit to drink. The provisions,
salt meat, cheese, biscuit, were found to be half putrid,
and a remarkable order was issued to serve out first
what was in worse condition, that the supplies might
hold out the longer. As the ships were to keep together,
the course and speed were necessarily governed by those
which sailed the worst. The galleons, high built, and
with shallow draught of water, moved tolerably before
the wind, but were powerless to work against it. The
north wind freshened. They were carried down as low
as Cape St. Vincent, standing out and in, and losing
ground on each tack. After a fortnight's labor they were
only in the latitude of Lisbon again. Tenders were sent
in every day to Philip, with an account of their progress. Instead of being in the mouth of the Channel,
the Duke had to report that he could make no way at
all, and, far worse than that, the entire ships' companies
were on their way to being poisoned. Each provision
cask which was opened was found worse than the last.
The biscuit was mouldy, the meat and fish stinking, the
water foul and breeding dysentery. The crews and companies were loud in complaint ; the officers had lost

heart, and the Duke, who at starting had been drawing pictures in his imagination of glorious victories, had already begun to lament his weakness in having accepted the command. He trusted God would help him, he said. He wished no harm to anyone. He had left his quiet, and his home, and his children, out of pure love to his Majesty, and he hoped his Majesty would remember it.* The state of the stores was so desperate, especially of the water, that it was held unsafe to proceed. The pilots said that they must put into some port for a fresh supply. The Duke feared that if he consented the men, in their present humor, would take the opportunity and desert.

At length, on June 10, after three weeks of ineffectual beating up and down, the wind shifted to the southwest, and the fleet could be laid upon its course. The anxiety was not much diminished. The salt meat, salt fish, and cheese were found so foul throughout that they were thrown overboard for fear of pestilence, and the rations were reduced to biscuit and weevils. A despatch was hurried off to Philip that fresh stores must instantly be sent out, or there would be serious disaster. The water was the worst of all, as when drunk it produced instant diarrhœa. On June 13 matters mended a little. The weather had cooled. The southwest wind had brought rain. The ships could be aired and purified. They were then off Finisterre, and were on a straight course for the Channel. Philip's orders had been positive that they were not to delay anywhere, that they were to hurry on and must not separate. They had five hundred men, however, down with dysentery, and the number of sick was increasing with appalling rapidity. A council was held on board the San Martin

* Medina Sidonia to Philip the Second, May 30.

3

and the Admirals all agreed that go on they could not. Part of the fleet, at least, must make into Ferrol, land the sick, and bring off supplies. The Duke could not come to a resolution, but the winds and waves settled his uncertainties. On the 19th it came on to blow. The Duke, with the Portugal squadron, the galleys and the larger galleons made in at once for Corunna, leaving the rest to follow, and was under shelter before the worst of the gale. The rest were caught outside and scattered. They came in as they could, most of them in the next few days, some dismasted, some leaking with strained timbers, the crews exhausted with illness; but at the end of a week a third part of the Armada was still missing, and those which had reached the harbor were scarcely able to man their yards. A hospital had to be established on shore. The tendency to desert had become so general that the landing-places were occupied with bodies of soldiers. A despatch went off to the Escurial, with a despairing letter from the Duke to the King.

" The weather," he said, " though it is June, is as wild as in December. No one remembers such a season. It is the more strange since we are on the business of the Lord, and some reason there must be for what has befallen us. I told your Majesty that I was unfit for this command when you asked me to undertake it. I obeyed your orders, and now I am here in Corunna with the ships dispersed and the force remaining to me inferior to the enemy. The crews are sick, and grow daily worse from bad food and water. Most of our provisions have perished, and we have not enough for more than two months' consumption. Much depends on the safety of this fleet. You have exhausted your resources to collect it, and if it is lost you may lose Portugal and the Indies.

The men are out of spirit. The officers do not understand their business. We are no longer strong. Do not deceive yourself into thinking that we are equal to the work before us. You remember how much it cost you to conquer Portugal, a country adjoining Castile, where half the inhabitants were in your favor. We are now going against a powerful kingdom with only the weak force of the Prince of Parma and myself. I speak freely, but I have laid the matter before the Lord ; you must decide yourself what is to be done. Recollect only how many there are who envy your greatness and bear you no good-will." *

On the 27th thirty-five ships were still absent, and nothing had been heard of them. The storm, however, after all, had not been especially severe, and it was not likely that they were lost. The condition to which the rest were reduced was due merely to rascally contractors and official negligence, and all could easily be repaired by an efficient commander in whom the men had confidence. But the Duke had no confidence in himself nor the officers in him. Four weeks only had passed since he had left Lisbon and he was already despondent, and his disquieted subordinates along with him. He had written freely to Philip, and advised that the expedition should be abandoned. He again summoned the Vice-Admirals to his cabin and required their opinions. Should they or should they not go forward with their reduced force ? The Inspector-General, Don George Manrique, produced a schedule of numbers. They were supposed, he said, to have twenty-eight thousand men besides the galley-slaves. Owing to sickness and other causes, not more than twenty - two or twenty - three thousand could be regarded as effective, and of these six

* Medina Sidonia to Philip the Second from Corunna, June 24.

thousand were in the missing galleons. The Vice-Admirals were less easily frightened than their leader.
None were for giving up. Most of them advised that
they should wait where they were till the ships came in,
repairing damages and taking in fresh stores. Pedro
de Valdez insisted that they should go on as soon as possible. While they remained in harbor fresh meat and
vegetables might be served out, and the crews would
soon recover from a sickness which was caused only by
bad food. With vigor and energy all that was wrong
could be set right. The missing ships were doubtless
ahead expecting them, and would be fallen in with somewhere.

Don Pedro was addressing brave men, and carried the
council along with him. He wrote himself to Philip to
tell him what had passed. " The Duke," he said, " bore
him no good-will for his advice, but he intended to persist in a course which he believed to be for his Majesty's
honor."

A day or two later the wanderers came back and restored the Duke's courage. Some had been as far as
Scilly, some even in Mount's Bay, but none had been
lost and none had been seriously injured. The fresh
meat was supplied as the Don Pedro advised. The sick
recovered ; not one died, and all were soon in health
again. Fresh supplies were poured down out of the
country. The casks were refilled with pure water. In
short, the sun began to shine once more, and the despondency fit passed away. Philip wrote kindly and cheer-
ily. " Everything would be furnished which they could
want. The Duke might spend money freely and need
spare nothing to feed the men as they ought to be fed.
If they had met with difficulties in the beginning they
would have greater glory in the end. There were diffi-

culties in every enterprise. They must overcome them and go on." The Duke still hesitated. He said truly enough that other things were wanting besides food: powder, cordage, and the thousand minor stores which ought to have been provided and were not. But the rest of the chief officers were now in heart again, and he found himself alone; Recalde only, like a wise man, begging Philip to modify his instructions and allow him to secure Plymouth or Dartmouth on their advance, as, although they might gain a victory, it was unlikely to be so complete as to end the struggle, and they might require a harbor to shelter the fleet.

Philip, unfortunately for himself, paid no attention to Recalde's suggestion, but only urged them to begone at their best speed. The ships were laid on shore to be scraped and tallowed. The gaps in the crews were filled up with fresh recruits. Another ship was added, and at the final muster there were a hundred and thirty-one vessels, between seven and eight thousand sailors and seventeen thousand infantry, two thousand slaves, and fourteen hundred officers, priests, gentlemen, and servants. With restored health and good-humor they were again commended to the Lord. Tents were set up on an island in the harbor, with an altar in each and friars in sufficient number to officiate. The ship's companies were landed and brought up man by man till the whole of them had again confessed and again received the Sacrament.

"This," said the Duke, "is great riches, and the most precious jewel which I carry with me. They now are all well, and content, and cheerful."

II.

Two months of summer were still left when the Armada made its second start out of Corunna on Friday, July 22, with fresh heart and better provision. On the 23d the last vessel in the fleet had passed Cape Ortegal, and the wind, as if to make amends for past persecution, blew fair and moderate from the south. Saturday, Sunday, and Monday the galleons swept easily along across the Bay of Biscay, and on the Monday night, the 25th, the Duke found himself with all his flock about him at the mouth of the English Channel. Tuesday broke calm and cloudy, with a draft of northerly air. Heavy showers fell. One of the galleys had sprung a leak, and was obliged to go home. On Wednesday the wind backed to the west, and rose into a gale, blowing hard with a high sea. The waves broke into the stern galleries of the galleons, and the fleet was hove to. On Friday the storm was over, but there was still a long, heavy roll. The ships were unmanageable, and from the maintop of the San Martin forty sail were again not to be seen. The remaining galleys, finding that in such weather they were like to be swamped, had made away for the coast of France ; the Santa Aña, the Capitana of the Biscay squadron, had disappeared completely, and was supposed to have been sunk. She had in fact lost her reckoning, and at last found her way into Havre. The rest of the missing ships proved only to be a few miles ahead. After a slight flutter, the Armada, shorn of its galleys and the Santa Aña, was again complete, and with the sky clearing from southwest went on upon its way. As yet they had seen nothing—not a sail or a

boat; but being on the enemy's coast they put themselves into fighting order. They were in three divisions.
The Duke was in the centre with the main battle. Alonzo
de Leyva led the advance as the post of honor. The
rear was under Martinez de Recalde, the formation being
like an oblique crescent, or like the moon when it lies
on its back, De Leyva and Recalde being at the two
horns.

In this order they sailed slowly on through the day,
still with nothing in sight, but knowing by observation
and soundings that they were coming up to land. The
sun on Friday, at noon, gave them 50 degrees, and the
lead 56 fathoms. At four in the afternoon the gray
ridge of the Lizard rose above the sea three leagues off.
They were now in sight of the den of the dragon which
they were to come to slay, and Medina Sidonia ran up
to his masthead a special flag of his own, which had
been embroidered for the occasion—Christ on the Cross,
and Our Lady and the Magdalen on either side of Him.
As the folds unrolled in the breeze, each ship in the fleet
fired a broadside, and the ships' companies gathered and
knelt on the deck to give thanks to the Almighty.

That evening the Duke despatched the last letter to
the King, which for a month he had leisure to write. So
far, he said, the enemy had not shown himself, and he
was going forward in the dark ; no word had come from
Parma; before him was only the silent sea, and the long
line of the Cornish coast, marked at intervals by columns
of smoke which he knew to be alarm beacons. The sea
that was so silent would soon be noisy enough. With a
presentiment of danger, the Duke told the King that
he must so far disregard his orders that, until Parma
had communicated with him, he proposed to halt at the
Isle of Wight and to go no further. Sail was taken in

that night. On the Saturday morning a despatch boat
was sent away with the letter to the King, and the fleet
crept on slowly and cautiously. They had hoped to fall
in with a fishing-smack, but none were to be discovered ;
nor was it till Saturday night, or rather at one o'clock
on the Sunday morning, that they were able to gather
any information at all. At that hour, and not before, a
pinnace that had gone forward to observe came back
with four Falmouth fishermen who had been fallen in
with at sea. From them the Duke and the admirals
learned that Drake and Howard had come out that morning from Plymouth Harbor, and were lying in the Sound,
or outside it, waiting for them. The burning beacons
had brought notice on the Friday evening that the
Armada was in sight, and the English had instantly got
under way. The Spanish records and diaries say distinctly that from these fishermen they had gathered their
first and only knowledge of the English movements.
The charge afterward brought against the Duke, therefore, that he had learned that Plymouth was undefended,
that Oquendo and Recalde urged him to go in and take
it, and that he refused and lost the opportunity, is proved
to be without foundation. Very likely a council of admirals did advise that Plymouth should be attacked if
they found Howard and Drake still in the Sound, for in
the narrow space the ships would be close together, and
the superior numbers of the Spaniards and their superior
strength in small arms and musketry would be able to
assert themselves. Medina Sidonia may have agreed, for
all that anyone can say to the contrary, but the opportunity was never allowed him. The English fleet was
already outside, and the Duke could not enter till he
had fought an action.

An hour after midnight, on the Sunday morning, the

Falmouth boatmen gave their information. Four hours later, directly off Ramhead, the two fleets were engaged. The air through the night had been light from the west. The water was smooth. At five o'clock, just after sunrise, eleven large vessels were seen from the deck of the San Martin three miles to leeward, outside the Mewstone, manœuvring to recover the wind, which was beginning to freshen. Forty others were counted between the Armada and the land to the west of the Sound. The squadron first seen consisted of the Queen's ships under Lord Howard; the others were Drake and the privateers. The breeze rose rapidly. The Duke flew the consecrated standard, and signalled to the whole fleet to brace round their yards and hold the wind between the two English divisions. Howard, however, with apparent ease, went on to windward and joined Drake. Both of them then stood out to sea behind the whole Armada, firing heavily into Recalde and the rearward Spanish squadron as they passed. Recalde tried hard to close, but Sir John Hawkins had introduced new lines into the construction of the English ships. The high castles at poop and stem had been reduced, the length increased, the beam diminished. They could sail perhaps within five points of the wind. They showed powers, at any rate, entirely new to Recalde, for they seemed to be able to keep at any distance which they pleased from him. They did not try to break his line or capture detached vessels. With their heavy guns, which he found to his cost to be of weightier metal and to carry farther than his own, they poured their broadsides into him at their leisure, and he could make no tolerable reply. Alonzo de Leyva and Oquendo, seeing that Recalde was suffering severely, went to his assistance, but only to experience themselves the effects

of this novel method of naval combat and naval construction. To fight at a distance was contrary to
Spanish custom, and was not held worthy of honorable
men. But it was effective ; it was perplexing, it was
deadly. The engagement lasted on these conditions
through the whole Sunday forenoon. The officers of
the Armada did all that gallant men could achieve.
They refused to recognize where the English superiority
lay till it was forced upon them by torn rigging and
shattered hulls. Recalde's own ship fired a hundred and
twenty shot, and it was thought a great thing. But the
English had fired five to the Spanish one, and the effect
was the greater because, as in Rodney's action at Do-
minica, the galleons were crowded with troops, among
whom shot and splinter had worked havoc. The Castilians and Biscayans were brave enough ; there were no
braver men in the world ; but they were in a position
where courage was of no use to them. They were perplexed and disturbed ; and a gentleman present who
describes the scene observes that " este dia mostra-
ronse de neustra Armada algunos officiales medrosos "
— this day some of the officers of our fleet showed
cowardice. The allusion was perhaps to the Duke, who
had looked on and done nothing.

No prizes were taken. Drake and Howard understood their business too well to waste life upon single
captures. Their purpose was to harass, shatter, and
weaken the entire Armada, as opportunity might offer,
with the least damage to themselves, till shot and
weather, and the casualties likely to occur under such
conditions, had reduced the fleets to something nearer
to an equality. Tactics so novel baffled the Spaniards.
They had looked for difficulties, but they had counted
with certainty on success if they could force the Eng-

lish into a general engagement. No wonder that they were unpleasantly startled at the result of the first experiment.

The action, if such it could be called when the Armada had been but a helpless target to the English guns, lasted till four in the afternoon. The southwest wind then was blowing up, and the sea was rising. The two fleets had by that time driven past the opening into the Sound. The Duke could not have gone in if he had tried, nor could De Leyva himself, under such circumstances, have advised him to try; so, finding that he could do nothing, and was only throwing away life, he signalled from the San Martin to bear away up Channel. The misfortunes of the day, however, were not yet over. The Spanish squadrons endeavored to resume their proper positions, De Leyva leading and Recalde covering the rear. The English followed leisurely, two miles behind, and Recalde's own vessel had suffered so much in the engagement that she was observed to be dropping back, and to be in danger of being left alone and overtaken. Pedro de Valdez, in the Capitana of the Andalusian squadron, one of the finest ships in the fleet, observing his old comrade in difficulties, bore up to help him. After such a day, the men, perhaps, were all of them disturbed, and likely to make mistakes in difficult manœuvres. In turning, the Capitana came into collision with the Santa Catalina and broke her own bowsprit; the fore-topmast followed, and the ship became an unmanageable wreck. She had five hundred men on board, besides a considerable part of the money which had been sent for the use of the fleet. To desert such a vessel, and desert along with it one of the principal officers of the expedition, on the first disaster, would be an act of cowardice and dishonor not to be looked for in a Spanish nobleman. But night was coming on. To bear up was to risk a renewal of the fighting, for which the Duke had no stomach. He bore Don Pedro a grudge for having opposed him at Corunna, when he had desired to abandon the expedition ; Diego Florez, his adviser, had also his dislike for Don Pedro, and, to the astonishment of everyone, the signal was made that the fleet was not to stop, and that Don Pedro was to be left to his fate. De Leyva and Oquendo, unable to believe the order to be serious, hastened on board the San Martin to protest. The Duke hesitated ; Diego Florez, however, said that to wait would be to risk the loss of the whole fleet, and by Diego Florez Philip had directed the Duke to be guided. Boats were sent back to bring off the Capitana's treasure and the crew, but in the rising sea boats could do nothing. Don Pedro was deserted, overtaken, and of course captured, after a gallant resistance. The ship was carried into Dartmouth, and proved a valuable prize. Besides the money, there was found a precious store of powder, which the English sorely needed. Among other articles, was a chest of swords, richly mounted, which the Duke was taking over to be presented to the English Catholic peers. Don Pedro himself was treated with the high courtesy which he deserved, to be ransomed at the end of a year, and to be spared the ignominy of further service under his extraordinary commander-in-chief.

The loss of Don Pedro was not the last, and not the worst, calamity of the night. Soon after dark the air was shaken and the sky was lighted by an explosion in the centre of the Spanish fleet. Oquendo's ship, Our Lady of the Rose, was blown up, and two hundred men, dead and wounded, were hurled into the sea. The wreck that was left was seen to be in a blaze, in which the rest on board were like to perish. Oquendo himself was absent. Some said it was an accident, others that it had been done by an Englishman in disguise, others that there had been some quarrel, and that one of the parties in a rage had flung a match into the magazine and sprung overboard. This time the Armada was rounded to ; the burning ship was covered by the main body. The money on board, for each galleon had its own treasury, was taken out with the survivors of the crew. The hull was then abandoned to the English. A few casks of stores were still found in her hold which had escaped destruction. Shortly afterward she sank.

From the day on which it sailed the fleet had been pursued by misfortune. Two such disasters following on the unexpected and startling features of the first engagement struck a chill through the whole force. The officers had no longer the least trust in a commander-in-chief whom they had ill liked from the first. The national honor was supposed to be touched by the desertion of Pedro de Valdez, who was universally loved and respected. The Duke was suspected to be no better than a poltroon. The next morning, August 1, broke heavily. The wind was gone, and the galleons were rolling in the swell. The enemy was hull down behind them, and the day was spent in repairing damages, knotting broken ropes, and nailing sheets of lead over the shot holes. Recalde's ship had been so roughly handled that the disposition of the squadrons was altered. De Leyva took charge of the rear in the Rata Coronada, where the danger was greatest. Don Martinez was passed forward into the advance, where he could attend to his hurts out of harm's way. The Duke in sour humor found fault all round, as incompetent commanders are apt to do. Orders were issued that each ship

should keep a position definitely laid down ; and any
captain found out of his place was to be immediately
hanged. Men will endure much from leaders whom
they trust. Severity at such a moment was resented as
ill-timed and undeserved. The day passed without incident. With the sunset the sea fell smooth, and not
an air was stirring. The English fleet had come up,
but was still a league behind. Both fleets were then off
Portland. An hour after midnight De Leyva, Oquendo,
and Recalde, burning with shame and indignation, came
on board the San Martin, woke the Duke out of his
sleep, and told him that now was the time for him to
repair his credit. By the light of the rising moon the
English ships could be seen drifted apart with the tide,
and deprived in the breathless calm of their superior
advantages. The galeasses, with their oars, should be
sent out instantly to attack single vessels. The dawn it
was likely would bring a breeze from the east, when the
galleons could gather way and support them. The
Duke roused himself. Oquendo himself carried the
orders to the captain of the galeasses, Don Hugo de
Monçada. The galeasses prepared for action. The
easterly air came up as was expected, and with the first
clear light Howard was seen dead to leeward standing
in for the land, and endeavoring, as he had done at
Plymouth, to recover the weather-gage. The galeasses
proved of small service after all, for the wind was soon
too fresh ; and they were useless. They could do nothing except in a calm. But the San Martin and her leading consorts bore down with all sail set. Howard
being near the shore, had to tack and stand off to sea.
He had thus to pass out through the centre of the whole
Spanish fleet. The ships became intermixed, the Ark
Raleigh was surrounded with enemies, and every Spanish

captain's heart was bounding with the hope of boarding her. If they could once grapple they were justly confident in the numbers and courage of their men. So near the chances were at one moment, that Martin De Bretandona, the Levantine commander, might have closed with one of the largest of the English ships "if he could have been contented with less than the vessel which carried Howard's flag." But the wind freshened up with the day, and Don Martin and his friends saw vessels handled in a style which they had never seen before. It has been often confidently urged, as a reason for reducing the naval estimates, that Howard's fleet was manned by volunteers, and not by professional seamen. It is true that the English crews were not composed of men who were in the permanent service of the Crown, but never in the history of the country were a body of sailors gathered together more experienced in sailing ships and fighting them. They were the rovers of the ocean. To navigate the wildest seas, to fight Spaniards wherever they could meet them, had for thirty years been their occupation and their glory. Tacking, wearing, making stern way where there was no room to turn, they baffled every attack by the swiftness of their movements, and cleared their way out of the throng. Once more they drew away to windward, took at their leisure such positions as suited them, and, themselves beyond the reach of the feeble Spanish artillery, fired into the galleons with their long heavy guns till five o'clock in the afternoon. This day the Duke personally behaved well. The San Martin was in the thickest of the fight, and received fifty shots in her hull. The famous standard was cut in two. The leaks were so many and so formidable that the divers were again at work all night plugging and stopping the holes. But the result was to show him, and to show them all, that the English ships were superior to theirs in speed and power and weight of artillery, and that to board them against their will was entirely hopeless. Another observation some of them made which was characteristic of the age. The galleons which had no gentlemen on board had been observed to hold off and keep out of range. In the evening the wind fell. With the last of it, Howard and Drake bore away and left them, as, with the calm, the galeasses might again be dangerous. Wednesday was breathless. The English wanted powder besides, having used what they had freely ; and they were forced to wait for fresh supplies, which came up in the course of the afternoon. The Duke, as has been seen, was superstitious. So far the nuns' and the hermits' visions had not been realized, but, perhaps, his past ill-success had been sent only as a trial of his faith.

The 4th of August, Thursday, was St. Dominic's Day. The house of Guzman de Silva claimed St. Dominic as a member of their family ; and St. Dominic, the Duke was assured, would now lend a hand to his suffering kinsman. The Isle of Wight, where he had announced to Philip that he intended to stop, was directly under his lee. Once anchored in St. Helen's Roads he would have the Armada in a safe shelter, where, if the English chose to attack him, they must come to closer quarters, as there would not be sea room for the manœuvres which had been so disastrous to him.* If he could land ten

---

* The Duke's intention of stopping at the Isle of Wight was expressed by him as clearly as possible. Writing on July 30 to the King, he said he must advance " poco a poco con toda el Armada junta en mis escuadrones hasta isla D'Wich y *no pasar* adelante hasta tener aviso del Duque de Parma. Porque si yo saliese de alli con esta, la costa de Flandes no habiendo en toda ella puerto ni abrigo ninguno para estas naves, con el primer temporal que les diese los echaria á los ban-

thousand men he might take the island ; and, perplexed, agitated, and harassed by the unexpected course which events had taken with him, he probably still intended to act on this resolution, which was the wisest which he could have formed. He would have another action to fight before he could get in, but with St. Dominic's help he might this time have better fortune.

Howard and Drake seemed willing to give St. Dominic an opportunity of showing what he could do. They had received their powder. They had been reinforced by a few privateers who had come out from the Needles, and they showed a disposition to engage at a nearer distance than they had hitherto ventured. They were so far at a disadvantage that the wind was light, but, using what there was of it, the Ark Raleigh led straight down on the San Martin, ranged alongside, and opened a furious fire from her lower ports, as it appeared to the Spaniards, with heavier guns than she had used in the previous actions. Again the San Martin was badly cut up. Many of her men were killed and more were wounded. Seeing her hard pressed, Recalde and Oquendo came to the Duke's support. Oquendo drove his own ship between the Ark and the San Martin, receiving the broadside intended for her, and apparently causing some confusion on board the Ark by a shot of his own. At this moment the wind dropped altogether. An eddy of the tide carried off the other English ships, leaving Howard surrounded once more by the enemy and in worse difficulties than in the fight off Portland. Three large galleons were close on board of him with Oquendo, the boldest officer of the Armada, in one of them. Eleven

cos, donde sin ningun remedio se habrian de perder ; y por excusar este peligro tan evidente, me ha parecido no pasar adelante de aquella isla hasta saber lo que el Duque hace," etc.— Duro, vol. ii., p. 221.

boats, to the amazement of the Spaniards, dropped over the Ark's side.   Hundreds of men sprang into them, seized their oars, and took the Ark in tow, careless of the storm of musketry which was rattling upon them. She was already moving when the breeze rose again. Her sails filled and she flew away, dragging her own boats, and leaving behind the swiftest of the pursuing galleons as if they were at anchor.*

Again the experience was the same.   St. Dominic had been deaf or impotent, and a long day of fighting at disadvantage ended as usual.   The ammunition of the Armada, which the Duke knew from the first to be insufficient, was giving out under the unprecedented demands upon it.   Had he been wise he would still have made a desperate attempt to force his way into St. Helen's.   His strength was not very much reduced. Though the loss of life had been considerable, Pedro de Valdez's ship was the only one which had been taken. To prevent him from entering the Solent the English must have closed with him, which they still hesitated to do, as they could not now tell how much hurt they had inflicted.   The Duke had still this single chance of recovering his credit.   He might have gone in.   Had he done it, he might have taken the Wight, have even taken Portsmouth or Southampton ; at all events he would have placed the Armada in a position out of which it would have been extremely difficult to dislodge it.   But the unfortunate man had lost his head.   He hated his work.   He determined to look neither right nor left, but stick to Philip's own instructions, go on to the Straits of Dover as he had been told to do, send Parma

* "Se fué saliendo con tanta velocidad que el galeon San Juan de Fernando y otro ligerísimo, con ser los mas veleros de la Armada, que le fuéron dando caza, en comparacion se quedaron surtos."

notice of his arrival, and leave the rest to fate. He despatched a messenger to tell the Prince to expect him and to have his army embarked ready to cross on the instant of his arrival. He asked for a supply of flyboats, gun-boats worked with oars, which Parma could not send him, and for ammunition of which the Prince had none to dispose, expecting himself rather to be furnished from the fleet. Then, taking the worst resolution possible, and going forward to inevitable ruin, he signalled to his flock to follow him and pursued his way up Channel, followed by the English as before.

The Isle of Wight once passed, the worst danger to England was over. Lord Henry Seymour's squadron was in the Downs. Howard and Drake would soon join hands with him, and they could then concert what was next to be done.

The Armada drifted on before a light west wind through Thursday night, all Friday, and till Saturday afternoon. They were then at Calais and dropped anchor in the roads. Like a shadow which they could not shake off, the English clung to them behind. As they anchored, the English anchored also, a mile and a half astern, as if the infernal devils, *esta endemoniada gente*, had known what the Duke was going to do. Philip's advice had been to avoid the French coast, to keep the other side, and to bring up behind the North Foreland. The Duke, like Sancho, in the night adventure with the fulling hammers, was flying for safety under the skirts of Parma's coat, and thought that the nearer he could be to him the better it would be. He had thus brought his charge to the most dangerous roadstead in the Channel, with an enemy close to him who had less cause to fear the weather than he, and almost within gunshot of the French shore, when he did not

know whether France was friend or foe. For the moment he thought himself secure. The wind was off the
land. He looked to see the Prince of Parma and his
boats coming out of Dunkirk at latest on the Monday
morning. The French Governor came off to call before
dark, expressed his surprise to see him in a position where a shift of weather might be inconvenient,
but offered him, meanwhile, the hospitalities of the port.
On the Sunday morning, August 7, the purveyor of the
fleet went on shore to buy vegetables. The men were
employed cleaning up the guns and setting the ships in
order after the confusion of the past week, and so much
work had to be done that the daily rations were not
served out and the Sunday holy day was a harassed
fast. As the day wore on messengers came in from
Parma. His transports were lying in Dunkirk, but
nothing was ready, and the troops could not be embarked for a fortnight. He was himself at Bruges, but
promised to hurry down to the port and to use all possible expedition. This was not consoling intelligence.
In the uncertain weather the Calais roadstead was no
place to linger in; and the Duke's anxieties were not
diminished when the English squadron of the Downs
under Seymour and Sir John Hawkins sailed in and
anchored with their consorts. Hawkins—Achines they
called him—was an object of peculiar terror to the
Spaniards from his exploits in the West Indies. Next
to Drake, or the Dragon, he was more feared than any
other English seaman. The galleons were riding with
two anchors on account of the tide. An English pinnace, carrying a light gun, ran down in the afternoon,
sailed up to the San Martin, lodged a couple of shots in
her hull, and went off again. Hugo de Monçada sent a
ball after her from the Capitana galeass which cut a hole

in her topsail, but she flew lightly away. The Spanish officers could not refuse their admiration for such airy impertinence.

If the Duke was uneasy the English commanders did not mean to give him time to recover himself. Calais Roads might be an awkward anchorage, but the weather might settle. August weather in the Channel often did settle. There had been a week of fighting and the Armada had got the worst of it, but still there it was, to outward appearance, not much damaged and within touch of the Prince of Parma. The backward state of Parma's preparations was unknown and unsuspected by the English commanders. Any morning he might be looked for, issuing out of Dunkirk with his fleet of gun-boats, his army on board his barges, and making his way across the Straits with the Armada to protect him. That Sunday evening Howard, Drake, Hawkins, Sey-mour, and Martin Frobisher held a consultation in the Ark's main cabin. The course which they intended to follow had probably been resolved on generally when Howard anchored so near the enemy on the previous evening, and the meeting must have been only to arrange the method and mode of action. After nightfall the flood tide would be running strong along the coast, and an intermittent but rising wind was coming up from the west. The Duke, as he restlessly paced his deck, ob-served lights moving soon after dark among the English vessels. He expected mischief of some kind and had ordered a strict look-out. About midnight eight large hulks were seen coming slowly down with tide and wind. Spars, ropes, and sails had been steeped in pitch, and as they approached nearer they burst out into flame and smoke. Straight on they came, for they had crews on board to direct the course, who only retreated to their boats when it was impossible to remain longer. The Spaniards, already agitated by the strange tricks of their English foes, imagined that the fireships were floating mines like those which had blown to pieces so many thousands of men at the bridge at Antwerp. The Duke, instead of sending launches to tow them clear, fired a signal for the whole fleet to get instantly under way. In the hurry and alarm, and with two anchors down, they had no time to weigh. They cut their cables, leaving buoys by which to recover them at daylight, and stood out into the Channel, congratulating themselves for the moment at having skilfully and successfully avoided a threatening danger. Medina Sidonia's intention had been to bring up again outside. He himself let go an anchor two miles off, and the best appointed galleons followed his example. The main body, unfortunately, had been sent to sea so ill provided that their third anchors, where they had any, were stowed away below and could not be brought up in time. Thus, when day dawned, the Duke found himself with less than half his force about him. The rest had drifted away on the tide and were six miles to leeward. The purpose of his enemy's "traicion," treason, as the Spaniards regarded it, was now apparent. The San Martin, and the vessels which remained with her, hoisted anchor and signalled to return to the roadstead. Seventy of the Duke's ships were far away, unable to obey if they had tried. The wind had drawn into the northwest; they were driving seemingly on the fatal banks, and when the Duke proposed to go after them the pilots told him that if he did they would probably be all lost together.

The spectacle on the shore was yet more dispiriting. The Capitana galeass, in clearing out from the fire-ships, had fouled the cable of another vessel. Monçada, who commanded her, knew as little of seamanship as his commander-in-chief. Her helm was jammed. An English crew with two hundred men at the oars would have found a way to manage her, but with galley slaves nothing could be done. She had drifted ashore under the town, and as the tide had gone back, was lying on her side on the sands, defending herself desperately against the crews of six English ships, one of them Howard's Ark, who were attacking her in their boats. Monçada fought like a hero till he was killed by a musket-shot, the slaves jumped overboard, the surviving sailors and soldiers followed their example, and the galeass was taken and plundered.

To the Duke such a sight was sad enough ; but he had little time to attend to it. While Howard was losing time over the galeass, Drake and Hawkins had stooped on a nobler quarry. The great fleet was parted ; forty ships alone were present to defend the consecrated banner of Castile which was flying from the mainmast of the San Martin. Forty only, and no more, were engaged in the battle which stripped Spain of her supremacy at sea. But in those forty were Oquendo, De Leyva, Recalde, Bretendona, all that was best and bravest in the Spanish service. The first burst of the storm fell on the San Martin herself. Drake, determined to make the most of his opportunity, no longer held off at long range, but closed up, yard-arm to yard-arm ; not to make prizes of the galleons, but to destroy, sink, or disable them. The force which the English brought into the action was no longer unequal to that of the enemy. The air was then so full of smoke that little could be seen from one ship of what was passing in another part of the action. Each captain fought his own vessel as he could, Medina giving no orders. He who, till the past few days, had

never heard a shot fired in anger, found himself in the
centre of the most furious engagement that history had
a record of. He was accused afterward of having shown
cowardice. It was said that his cabin was stuffed with
woolpacks, and that he lay himself during the fight in
the middle of them. It was said, also, that he charged
his pilot to take his ship where the danger was least. If
he did, his pilot disobeyed his orders, for the San Martin
was in the hottest part of the battle. It could not be
otherwise. The flag which she carried to the end of it
necessarily drew the heaviest fire upon her. The accounts of eye-witnesses charge the Duke only with the
helpless incapacity which he had himself been the first
to acknowledge. Though the San Martin's timbers were
of double thickness, the shot at close range went through
and through her, " enough to shatter to pieces a rock."
Her deck became a slaughter-house. Half her crew
were killed or wounded, and she would have been sunk
altogether had not Oquendo and De Leyva dashed in
and forced the English to turn their guns upon them, and
enable the unhappy Duke to crawl away and stop his
leaks again. This was about noon ; and from that time
he himself saw no more till the engagement was over.
Even from his maintop nothing could be made out for
the smoke ; but the air was shaking with the roar of the
artillery. The Spanish officers behaved with the desperate heroism which became the countrymen of Cortez
and Santa Cruz, and never did Spanish soldier or seaman distinguish himself more than on this tremendous
day. There was no flinching, though the blood was
seen streaming out of the scuppers. Priests went up
and down under the hottest fire, crucifix in hand, con-
fessing and absolving the dying. Not a ship struck
her colors. They stood to their guns till their powder

was all gone, and in half the ships not a round was left.

Happily for them, the English were no better furnished; Howard's ammunition was all exhausted also; and the combat ended from mere incapacity to continue it. But the engagement from the first preserved the same character which had been seen in those which had preceded it. The Spaniards' courage was useless to them. Their ships could not turn or sail; their guns were crushed by the superior strength of the English artillery; they were out-matched in practical skill, and, close as the ships were to one another, they could not once succeed in fixing a grappling-iron in an English rigging. Thus, while their own losses were terrible, they could inflict but little in return. They had endured for five hours to be torn to pieces by cannon-shot—and that was all.

Before sunset the firing had ceased; the wind rose, the smoky canopy drifted away, and the San Martin and her comrades were seen floating, torn and tattered, *casi sin poder hacer mas resistencia,* almost powerless to resist longer. If the attack had continued for the two hours of daylight that remained, they must all have sunk or surrendered. A galleon in Recalde's squadron had gone down with all hands on board. The San Philip and the San Matteo were falling away dismasted and helpless toward the Dutch coast, where they afterward went ashore. The condition of the rest was little better. The slaughter had been appalling from the crowd of soldiers who were on board. They had given themselves up as lost when it pleased God, for they could give no other explanation, that the enemy ceased to fire, drew off and left them, to bring their vessels to the wind, throw their dead overboard, and see to the hurts of the wounded, who were counted by thousands. They were so crippled that they could not bear their canvas, and unless they could repair their damages swiftly, the northwest wind which was rapidly rising would drive them on the banks above Dunkirk. From the day on which they left Lisbon an inexorable fatality had pursued them. They had started in an inflated belief that they were under the especial care of the Almighty. One misfortune had trod on another's heel; the central misfortune of all, that they had been commanded by a fool, had begun to dawn on the whole of them. But the conviction came too late to be of use, and only destroyed what was left of discipline. The soldiers, finding that they outnumbered the seamen, snatched the control, chose their own course, and forced the pilots to steer as they pleased. The night passed miserably in examining into injuries, patching up what admitted of being mended, and discovering other hurts which could not be mended. The fresh water which they had brought from Corunna had been stowed on deck. The casks had been shot through in the action, and most of it was gone. The Ave Maria, if it was sung that evening, must have been a dirge, and the Buenos Dias of the ship boys in the morning a melancholy mockery. Yet seventy vessels out of the great fleet were still entire. They had not come up to join in the fight, because they could not. Their hulls were sound, their spars were standing, their crews untouched by any injury worse than despondency. The situation was not really desperate, and a capable chief with such a force at his disposition might have done something still to retrieve his country's credit, if only these ships could be made use of. Yet when day broke it seemed that a common fate would soon overtake those who had fought and those who so far had escaped.

They came together in the night. The dawn found them dragging heavily into the North Sea. The north-west wind was blowing hard, and setting them bodily on the banks. The bad sailers could not go to wind-ward at all. Those which had been in the fight could not bear sail enough to hold a course which, when sound, they might have found barely possible. The crews were worn out. On the Sunday they had been dinnerless and supperless. All Monday they had been fighting, and all Monday night plugging shot-holes and fishing spars. The English fleet hung dark and threatening a mile distant on the weather quarter. The water was shoaling every moment. They could see the yellow foam where the waves were breaking on the banks. To wear round would be to encounter another battle, for which they had neither heart nor strength, while the English appeared to be contented to let the elements finish the work for them. The English vessels drew more water, and would have grounded while the galleons were still afloat. It was enough for them if they could prevent the Armada from turning round and could force it to continue upon a course of which an hour or two would probably see the end. The San Martin and Oquendo's ship, the San Juan, were farthest out. The sounding-line on the San Martin gave at last but six fathoms ; the vessels to leeward had only five. Someone, perhaps Diego Florez, advised the Duke to strike his flag and surrender. Report said that a boat was actually lowered to go off to Howard and make terms, and that Oquen-do had prevented it from pushing off, by saying savage-ly that he would fling Diego Florez overboard. The Duke's friends, however, denied the charge, and insisted that he never lost his faith in God and God's glorious mother. Certain it is, that with death staring them

in the face and themselves helpless, men and officers be-
took themselves to prayer as the only refuge left, and
apparently the prayer was answered. A person who was
on the San Martin describes the scene. Everyone was
in despair, he said, and only looking for destruction.
Had the enemy known the condition in which they were,
and borne down and attacked them, they must all have
given in, for they were without power to defend themselves. At the last extremity, somewhere about noon,
" God was pleased to work a miracle." The wind shifted, backing to the southwest, and ceased to jam them
down upon the sands. With eased sheets they were able
to point their heads northward and draw out into the
deep water. The enemy followed, still keeping at the
same distance, but showed no further disposition to
meddle with them ; and the Armada breathed again,
though huddled together like a flock of frightened sheep.
A miracle they thought it. Being pious Catholics and
living upon faith in the supernatural they recovered
heart, and began to think that God's anger was spent,
and that He would now be propitious. He had been
with them when they thought they were deserted. He
had brought the survivors of them "through the most
terrible cannonade ever seen in the history of the world"
(la mas fuerte bateria y major que los nacidos han visto
ni los escriptores han escrito). He had perhaps been
disciplining them to do His work after all. Death at
any rate was no longer before their eyes.

Alas ! if the change of wind was really an act of Providence in answer to prayer, Providence was playing with
their credulity, and reserving them deliberately for an
end still more miserable. This Tuesday, August 9,
was the day of Philip's patron saint, St. Lawrence, whose
arm he had lately added to his sacred treasures in the

Escurial. In the afternoon a council of war was again held on board the flag-ship, consisting of the Duke, Alonzo de Leyva, Recalde, Don Francisco de Bobadilla, and Diego Florez. They had little pleasant to say to each other. Oquendo was at first absent, but came in while they were still deliberating. "O Señor Oquendo," they cried, "que haremos," "What shall we do?" "Do!" he replied; "bear up and fight again." It was the answer of a gallant man who preferred death to disgrace. But the Duke had to consider how to save what was left of his charge, and the alternatives had to be considered. They were before the wind, running right up the North Sea. The Duke explained that every cartridge had been spent in the vessels which had been engaged, and that, although some were left in the rest of the fleet, the supply was miserably short. Their ships were leaking. Half the sailors and half the artillerymen were killed or wounded. The Prince of Parma was not ready, and they had found by experience that they were no match for the English in fighting. The coast of Spain was at present unprotected, and unless they could carry the fleet home in safety would be in serious danger. The Duke's own opinion was that they ought to make haste back, and by the sea route round the North of Scotland and Ireland. To return through the Straits implied more battles, and in their battered state it was doubtful whether they could work their way as the wind stood, even if the enemy left them alone.

Flight, for it was nothing else, after such high expectations and loud prayers and boastings, flight after but a week's conflict, seemed to the old companions of Santa Cruz an intolerable shame. De Leyva was doubtful. He admitted, as the Duke said, that the English were too strong for them. They had done their best and it had

not availed. His own ship would hardly float, and he
had not thirty cartridges left. Recalde and Bobadilla
supported Oquendo, and insisted that, at whatever risk,
they must endeavor to recover Calais Roads. They
were old sailors, who had weathered many a storm, and
fought in many a battle. The chances of war had been
against them so far, but would not be against them always. If the English fleet could go down Channel, it
was not to be supposed that a Spanish fleet could not,
and if they were to return home, the Channel was the
nearest road. If the worst came, an honorable death
was better than a scandalous retreat.

. Spanish history has accused Medina Sidonia of having
been the cause that the bolder course was rejected. Independent contemporary witnesses say that it was made
impossible by the despondency of the men, who could
not be induced to encounter the English again.

Though he determined against returning through the
Channel, more than one alternative was still open to
him. The harbors of Holland and Zealand were in the
hands of Dutch rebels. But there was the Elbe, there
was the Baltic, there was Norway. If the Duke had
been a man of daring and genius there was the Frith
of Forth. Had he anchored off Leith and played his
cards judiciously, there was still a possibility for him to
achieve something remarkable. The Duke, however,
probably knew that his master had intended to exclude
the King of Scots from the English succession, and may
have doubted the reception which he might meet with.
Or, and perhaps more probably, he was sick of a command which had brought him nothing but defeat and
distraction, and was only eager to surrender his trust at
the earliest possible moment.

Thus forlorn and miserable, the great Armada, which

was to have made an end of the European Reformation,
was set upon its course for the Orkneys, from thence to
bear away to the west of Ireland, and so round to Spain.
Drake and Howard, not conceiving that their object
would be so lightly abandoned, and ignorant of the condition to which the enemy was reduced, followed them
at a distance to see what they would do, and on the
Wednesday had almost taken Recalde, whose disabled
ship was lagging behind. The Duke, however, did not
dare to desert a second admiral. He waited for Recalde
to come up, and the English did not interfere. In fact
they could not. Owing to Elizabeth's parsimony, their
magazines were hardly better furnished than the Spanish.
In pursuing the Armada they acknowledged that they
were but "putting on a brag" to frighten the Duke out
of turning back. They could not have seriously attacked
him again, at all events for many days, and the bravest
course would after all have proved the safest for him.
As it was, he saved Recalde, and went on thanking
Providence for having induced the English to let him
alone.

III.

On Friday the 12th the Armada passed the mouth of
the Forth. Howard had followed so far, expecting that it
might seek shelter there. But it went by with a leading
wind. He knew then that till another season they would
see no more of it, so put about and returned to Margate.

Relieved of his alarming presence, the Spaniards were
able to look into their condition and to prepare for a
voyage which might now be protracted for several

weeks. The Duke himself was short and sullen, shut himself in his state-room and refused to see or speak with anyone. Diego Florez became the practical commander, and had to announce the alarming news that the provisions taken in at Corunna had been wholly inadequate, and that at the present rate of consumption they would all be starving in a fortnight. The state of the water-supply was worst of all, for the casks had most of them been destroyed by the English guns. The salt meat and fish were gone or spoiled. The rations were reduced to biscuit. Half a pound of biscuit, a pint of water, and half a pint of wine was all that each person could be allowed. Men and officers fared alike ; and on this miserable diet, and unprovided with warm clothing, which they never needed in their own sunny lands, the crews of the Armada were about to face the cold and storms of the northern latitudes.

They had brought with them many hundreds of mules and horses. They might have killed and eaten them, and so mitigated the famine. But they thought of nothing. The wretched animals were thrown overboard to save water, and the ships in the rear sailed on through floating carcasses—a ghastly emblem of the general wreck. The Duke felt more than the officers gave him credit for. In a letter which he despatched to Philip on August 21, in a forlorn hope that it might reach Spain somehow, he described the necessity which had been found of cutting down the food, and the consequent suffering.* That alone would have been enough,

* " Por ser tan pocos los bastimentos que se llevan, que, para que puedan durar un mes, y el agua, se han acortado las raciones generalmente sin exceptuar persona, porque no perezcan, dando se media libra de biscocho, y un cuartillo de agua, y medio de vino sin ninguna otra cosa, con que se va padeciendo lo que V.M. podra juzgar."—Medina Sidonia to Philip, August 21. Duro, vol. ii., p. 226.

for the men were wasting to a shadow of themselves, but besides there were three thousand sick with scurvy and dysentery, and thousands more with wounds uncured.

But if he sympathized with the men's distresses he did not allow his sympathy to be seen. He knew that he was blamed for what had happened, that he was distrusted and perhaps despised ; and while keeping aloof from everyone, he encouraged their resentment by deserving it. Many persons might have been in fault. But there is a time for all things, and those wretched days, wretched mainly through the Duke's own blunders, were not a time for severity ; yet it pleased him, while secluded in his cabin, to order an inquiry into the conduct of the commanders who had lost their anchors at Calais, and had failed to support him in the action which followed. He accused them of cowardice. He held a court-martial on them and ordered twenty to be executed. Death with most was exchanged for degradation and imprisonment, but two poor wretches were selected on whom the sentence was to be carried out, as exceptionally culpable. When he had decided to fly, the Duke had ordered that the whole fleet should follow and not go in advance of the San Martin. A Captain Cuellar and a Captain Christobal de Avila had strayed for a few miles ahead, intending, as the Duke perhaps supposed, to desert. Don Christobal, to the disgust of the fleet, was executed with a parade of cruelty. He was hung on the yard of a pinnace, which was sent round the squadrons with Don Christobal's body swinging upon it before it was thrown into the sea. Cuellar's fate was to have been the same. He commanded a galleon called the San Pedro. He had been in the action and had done his duty. His ship had been cut up. He himself had not slept for ten days, having been in every

5

fight since the Armada entered the Channel. When all
was over, and the strain had been taken off, he had
dropped off exhausted. His sailing master, finding the
San Pedro leaking, had gone in advance to lay-to and examine her hurts. Exasperated at the disobedience to
his directions, the Duke sent for Cuellar, refused to
listen to his defence, and ordered him to be hanged.
Don Francisco de Bobadilla with difficulty obtained his
life for him, but he was deprived of his ship and sent
under arrest to another galleon, to encounter, as will be
seen, a singular adventure.

The display of temper, added to the general conviction
of the Duke's unfitness for his place, may have been the
cause of the dispersal of the Armada which immediately
followed. The officers felt that they must shift for themselves. The fleet held together as far as the Orkneys.
The intention was to hold a northerly course till the
60th parallel. Assuming the wind to remain in the
west, the pilots held that from this altitude the galleons
could weather the Irish coast at sufficient distance to be
out of danger—to weather Cape Clear, as they described
it, but the Cape Clear which they meant—a glance at
the map will show it—was not the point so named at
present, but Clare Island, the extreme western point of
Mayo. The high-built, broad and shallow galleons were
all execrable sailers, but some sailed worse than others,
and some were in worse condition than others. They
passed the Orkneys together, and were then separated
in a gale. The nights were lengthening, the days were
thick and misty, and they lost sight of each other. Two
or three went north as far as the Faroe Islands, suffering pitifully from cold and hunger. Detachments,
eight or ten together, made head as they could, working
westward, against wind and sea, the men dying daily in

hundreds. The San Martin, with sixty ships in company, kept far out into the Atlantic, and they rolled down toward the south, dipping their mainyards in the tremendous seas. On August 21, the day on which the Duke wrote to Philip, they were two hundred miles west of Cape Wrath, amid the tumult of the waters. "The Lord," he said, "had been pleased to send them a fortune different from that which they had looked for ; but since the expedition had been undertaken from the beginning in the Lord's service, all doubtless had been ordered in the manner which would conduct most to the King's advantage and the Lord's honor and glory. The fleet had suffered so heavily that they had considered the best thing which they could do would be to bring the remains of it home in safety. Their finest ships had been lost, their ammunition had been exhausted, and the enemy's fleet was too strong for what was left. The English guns were heavier than the Spanish ; their sailing powers immeasurably superior. The sole advantage of the Spaniards was in small arms, and these they could not use, as the enemy refused to close. Thus, with the assent of the vice-admirals, he was making for home round the Scotch Isles. The food was short ; the dead were many ; the sick and wounded more. He himself could but pray that they might soon reach a port, as their lives depended on it."

This letter, though sent off out of the Western Ocean, did eventually reach the King's hands. Meanwhile the weather grew wilder and wilder. The number of vessels which could bear up against the gales diminished daily, and one by one they fell to leeward on the fatal Irish shore. Leaving Medina Sidonia and the survivors which reached home along with him, the story must follow those which were unequal to the work required of them.

The Spaniards were excellent seamen. They had navigated ships no worse than those which were lumbering through the Irish seas, among West Indian hurricanes and through the tempests at Cape Horn. But these poor wretches were but shadows of themselves ; they had been poisoned at the outset with putrid provisions ; they were now famished and sick, their vessels' sides torn to pieces by cannon-shot and leaking at a thousand holes, their wounded spars no longer able to bear the necessary canvas ; worst of all, their spirits broken. The superstitious enthusiasm with which they started had turned into a fear that they were the objects of a malignant fate with which it was useless to struggle. Some had been driven among the Western Islands of Scotland ; the ships had been lost ; the men who got on shore alive made their way to the Low Countries. But these were the few. Thirty or forty other vessels had attempted in scattered parties to beat their way into the open sea. But, in addition to hunger, the men were suffering fearfully for want of water and perhaps forced the pilots either to make in for the land, or else to turn south before they had gained sufficient offing. Thus, one by one all these drove ashore, either on the coast of Sligo or Donegal, or in Clew Bay or Galway Bay, or the rocks of Clare and Kerry, and the wretched crews who escaped the waves found a fate only more miserable. The gentlemen and officers, soiled and battered though they were, carried on land such ornaments as they possessed. The sailors and soldiers had received their pay at Corunna, and naturally took it with them in their pockets. The wild Irish were tempted by the plunder. The gold chains and ducats were too much for their humanity, and hundreds of half-drowned wretches were dragged out of the waves only to be stripped and knocked on the head, while those who escaped the Celtic skenes and axes, too weak and exhausted to defend themselves, fell into the hands of the English troops who were in garrison in Connaught. The more intelligent of the Irish chiefs hurried down to prevent their countrymen from disgracing themselves. They stopped the robbing and murdering, and a good many unfortunate victims found shelter in their castles. Such Spaniards as were taken prisoners by the English met a fate of which it is impossible to read without regret. Flung as they were upon the shore, ragged, starved, and unarmed, their condition might have moved the pity of less generous foes. But the age was not pitiful. Catholic fanaticism had declared war against what it called heresy, and the heretics had to defend their lives and liberties by such means as offered themselves. There might be nothing to fear from the Spanish prisoners in their present extremity, but if allowed to recover and find protection from Irish hospitality, they might and would become eminently dangerous. The number of English was small, far too small, to enable them to guard two or three thousand men. With the exception, therefore, of one or two officers who were reserved for ransom, all that were captured were shot or hanged on the spot.

The history of these unfortunates must be looked for in the English records rather than the Spanish. They never returned to Spain to tell their own story, and Captain Duro has little to say about them beyond what he has gathered from English writers. Among the documents published by him, however, there is an extraordinary narrative related by the Captain Cuellar who so nearly escaped hanging, a narrative which not only contains a clear account of the wreck of the gal-

leons, but gives a unique and curious picture of the
Ireland of the time.

The scene of the greatest destruction among the ships
of the Armada was Sligo Bay. It is easy to see why.
The coast on the Mayo side of it trends away seventy
miles to the west as far as Achill and Clare Island, and
ships embayed there in heavy southwesterly weather
had no chance of escape. On one beach, five miles in
length, Sir Jeffrey Fenton counted eleven hundred dead
bodies, and the country people told him, " the like was
to be seen in other places." Sir William Fitzwilliam
saw broken timber from the wrecks lying between Sligo
and Ballyshannon "sufficient to have built five of the
largest ships in the world," besides masts and spars and
cordage, and boats bottom uppermost. Among the vessels which went ashore at this spot to form part of the
ruin which Fitzwilliam was looking upon was a galleon
belonging to the Levantine squadron, commanded by
Don Martin de Aranda, to whose charge Cuellar had been
committed when Bobadilla saved him from the yard-arm.
Don Martin, after an ineffectual struggle to double
Achill Island, had fallen off before the wind and had
anchored in Sligo Bay in a heavy sea with two other
galleons. There they lay for four days, from the first
to the fifth of September, when the gale rising their
cables parted, and all three drove on shore on a sandy
beach among the rocks. Nowhere in the world does the
sea break more violently than on that cruel, shelterless
strand. Two of the galleons went to pieces in an hour.
The soldiers and sailors, too weak to struggle, were most
of them rolled in the surf till they were dead and then
washed up upon the shingle. Gentlemen and servants,
nobles and common seamen, shared the same fate.
Cuellar's ship had broken in two, but the forecastle held

a little longer together than the rest, and Cuellar, clinging to it, watched his comrades being swept away and
destroyed before his eyes. The wild Irish were down
in hundreds stripping the bodies. Those who had come
on shore with life in them fared no better. Some were
knocked on the head, others had their clothes torn off
and were left naked to perish of cold. Don Diego Enriquez, a high-born patrician, passed, with the Conde de
Villafranca and sixty-five others, into his ship's tender,
carrying bags of ducats and jewels. They went below
and fastened down the hatchway, hoping to be rolled
alive on land. A huge wave turned the tender bottom
upward, and all who were in it were smothered. As
the tide went back the Irish came with their axes and
broke a hole open in search of plunder; while Cuellar
looked on speculating how soon the same fate would be
his own, and seeing the corpses of his comrades dragged
out, stripped naked, and left to the wolves. His own
turn came at last. He held on to the wreck till it was
swept away, and he found himself in the water with a
brother officer who had stuffed his pockets full of gold.
He could not swim, but he caught a scuttle board as it
floated by him and climbed up upon it. His companion
tried to follow, but was washed off and drowned. Cuellar, a few minutes later, was tossed ashore, his leg
badly cut by a blow from a spar in the surf. Drenched
and bleeding as he was, he looked a miserable figure.
The Irish, who were plundering the better dressed of the
bodies, took no notice of him. He crawled along till
he found a number of his countrymen who had been left
with nothing but life, bare to their skins, and huddled
together for warmth. Cuellar, who had still his clothes,
though of course drenched, lay down among some
rushes. A gentleman, worse off than he, for he was en-

tirely naked, threw himself at his side too spent to speak.
Two Irishmen came by with axes who, to Cuellar's surprise, cut some bushes, which they threw over them for a
covering, and went on to join in the pillage on the shore.
Cuellar, half dead from cold and hunger, fell asleep. He
was woke by a troop of English horsemen galloping by
for a share in the spoil. He called his comrade, but
found him dead, while all round the crows and wolves
were busy over the naked carcasses. Something like a
monastery was visible not far off. Cuellar limped along
till he reached it. He found it deserted. The roof of
the chapel had been lately burned. The images of the
saints lay tumbled on the ground. In the nave twelve
Spaniards were hanging from the rafters. The monks
had fled to the mountains.

Sick at the ghastly spectacle, he crept along a path
through a wood, when he came upon an old woman who
was hiding her cattle from the English. Her cabin was
not far distant, but she made signs to him to keep off,
as there were enemies in occupation there. Wandering
hopelessly on, he fell in with two of his countrymen,
naked and shivering. They were all famished, and they
went back together to the sea, hoping to find some fragments of provisions washed on land. On the way they
came on the body of Don Enriquez and stopped to
scrape a hole in the sand and bury it. While they were
thus employed a party of Irish came up, who pointed to
a cluster of cabins and intimated that if they went there
they would be taken care of. Cuellar was dead lame.
His companions left him. At the first cottage which he
reached, there was an old Irish " savage," an Englishman, a Frenchman, and a girl. The Englishman struck
at him with a knife and gave him a second wound. They
stripped him to his shirt, took a gold chain from

him, which they found concealed under it, and a purse of ducats. They would have left him *en cueros*, like the rest, without a rag upon him, had not the girl interposed, who affected to be a Christian, " though she was no more a Christian than Mahomet." The Frenchman proved to be an old sailor who had fought at Terceira. In him the Spanish captain found some human kindness, for he bound up his leg for him and gave him some oatcakes with butter and milk. The Frenchman then pointed to a ridge of distant mountains. There, he said, was the country of the O'Rourke, a great chief, who was a friend of the King of Spain. O'Rourke would take care of him ; many of his comrades had already gone thither for protection. With his strength something restored by the food, Cuellar crawled along, stick in hand. At night he stopped at a hut where there was a lad who could speak Latin. This boy talked with him, gave him supper and a bundle of straw to sleep upon. About midnight the boy's father and brother came in, loaded with plunder from the wrecks. They, too, did him no hurt, and sent him forward in the morning with a pony and a guide. English soldiers were about, sent, as he conjectured, probably with truth, to kill all the Spaniards that they could fall in with. The first party that he met did not see him. With the second he was less fortunate. His guide saved his life by some means which Cuellar did not understand. But they beat him and took his shirt from him, the last of his garments that had been left. The boy and pony went off, and he thought then that the end was come and prayed God to finish with him and take him to His mercy. Forlorn as he was, however, he rallied his courage, picked up a piece of old matting, and with this and some plaited ferns made a shift to

cover himself; thus costumed he went on to a hamlet at
the side of a lake; the hovels of which it consisted were
all empty; he entered the best-looking of them, found
some fagots of oat-straw, and was looking about for a
place to sleep among them, when three naked figures
sprang suddenly up. He took them for devils, and in his
extraordinary dress they thought the same of him; but
they proved to have belonged to the wrecked galleons;
one of them a naval officer, the other two soldiers.
They explained mutually who they were, and then
buried themselves in the oat-sheaves and slept. They
remained there for warmth and concealment all the
next day. At night, having wrapped themselves in
straw, they walked on till they reached the dominions
of the chief to whom they had been directed. O'Rourke
himself was absent " fighting the English," but his wife
took them in, fed them, and allowed them to stay. As
a particular favor she bestowed an old cloak upon
Cuellar, which he found, however, to be swarming with
lice.   The hospitality was not excessive.   A report
reached him that a Spanish ship had put into Killybegs
Harbor, was refitting for sea, and was about to sail. He
hurried down to join her, but she was gone. He learned
afterward that she had been wrecked and that all on
board had perished.

He was now like a hunted wolf.   The English deputy
had issued orders that every Spaniard in the country
must be given up to the Government.   The Irish did not
betray Cuellar, but they did not care to risk their necks
by giving him shelter, and he wandered about through
the winter in Sligo and Donegal, meeting with many
strange adventures.   His first friend was a poor priest,
who was performing his functions among the Irish, in
spite of the law, disguised as a layman.   From this man

he met with help. He worked next as a journeyman
with a blacksmith, whose wife was a brute. The priest
delivered him from these people, and carried him to a
castle, which, from the description, appears to have been
on Lough Erne, and here, for the first time he met with
hearty hospitality, in the Irish understanding of the
term. The owner of the castle was a gentleman. He
recognized an ally in every enemy of England. He took
Cuellar into his troop of retainers, and dressed him in
the saffron mantle of the Irish gallowglass. For some
weeks he was now permitted to rest and recover himself,
and he spent the time in learning the manners of the
people. The chief's wife was beautiful, unlike the
blacksmith's, and the handsome and unfortunate Spanish officer was an interesting novelty. Besides the lady
there were other girls in the castle, who came about him
perhaps too ardently, asked him a thousand questions,
and at length insisted that he should examine their
hands and tell their fortunes. He had learned palmistry
from the gypsies in his own land. His invention was
ready. He spoke Latin, which they could understand,
and he gathered from their lips broken fragments of
their own Irish. At length, with his art and his attrac-
tiveness, he gives the reader to understand that he was
inconveniently popular ; men and women persecuted
him with demands and attentions, and he had to throw
himself on the protection of the chief himself. He describes the habits and character of the people as if he
was writing of a fresh discovered island in the New
World.

They lived, he said, like mere savages about the mountains. Their dwelling-places were thatched hovels. The
men were large-limbed, well-shaped, and light as stags
(sueltos como corzos). They took but one meal a day,

and that at night. Their chief food was oatmeal and butter; their drink sour milk, for want of anything better, and never water, though they had the best in the world. The usquebaugh Cuellar does not mention. On feast days they dined on underdone boiled meat, which they ate without bread or salt. The costume of the men was a pair of tight-fitting breeches with a goatskin jacket; over this a long mantle. Their hair they wore low over their eyes. They were strong on their legs, could walk great distances, and were hardy and enduring. They, or such of them as he had known, paid no obedience to the English. They were surrounded by swamps and bogs, which kept the English at a distance, and there was constant war between the races. Even among themselves they were famous thieves. They robbed from each other, and every day there was fighting. If one of them knew that his neighbor had sheep or cow, he would be out at night to steal it, and kill the owner. Occasionally a fortunate robber would have collected large herds and flocks, and then the English would come down on him, and he had to fly to the hills with wife, and children, and stock. Sheep and cattle were their only form of property. They had no clothes and no furniture. They slept on the ground on a bed of rushes, cut fresh as they wanted them, wet with rain or stiff with frost. The women were pretty, but ill-dressed. A shift or a mantle, and a handkerchief knotted in front over the forehead, made their whole toilet; and on the women was thrown all the homework, which, after a fashion, they managed to do. The Irish professed to be Christians. Mass was said after the Roman rule. Their churches and houses of religion had been destroyed by the English, or by such of their own countrymen as had joined the English. In short, they were a wild, lawless race, and everyone did as he liked. They wished well to the Spaniards because they knew them to be enemies of the English heretics, and had it not been for the friendliness which they had shown, not one of those who had come on shore would have survived. It was true at first they plundered and stripped them naked, and fine spoils they got out of the thirteen galleons which were wrecked in that part of the country; but as soon as they saw that the Spaniards were being killed by the English, they began to take care of them.

Such was Cuellar's general picture, very like what was drawn by the intruding Saxon, and has been denounced as calumny. Cuellar was, at any rate, impartial, and rather liked his hosts than otherwise. The Lord Deputy was alarmed at the number of fugitives who were said to be surviving. As the orders to surrender them had not been attended to, he collected a force in Dublin and went in person into the West to enforce obedience. Cuellar's entertainer had been especially menaced, and had to tell his guests that he could help them no further. He must leave his castle and retreat himself with his family into the mountains, and the Spaniards must take care of themselves. Cuellar calls the castle Manglana; local antiquaries may be able to identify the spot. It stood on a promontory projecting into a long, deep, and broad lake, and was covered on the land side by a swamp. It could not be taken without boats or artillery, and the Spaniards offered to remain and defend it if the chief would leave them a few muskets and powder, with food for a couple of months. There were nine of them. The chief agreed, and let them have what they wanted; and, unless Cuellar lies, he and his friends held "Manglana" for a fortnight against a force of eighteen hundred English, when God came to their help by sending such weather that the enemy could not any longer keep the field.

The chief, finding the value of such auxiliaries, wished to keep them permanently at his side, and offered Cuellar his sister for a wife. Cuellar, however, was longing for home. He supposed that if he could reach Scotland he could cross easily from thence to Flanders. One night after Christmas he slipped away and made for Antrim, travelling, seemingly, only in the dark, and hiding during day. He was in constant danger, as the tracks were watched, and suspected persons were seized and searched. He got as far as the Giant's Causeway; there he heard particulars of the wreck of the ship which he had tried to join at Killybegs. It was a galeass with Alonzo de Leyva on board and two or three hundred others with him. They were all dead, and Cuellar saw the relics of them which the people had collected on the shore. Alonzo de Leyva was the best loved of all the Spaniards in the fleet, and the sight of the spot where he had perished was a fresh distress. He was afraid to approach a port lest he should be seized and hanged. For six weeks he was hid away by some women, and after that by a bishop, who was a good Christian, though dressed like a savage. This bishop had a dozen Spaniards with him, fed, clothed, and said Mass for them, and at last found a boat to carry them across the Channel. They went, and after a three days' struggle with the sea contrived to land in Argyllshire. They had been led to hope for help from James. Cuellar says that they were entirely mistaken. James never gave them a bawbee, and would have handed them over to the English if he had not been afraid of the resentment of the Scotch Catholic nobles. The Calvinist Lowlanders showed them scanty hospitality. The

Prince of Parma was informed of their condition, and agreed with a Flemish merchant to bring over to him all the Spaniards, now numerous, who were on Scotch soil, at five ducats a head. Even yet misfortune had not tired of persecuting them. In their passage they were chased and fired on by a Dutch frigate. They had to run ashore, where they were intercepted by the Hollanders, and all but Cuellar and two of his companions were killed.

So ends the Spanish captain's story. The wide calamities involving multitudes are but the aggregate of the sufferings of each individual of whom the multitude is composed. Cuellar came off luckily compared with most of his companions. Each of the twenty-nine thousand men who sailed in July from Corunna would have had to relate a tale of misery at least as pitiful as his, and the worst of all was, that no one's neck was wrung for it.

The sixty galleons who remained with the Duke till the end of August were parted again by a southwesterly gale, off the point of Kerry. The Duke himself passed so far out to sea that he did not see the Irish coast at all. Recalde, with two large ships besides his own, had come round Dunmore Head, near the land. His crews were dying for want of water. He seems to have known Dingle. Dr. Sanders, with the Pope's contingent, had landed there eight years before, and a statement in an account of Recalde's life that he had once carried a thousand men to the coast of Ireland, refers probably to that occasion. At all events, he was aware that there was a harbor in Dingle Bay, and he made for it with his consorts. One of them, Our Lady of the Rosary, was wrecked in Blasket Sound. She carried seven hundred men when she sailed out of Lisbon. Two hundred out of the seven were alive in her when she struck the rock, and every one of them perished, save a single lad. Recalde, with the other galleon, anchored in the Dingle estuary, and sent in to the town a passionate entreaty to be allowed to fill his water-casks. The fate of the Papal troops, who had been all executed a few miles off, had so frightened the Irish there that they did not dare to consent. The English account states that Recalde had to sail as he was, to live or die. The belief in Spain was that he took the water that he wanted by force. Perhaps the inhabitants were not entirely inhuman, and did not interfere. He saved the lives for the moment of the wretched men under his charge, though most of them perished when they reached their homes ; he brought back his ship to Corunna, and there died himself two days after his arrival, worn out by shame and misery.

Oquendo also reached Spain alive. The persevering west winds drove him down the Bay of Biscay, and he made his way into St. Sebastian, where he had a wife and children ; but he refused to see them ; he shut himself into a solitary room, turned his face to the wall, and ended like Recalde, unable to outlive the disgrace of the gallant navy which he had led so often into victory. They had done all that men could do. On the miserable day when their commander decided to turn his back and fly they would have forced him upon a more honorable course, and given the forlorn adventure an issue less utterly ignominious. But their advice had been rejected. They had sailed away from an enemy whose strength at most was not greater than theirs. They had escaped from a battle with a human foe to a more fatal war with the elements, and they had seen their comrades perish round them, victims of folly and weakness.

The tremendous catastrophe broke their hearts, and they lay down and died. Oquendo's Capitana had been blown up after the fight at Plymouth. By a strange fatality the ship which brought him home blew up also in the harbor at St. Sebastian. The explosion may have been the last sound which reached his failing sense. The stragglers came in one by one; sixty-five ships only of the hundred and thirty who, in July, had sailed out of Corunna full of hope and enthusiasm. In those hundred and thirty had been twenty-nine thousand human creatures, freshly dedicated to what they called the service of their Lord. Nine or ten thousand only returned; a ragged remnant, shadows of themselves, sinking under famine and fever and scurvy, which carried them off like sheep with the rot. When they had again touched Spanish soil, a wail of grief rose over the whole peninsula, as of Rachel weeping for her children; yet above it all rose the cry, Where was Alonzo de Leyva? Where was the flower of Spanish chivalry? Cuellar knew his fate; but Cuellar was with his Irish chief far away. Weeks, even months, passed before certain news arrived, and rumor invented imaginary glories for him. He had rallied the missing galleons, he had fallen in with Drake, had beaten and captured him, and had sunk half the English fleet. Vain delusion! De Leyva, like Oquendo and Recalde, had done all which could be done by man, and God had not interposed to help him. He had fought his Rata Coronada till her spars were shot away and her timbers pierced like a sieve. She became waterlogged in the gales on the Irish coast. A second galleon and a surviving galeass were in his company. The Rata and the galleon drove ashore. De Leyva, in the galeass, made Killybegs Harbor, and landed there with fourteen hundred men. It was the country of the O'Neil. They

were treated with the generous warmth which became
the greatest of the Irish chieftains. But their presence
was known in Dublin. O'Neil was threatened, and De
Leyva honorably refused to be an occasion of danger to
him. He repaired the galeass at Killybegs. The October weather appeared to have settled at last, and he
started again with as many of his people as the galeass
would carry to make the coast of Scotland. She had
passed round the north of Donegal, she had kept
along the land and had almost reached the Giant's
Causeway, when she struck a rock and went to pieces,
and De Leyva and his companions went the way of the
rest.

The men who came back seemed as if they had been
smitten by a stroke from which they could not rally.
One of them describes pathetically the delight with
which, after those desperate storms, and hunger and
cold and thirst, they felt the warmth of the Spanish sun
again ; saw Spanish grapes in the gardens at Santander,
and the fruit hanging on the trees ; had pure bread to
eat and pure water to drink. But the change brought
no return of health. For the first weeks they were left
on board their ships, no preparation on shore having
been made to receive them. When the mortality was
found rather to increase than diminish, they were moved
to hospitals, but they died still by hundreds daily, as if
destiny or Providence was determined to sweep off the
earth every innocent remnant of the shattered expedition, while those who were really to blame escaped un-
punished.

Medina Sidonia had been charged by Philip to report
his progress to him as often as messengers could be
sent off. He had written when off the Lizard before
his first contact with the enemy. He had written again

on August 21 among the Atlantic rollers, when he believed that he was bringing home his charge at least safe if not victorious. On September 22 he arrived at Santander, and on the 23d reported briefly the close of the tragedy so far as it was then known to him. The weather, he said, had been terrible since he last wrote. Sixty-one vessels were then with him. They had held tolerably well together till September 18, when they were caught in another gale, and fifty of them had gone he knew not where. Eleven only had remained with himself. They had made the coast near Corunna, and had signalled for help, but none had come off. They had then struggled on to Santander and were lying there at anchor. He had himself gone on shore, being broken down by suffering. The miseries which they had experienced had exceeded the worst that had ever before been heard of. In some ships there had not been a drop of water for fourteen days. A hundred and eighty of the crew of the San Martin had died, the rest were down with putrid fever. Of his personal attendants all were dead but two. There was not food enough left on board for those who were alive to last two days. The Duke "blessed the Lord for all that He had ordained;" but prayed the King to see instantly to their condition, and to send them money, for they had not a maravedi in the fleet. He was himself too ill to do anything. There was no person whose duty it was to help them, neither inspector, purveyor, nor paymaster. They could obtain nothing that they wanted. He had written to the Archbishop of Burgos for assistance in establishing a hospital.*

The opinion in Spain was savagely hostile to the Duke.

---

* The Duke of Medina Sidonia to Philip, September 23, from Santander.

It was thought that if he had possessed the feelings of
a gentleman, he would have died of the disgrace like
Oquendo and Recalde. The Duke, so far from feeling
that he was himself to blame, considered that he above
the rest had most reason to complain of having been
forced into a position which he had not sought and for
which he had protested his unfitness. Being Lord High
Admiral, his business was to remain with the fleet, however ill he might be, till some other responsible officer
could be sent to relieve him. His one desire was to
escape from the sight of ships and everything belonging
to them, and hide himself and recover his spirits in his
palace at San Lucar. Not Sancho, when he left his isl-
and, could be in greater haste to rid himself of his office
and all belonging to it.

On September 27, before an answer could arrive from
Philip, he wrote again to Secretary Idiaquez. Almost
all the sailors were dead, he said. Many of the ships
were dismasted ; no one could believe the state in which
they were. Idiaquez must look to it. For himself, his
health was broken ; he was unfit for further duty, and
even if he was perfectly well he would never go on ship-
board again. He was absolutely without any knowledge
either of navigation or of war, and the King could have
no object in forcing him to continue in a service from
which the State could derive no possible advantage. He
begged that he might be thought of no more in connection with the navy, and that, since the Lord had not
been pleased to call him to that vocation, he might not
be compelled to return in a situation of which he could
not, as he had many times explained, conscientiously
discharge the duties. His Majesty, he said, could not
surely wish the destruction of a faithful subject. With
sea affairs he neither could nor would meddle any fur-

ther, though it should cost him his head.* Better so than fail in an office of the duties of which he was ignorant, and where he had to be guided by the advice of others, in whose honesty of intention he could feel no confidence.

The last allusion was of course to Diego Florez, on whom, since it was necessary to punish someone, the blame was allowed to fall. In justice, if justice was to have a voice in the matter, the person really guilty was Don Philip. Of the subordinates, Diego Florez was probably the most in fault, and he was imprisoned in the Castle of Burgos. For the rest, Philip was singularly patient, his conscience perhaps telling him that if he was to demand a strict account he would have to begin with himself. The popular story of the composure with which he heard of the fate of the Armada is substantially true, though rather too dramatically pointed. The awful extent of the catastrophe became known to him only by degrees, and the end of Alonzo de Leyva, which distressed him most of all, he only heard of at Christmas.

To the Duke's letter he replied quietly and affectionately, without a syllable of reproach. Unlike Elizabeth, who left the gallant seamen who had saved her throne to die of want and disease in the streets of Margate, and had to be reminded that the pay of those who had been killed in her service was still due to their relations, Philip ordered clothes, food, medicine, everything that was needed, to be sent down in hottest haste to Corunna and Santander. The widows and orphans of the dead sailors and soldiers were sought out and pensioned at the cost of the State. To Medina Sidonia he

* "En las cosas de la mer, por ningun caso ni por alguna via trataré dellas, aunque me costase la cabeza."

sent the permission which the Duke had asked for, to leave the fleet and go home. He could not in fairness have blamed the commander-in-chief for having failed in a situation for which he had protested his incompetence. The fault of Philip as a king and statesman was a belief in his own ability to manage things. In sending out the Armada he had set in motion a mighty force, not intending it to be used mightily, but that he might accomplish with it what he regarded as a master-stroke of tame policy. He had selected Medina Sidonia as an instrument who would do what he was told and would make no rash experiments. And the effect was to light a powder-magazine which blew to pieces the naval power of Spain. It is to his credit, however, that he did not wreak his disappointment upon his instruments, and endured patiently what had befallen him as the Will of God. The Will of God, indeed, created a difficulty. The world had been informed so loudly that the Armada was going on the Lord's work, the prayers of the Church had been so long and so enthusiastic, and a confidence in what the Lord was to do had been generated so universally, that when the Lord had not done it, there was at once a necessity for acknowledging the judgment, and embarrassment in deciding the terms in which the truth was to be acknowledged. Philip's formal piety provided a solution which might have been missed by a more powerful intellect, and on October 13 the following curious letter was addressed by him to the bishops and archbishops throughout his dominions:

"Most Reverend :—The uncertainties of naval enterprises are well known, and the fate which has befallen the Armada is an instance in point. You will have already heard that the Duke of Medina Sidonia has returned to Santander, bringing back with him part of the fleet. Others of the ships have reached various ports, some of them having suffered severely from their long and arduous voyage. We are bound to give praise to God for all things which He is pleased to do. I on the present occasion have given thanks to Him for the mercy which He has shown. In the foul weather and violent storms to which the Armada has been exposed, it might have experienced a worse fate; and that the misfortune has not been heavier is no doubt due to the prayers which have been offered in its behalf so devoutly and continuously.

"These prayers must have entailed serious expense and trouble on those who have conducted them. I wish you, therefore, all to understand that while I am, so far, well pleased with your exertions, they may now cease. You may wind up in the cathedrals and churches of your dioceses with a solemn Thanksgiving Mass on any day which you may appoint, and for the future I desire all ecclesiastics and other devout persons to continue to commend my actions to the Lord in their secret devotions, that He may so direct them as shall be for His own service, the exaltation of His Church, the welfare and safety of Christendom, which are the objects always before me.

"From the Escurial: October 13, 1588.*

Medina Sidonia reconsidered his resolution to have no more to do with ships and fighting. He was continued in his office of Lord High Admiral; he was again appointed Governor of Cadiz, and he had a second opportunity of measuring himself against English seamen, with the same result as before. Essex went into Cadiz in 1596, as Drake had gone in 1587. The Duke acted in the same manner, and withdrew to Seville to seek for reinforcements. He ventured back only after the

---

* Duro, vol. ii., p. 314.

English had gone, and was again thanked by his master
for his zeal and courage. As if this was not enough,
Philip, in 1598, raised him to the rank of Consejero
altísimo de Estado y Guerra, Supreme Councillor in
Politics and War. Who can wonder that under such a
king the Spanish Empire went to wreck?

The people were less enduring. Clamors were raised
that he had deserted the fleet at Santander, that he had
shown cowardice in action, that he had neglected the
counsels of his wisest admirals, that he was as heartless
as he was incapable, and that, leaving the seamen and
soldiers to die, he had hastened home to his luxuries at
San Lucar. In reality he had gone with the King's permission, because he was useless and was better out of
the way. He was accused of having carried off with him
a train of mules loaded with ducats. He had told Philip
that he had not brought home a maravedi, and if he had
really taken money he would have done it less ostenta-
tiously and with precautions for secrecy.

But nothing could excuse him to Spain. Every calumny found credit. He had shown "cobardia y con-
tinual pavor y miedo de morir, avaricia, dureza y cru-
eldad"—cowardice, constant terror, and fear of death,
avarice, harshness, and cruelty. His real faults were
enough without piling others on him of which he was
probably innocent. With or without his will, he had
been in the thickest and hottest parts of the hardest
engagements, and the San Martin had suffered as
severely as any ship in the fleet. He knew nothing of
the work which he was sent to do ; that is probably the
worst which can justly be said of him ; and he had not
sought an appointment for which he knew that he was
unfit. But an officer who tried to defend him was
obliged to admit that it would have been happy for his

country if the Duke had never been born ; that he threw away every chance which was offered him, and that he talked and consulted when acts and not words were wanted.

His journey home across Castile was a procession of ignominy. The street boys in Salamanca and Medina del Campo pelted him with stones ; crowds shouted after him " A las gallinas, á las almadradas "—" To the hens and the tunnies "—the tunnies being the fattest and the most timid of fish, and the tunny fishing being a monopoly of his dukedom. He was told that he had disgraced his illustrious ancestors, and that had he the spirit of a man he would not have outlived his shame.

History does not record the reception which he met with from his wife when he reached his palace.

ANTONIO PEREZ: AN UNSOLVED HISTORICAL RIDDLE *

ONE day early in the spring of the year 1590, while
Spain was still bleeding from the destruction of the
Great Armada, Mass was being sung in the Church of
the Dominican Convent at Madrid. The candles were
burning, the organ was pealing, the acolytes were swinging the censers, and the King's confessor was before the
altar in his robes, when a woman, meanly dressed, rushed
forward amid the fumes of the incense. Turning to
the priest, she said: "Justice! I demand justice; I demand that you hear me! Are you deaf, that I come so
often to you and you will not listen? Then I appeal to
One who will listen; I appeal to thee my God who art
here present; I call on God to be my witness and my
judge; He knows the wrongs which I suffer. Let Him
punish yonder man, who is my oppressor."

The confessor turned pale as death. He stood speech-
less for a few moments. He then beckoned to the attendants. "Bid the lady prioress come hither," he said,
"and the sisterhood, and this woman's sister, who is one
of them. Say I require their presence."

The lady mother came fluttering with her flock behind
her. They gathered to the grating which divided the
chancel from the convent precincts.

"Holy mother," the confessor said, "this lady here
present charges me on my soul and conscience. She calls

* Nineteenth Century, April, May, 1883.

on God to judge her cause, and she clamors for redress. I do not wonder ; I should wonder rather if she held her peace. But what can I do that I have left undone ? I have told the King that it is his duty to despatch the business of the lady's husband and restore him to his family ; what would she have from me more ? "

" I would have this much more, señor," the lady replied. " If the King will not do what you command him, refuse him absolution and withdraw to your cell. You will be nearer heaven there, than where you now stand. As the King's confessor you are his judge. The King is the offender ; I am the injured woman of St. Luke's Gospel. The King may wear the crown on his head ; but you are higher than he."

The confessor could not answer her.

The scene shifts to the reception - hall of Rodrigo Vasquez, the President of the High Court of Justice. The president was a grave, dignified man, seventy years old. Before him stood a family of children, the eldest a girl of sixteen, the little ones holding her hands or clinging to her dress.

The girl did not seem daunted by the presence in which she stood. "Your lordship," she said, "has promised us this, that, and the other ; you tell us one day that something shall be done on the morrow, and then the next, and the next, as if a last 'morrow' there would never be. You have brought our home to desolation. You have deceived a girl like me, and you think it a grand victory, a glorious distinction. You thirst, it seems, for our blood ; well, then, you shall have it. Old men, it is said, go again to the breast for milk to keep the life in them. You require blood, fresh from the veins of its owners. We had rather not be swallowed piecemeal, so we are come all to you together. You per-

haps would prefer to linger over us, but we cannot wait.
Let your lordship make an end with us.   Here we are."

Don Rodrigo started out of his chair.   He marched up
the hall, and down, and then to the four corners.   He
twisted his fingers, he crossed his arms.   He appealed
to an old aunt and uncle who had brought the children.

"Señora, señor," he said, "I beseech you make that
young woman hold her peace and say no more."

The young woman would not hold her peace.

"Pray, sit down, your lordship," she said ; "pray, be
calm.   We are young ; some of us were born, so to say,
but yesterday.   But you have made our lives a burden
to us.   Finish the work ; take our blood, and let our
souls depart from this miserable prison."

These two incidents, if the children's father wrote the
truth, happened precisely as I have described them, and
are as literal facts as usually pass for history.   Perhaps
they are not exaggerated at all.   The priest in the
Dominican convent was Diego de Chaves, spiritual adviser to Philip the Second.   The woman before the altar
was Juana de Coello, wife of Antonio Perez, his Majesty's
Secretary of State and confidential minister.   The girl
in the Court of Justice was his daughter, Doña Gregoria,
and the little ones were her brothers and sisters.

What strange cause could have wrought a mother and
child into a state of passion so unnatural ?

For three centuries after the Reformation, Philip the
Second was the evil demon of Protestant tradition.   Every
action which could be traced to him was ascribed to the
darkest motives.   He was like some ogre or black enchanter sitting in his den in the Escurial, weaving plots
for the misery of mankind, in close communion and correspondence with his master, the Antichrist of Rome.
He was the sworn enemy of the light which was rising

over Europe ; he was the assassin of his subjects abroad ;
he was a tyrant at home, and even in his own household ;
he was believed universally to have murdered his own
son, and if not to have murdered his wife, to have driven
her to death with a broken heart. The Inquisition was
his favorite instrument, and his name has been handed
down through modern history by the side of the most
detestable monsters who ever disgraced a throne.

All this violence of censure was perfectly natural.
Men engaged in a deadly struggle for what they regard
as a sacred cause are seldom charitable to their adver-
saries. It was the Spanish power indisputably which
stemmed the Reformation, and more than once was near
extinguishing it. The conflict was desperate and at last
savage, and deeds were done which have left a stain on
all who were concerned in them.

But as time has gone on, and as it has appeared that
neither Lutheranism nor Calvinism nor Anglicanism can
be regarded as a final revelation, we have been able to
review the history of the sixteenth century in a calmer
temper. For a thousand years the doctrines of the
Catholic Church had been guarded by the civil power as
the most precious of human possessions. New ideas on
such subjects, shaking as they do the foundations of
human society, may be legitimately resisted on their
first appearance from better motives than hatred of
truth ; and although, in a strife so protracted and so
deadly, evil passions dressed themselves in sacred
colors, and crimes were committed which we may legitimately assign to the devil, yet it has been recognized
that, on fair grounds of principle, right-thinking men
might naturally have taken opposite sides, and that
Catholics as well as Protestants might have been acting
on conscientious convictions. The dust has settled a

little, the spiritual atmosphere has cleared itself, and among the consequences the cloud which hung over Philip the Second has partially lifted. The countrymen of Cervantes were not a nation of mere bigots; yet it is clear that the whole Spanish people went with the King enthusiastically in defence of the Church, and complained only when his *pié de plomo*, his foot of lead that he was so proud of, would not move fast enough. The romance of Don Carlos has gone into the air of which it was made. Don Carlos is known now to have been a dangerous lunatic, whom it was necessary to cage like a wild animal; the exact manner of his death is unknown; but his father acted throughout by the advice of the Council of State, and it was by their advice also that so distressing a secret was concealed from public curiosity. As we look at Philip with more impartial attention, the figure comes out before us of a painstaking, laborious man, prejudiced, narrow-minded, superstitious, with a conceit of his own abilities not uncommon in crowned heads, and frequently with less justification, but conscientious from his own point of view, and not without the feelings of a gentleman.

I purpose to reconstruct on these more tolerant lines the story of the relations between Philip the Second and Antonio Perez which have so long perplexed historical inquirers—on the surface a mere palace intrigue, but developing from its peculiar features into a nine days' wonder throughout Europe, and occasioning, if not causing, the overthrow of the constitutional liberties of Aragon.

Students of the history of the sixteenth century must be familiar with the name of Gonzalo Perez. He was State Secretary to Charles the Fifth, and his signature stands at the bottom of the page on thousands of Charles's despatches which are now extant. When the Emperor abdicated, Gonzalo remained in office with Philip, and had been forty years in the public service when he died. Antonio Perez passed as Gonzalo's natural son. He was born in 1542, and was legitimatized immediately by an imperial diploma. There were those who said, and spoke of it as notorious, that Antonio was not Gonzalo's son at all, but the son of Ruy Gomez, Prince of Eboli and Duke of Pastraña, Philip's favorite minister. Ruy Gomez, at any rate, took charge of the boy, removed him from school, brought him up in his own family, and introduced him into a public department. Being quick and brilliant, he was rapidly promoted; and when Ruy Gomez died in 1567 he left Antonio, at the age of twenty-five, chief secretary to the Council of State, with a salary of four thousand ducats a year, in addition to which, and as a sinecure, he was Protonotary of Sicily with two thousand ducats a year. A rise so swift implied extraordinary private influence, or extraordinary personal qualities; and this was but the beginning of his fortunes. On losing Ruy Gomez, Philip took Perez as his own confidential secretary; and along with him another youth, Juan de Escovedo, who had also been a pupil of Ruy Gomez, and had been brought up at Perez's side. The two young men had been, and still continued, intimate personal friends.

The Spanish administration was divided into separate councils, the secretaries of which were each in close relation with the King, who insisted on knowing all that was going on. Besides these there were the secretaries who deciphered despatches, who were thus admitted into State mysteries, and were necessarily treated with confidence. But of the whole number Antonio Perez and Escovedo were nearest to the King, and Perez the closer of the two. He and he alone was admitted into the interior labyrinths of Philip's mind.

He was thus a person of extraordinary consequence. He was courted by great men in Church and State. The Italian princes sent him presents to advance their interests. He was the dispenser of royal favors. He treated dukes as his equals, and the splendor in which he lived was envied and criticised ; but his legitimate income was considerable ; in all countries in that age influential statesmen accepted homage in the shape of offerings ; and, considering the opportunities the favored secretary had, he does not seem to have exceptionally abused them.

Perez being thus upon the stage, we introduce a more considerable figure, Don John of Austria, the King's brother, illegitimate son of Charles the Fifth. An illegitimate prince is always in a delicate position, especially when his father happens to have brought him up as a real one. He is of royal blood, but without the rights belonging to it. He is uncertain of his rank, and may generally be presumed to be discontented. But Philip had shown no suspicion of his brother. He had trusted him, employed him, refused him no opportunities which he could have desired had he come more regularly into the world. Don John was ˙chivalrous, ardent, ambitious. He had every quality which promised distinction, if in his youth he had been wisely guided. Ruy Gomez had furnished him with a secretary supposed to be prudence itself, Juan de Soto, who had been trained in the War Office. Thus accompanied when the Moors broke into insurrection, Don John was sent to Granada to reduce them. He did his work well ; he became a popular favorite, and went next to command the allied Catholic fleet in the Mediterranean. De Soto only had given imperfect satisfaction. Don John had high-flying views for himself, and De Soto, it was feared, had not sufficiently discouraged them. Perez and Escovedo were instructed to give him an admonition, which they did, and with this friendly warning Don John and his secretary went their way into Italy. The battle of Lepanto followed, and the young irregular Spanish prince blazed out into a hero of romance. Philip was a faithful son of the Church, and of the Pope in his spiritual capacity ; but he was King of Naples and Sicily, with interests in the Peninsula not always identical with the interests of the court of Rome. Pius the Fifth, who had just then absolved England from its allegiance to Queen Elizabeth and believed it his mission to sweep away heresy, found in Don John a child much nearer to his heart. Don John was to be the Church's knight, the chosen soldier of the Lord, and immediately after Lepanto Pius had formed views for constituting him an independent sovereign. Tunis was to be the first scene of his greatness. The Emperor Charles had won immortal glory in his African campaign. De Soto had studied history and dreamt of the possibility of reviving the Carthaginian empire. Don John, set on by the Pope, refortified the Goleta, and transported on his own authority, out of Italy, the best part of the Spanish troops there, while the Papal Nuncio at Madrid requested Philip in Pope Pius's name to allow his brother to take the title of King of Tunis. The Spanish council knew better than his Holiness the value of the Emperor's African conquests. They had been a drain upon the treasury and the grave of thousands of their bravest men. Instead of indulging Don John they sent orders that the fortresses should be demolished and the troops withdrawn. But the order came too late. The Goleta

7

was assaulted by the Turks in overwhelming numbers, and the garrison was cut off to a man. Philip had good reason to be displeased. The independent action of a commander cannot expect to be regarded, when unsuccessful, with especial leniency, nor were matters mended by the signs which his brother was manifesting of a restless ambition. He replied politely to the Pope, however, that the establishment of a kingdom in Tunis was not at the time expedient. He found no fault with Don John, but laid the blame on bad advisers. He gently removed De Soto, leaving him as commissary-general of the army ; and secretary Escovedo, who had been especially eloquent in the cabinet on De Soto's rashness, was sent to take his place as a safer companion to the prince.

Philip, however, was again unfortunate. The mischance at the Goleta had not been sufficient to dim the glories of Lepanto, or cool the hopes which so brilliant a victory had inspired. Don John was still persuaded that there were great things in store for him. It seemed as if he had an especial power of turning the heads of the secretaries, and Escovedo himself was soon embarked with him in a yet wilder scheme, to which the Pope and the Fates were beckoning the way.

After a struggle of ten years with his revolted subjects in the Low Countries, experience was beginning to teach Philip that it might be expedient to try milder ways with them. The Duke of Alva with his blood and iron had succeeded only in enlisting the whole of the seventeen provinces in a common rebellion, and if the war continued, the not unlikely end of it would be that Spain would finally lose them all. Holland and Zealand might become English, Belgium be absorbed into France, and the rest drift away into Germany. Bitter

Catholic as he was, Philip had some qualities of a statesman. He had determined on an effort to make up the
quarrel. The provinces were to be left with their constitutional rights, securities being given for the safety
of religion. The Spanish army was to be withdrawn,
and by abandoning attempts at coercion he hoped that
it might not be too late to recover the hearts of the
people.

To carry out this purpose he had pitched upon his
brother Don John. The Emperor's memory was still
honored in the Low Countries. Charles had always
been more a Fleming than a Spaniard. Don John, with
his high rank and chivalrous reputation, was likely to
be welcome there, or at least more welcome than any
other person who could be selected ; and an opportunity was thrown in his way, if he could use it, of win-
ning laurels for himself more enduring than those which
grow on battle-fields.

The opportunity, however, was one which a wise
man only could appreciate. Young soldiers, especially
soldiers who have been distinguished in arms, are seldom in love with constitutions ; and to be governor at
Brussels, with a council of successful rebels to tie his
hands, was a situation which would have had no attrac-
tion for the victor of Lepanto, had there not been attached to it a more interesting possibility, the *empresa de
Inglaterra*, the invasion and conquest of England. Philip
himself had for a few years been called King of England. His name remains in our Statute Book. It was
asserted by the Jesuits, it was believed by nine-tenths
of the orthdox world, that the English Catholics, who
were two-thirds of the nation, were waiting only for
the help of a few thousand Spaniards to hurl from the
throne the excommunicated usurper. The Queen of

Scots, the Lady of Romance, was lying a prisoner in
Sheffield Castle.   To carry over the army when it left
the Netherlands, to land in Yorkshire, to deliver the
enchanted princess, and reign at her side with the
Pope's blessing over an England restored to the faith
—this was a glorious enterprise, fit to fire the blood of a
Christian knight who was also the countrymen of Don
Quixote.

Don John was still in Italy when the offer of the appointment was made.   If it was accepted, the King's
order to him was to proceed with his secretary directly
to Brussels without returning to Spain.   Not the pacification of Flanders, but the *empresa de Inglaterra* was
the thought which rushed into the minds of Don John
and Escovedo.   Instead of setting out as they were enjoined, they went to Rome to consult Pope Pius's successor, to ask for his sanction, to ask for men, to ask
for the title which had been borne by his brother, and
all this without so much as going through the form of
consulting his brother on the subject.

The Pope was of course delighted.   If the attempt
was made, God would not allow it to fail.   The Jesuits
had all along insisted that Philip's dilatoriness had alone
allowed heresy to take root in England.   Philip himself,
who knew something of the country, wasunder no such
illusion.   Five years before he had consented unwillingly to the Ridolfi conspiracy.   Elizabeth was then to
have been assassinated ; Spanish troops were to have
landed, and the Queen of Scots was to have had the
crown.   The end of this fine project had been the execution of the Duke of Norfolk, the near escape from
execution of Mary Stuart, a plague of pirates and privateers on the shores of Spanish America, and increased
severities against the English Catholics.   Of the Queen

of Scots Philip had the very worst opinion. To strike
a blow at that moment at Elizabeth could not fail to re-
exasperate the Low Countries. English soldiers would
land in Holland, English corsairs would swarm in the
Atlantic and seize his treasure ships.

None of these considerations occurred to Don John
or his fiery adviser. Escovedo was even hotter than his
master, and audacious even to insolence. From Rome,
in spite of his orders, he went to Madrid; and Don
John soon after followed him thither, leaving their purposes to reach Philip indirectly from another quarter.
This was in the summer of 1576, and we now approach
the critical part of the story. Shortly after Escovedo
arrived at the court, the Nuncio sent one morning for
Antonio Perez and inquired who a certain Escoda was.
He had been all night, he said, deciphering a despatch
from his Holiness. It referred to the "enterprise of
England" which was to be undertaken, if the king
would allow it, by Don John. Escoda would inform
him of the particulars.

"Escoda" could be no one but Escovedo. Perez carried his information to the King, who was again naturally
extremely dissatisfied; the more so perhaps that Don
John's popularity, and the general favor with which
Spanish sentiment was likely to take up the adventure,
obliged him to keep his displeasure to himself. Escovedo evidently thought himself secure. He addressed
Philip in so rude a letter that Philip complained of it to
Perez. "If he had spoken to me as he has written,"
the King said, "I believe I could not have contained
myself." Words still more rash had fallen from Escovedo's lips. "Don John, when master of England, was
afterward to take charge of Spain."

Philip, like most small-minded men, shrank from

meeting difficulties openly. He took no notice of Escovedo's impertinence, and he was afraid or unwilling to
quarrel with his brother. He allowed the Nuncio to
give him the Pope's message, and put him off with a
vague answer. Don John ventured on ground still more
delicate by asking for the "chair and canopy," the in-
signia of a legitimate prince of the blood royal. Even
this Philip did not refuse. He required only that Don
John should repair first to his government, compose the
provinces, and withdraw the army. When this was done
it would be time to think of "English enterprises" and
chairs and canopies.

Don John went, and it seemed as if all was smooth
again. Escovedo was left at Madrid professedly to complete some defective arrangements for his master. Perhaps Philip was uncertain whether he would trust so
doubtful an adviser at his brother's side any more.

I am not writing the history of the wars in the Netherlands; it is enough to say that any hopes which had
been built on the popularity of Don John were disappointed. The Estates refused to admit him as governor
while the Spanish troops were in the fortresses; the
troops were sullen, and would not move till they were
paid their wages. Don John wished to remove them by
sea, meaning, when they were in the Channel, to fly at
England permitted or unpermitted; but Elizabeth and
the Prince of Orange had their eyes open; the Estates
insisted that the army should retire by land, and declined to advance a dollar till they were on the march.
Don John, being without a friend whom he could trust,
begged that Escovedo might rejoin him; and Escovedo,
not without emphatic warnings and reiterated instructions, was allowed to go. The demands of the Estates
were to be complied with to the letter. The army, at

whatever sacrifice of bolder purposes, was to retire as
the Estates desired. Philip required peace and was prepared for the price that was to be paid for it. The
humiliation was too deep for Don John. For the knight
errant of the Church to retreat before a burgher council
was ignominy. Something, he knew not what, must be
done to repair it, and his thoughts went everywhere
except where they ought to have been. Escovedo had
no sooner arrived than a secret correspondence began
again with the Pope. The religious war was raging in
France. Don John might join the Duke of Guise and
the Catholic League, and they might manage England
between them. Then again he thought how he might
satisfy his ambition at home. On February 3, 1577,
Escovedo wrote to Perez to revive the request for the
chair and canopy. It would give Don John a seat in the
Council of State. He and Perez and their friends, the
Archbishop of Toledo and the Marques de los Velez,
could rule the country as they pleased, and relieve his
brother of the cares of government. On reflection he
perhaps remembered that Philip might not be so anxious
to be relieved ; for some days after the purpose was
changed ; Don John was to take his army into France
as an adventurer, and help the Duke of Guise to destroy
the Huguenots. Victorious there, he could hold the
Estates in check, the shame of the retreat would be
covered, and the "great design" on England could go
forward. Royal princes are excused their follies at the
expense of their servants. These feverish dreams were
set down at the Escurial to Escovedo's account, and
probably with excellent reason.

Meanwhile, Philip's orders were being obeyed. He
had agreed to all which the Estates demanded. On
February 12 the arrangement known as the "Perpetual

Edict" was provisionally accepted, and was forwarded to
Madrid for ratification. Don John was distracted. He
believed that he might write to Perez confidentially; for
Perez, by Philip's order, had encouraged him to suppose
so ; and much eloquence has been expended on the assumed treachery. But kings may be judged too harshly
in such matters, when they have reason to fear that persons whom they have trusted are playing tricks with them.
If Don John was acting loyally, he had nothing to fear.
After the edict was sent off, Don John wrote again to
Perez that he must resign. Sooner than remain to govern
Flanders on such conditions, he would turn hermit. If
the King insisted on keeping him there he would become desperate, fling up the reins and go home, though
he lost his life for it. He implored that he might not be
driven to choose between disobedience and infamy.

Perez showed Philip all these letters ; and they were
considered in the cabinet. The blame was laid on Escovedo, who was held to have betrayed his trust. Don
John was informed kindly, but peremptorily, that his
return at such a time would be prejudicial to the public
service. No one could be so fit as the King's brother to
recover the loyalty of the Estates. The King said that
he understood his feelings, and could sympathize with
him ; but he must try to be patient ; least of all must
he rush off into France where the Government had not
asked for his assistance. The English project and his
other wishes should be considered when the time for
them was come ; but his present duty was to reconcile
Flanders, and there he must remain. Escovedo had
spoken of returning himself to speak to the King.
Perez told him that if he came back without permission
it would be taken as a serious offence, and was not to
be thought of.

Don John acquiesced, or seemed to acquiesce. The Perpetual Edict was ratified. The troops began the evacuation, and on May 2 Don John was received at Brussels, and installed as governor. Had he been sincere, the storm would have blown over; but the next news which arrived about him at Madrid was that he had actually made a private treaty with the Court of Rome. The Pope had promised him 6,000 men and 150,000 ducats for the English expedition, while before the Brussels settlement had lasted a fortnight he was again in correspondence with the Duke of Guise, and was threatening open hostilities against Holland and Zealand, which were making difficulties about liberty of worship. The difficulty need not have been insuperable; and the Estates refused to sanction immediate violence. Don John snatched at the excuse to break with them on his own authority; with such regiments as had not yet gone, he seized Namur; and Escovedo, in spite of his positive orders, rushed home after all, to press Philip to allow the army to return. The war should then be carried on in earnest. The Spanish forces could live in the rebel provinces as in an enemy's country, and lay them waste with fire and sword.

Information more unwelcome never reached Philip. He longed for peace; he had been acting in good faith; he refused to counter-order the troops; he blamed the seizure of Namur, and abhorred the very mention of fire and sword. Still at the eleventh hour he clung to the hope of reconciliation. The Estates declared Don John a public enemy, and invited the Archduke Matthias to take his place. Even so, Philip persevered. He sent a commission to offer a complete amnesty, with the instant and perpetual removal of the army. The Estates might choose their own governor, either the Archduke Mat-

thias, or the Archduke Ferdinand, or the Prince of
Parma. But it was too late ; the day for peace was gone.
Confidence was irrecoverably lost, and the quarrel had
to be fought out to the end. The army went back—
there was no help for it—with the Prince of Parma at
its head ; while it was said and believed that Don John
was treating with the Duke of Guise for an open alliance, without regard to their respective sovereigns—
a very strange and questionable performance. Both
Guise and Philip were no doubt defending the Catholic
religion. But respect for forms and secular interests
were not to pass for nothing. Spain and France were
the rivals for Continental supremacy. They had been
at war off and on for three-quarters of a century, and, if
the religious question was settled, might at any time be
at war again. Philip had not forgotten that it was a
Duke of Guise who had defended Metz against his
father ; and for his brother to take on himself to settle
points of international policy with the subject of another
sovereign, was something not very far removed from
treason.

But we must now return to the scapegoat who was to
bear the blame for all these things, the unlucky Escovedo. Flying home, as we saw him, in the teeth of a
positive command, he landed at Santander on July 21.
The worst had not yet happened ; for it was not till the
January following that the commission went with the
last overtures for peace, nor was the treating with Guise
as yet more than an unpleasant rumor. But Philip was
legitimately incensed with Escovedo, and, if we can believe M. Mignet, had prepared a peculiar reception for
him ; nay, was expecting that Escovedo was coming
with murderous intentions against himself. Perez having informed the King in a note of Escovedo's approach,

Philip, according to his habit, and in his well-known abominable hand, scrawled on the margin, " Menester será prevenir nos bien de todo y dar nos mucha priesa á despacharle antes que nos maté." The verb "de-spachar," like its English correspondent " despatch," has two meanings, and " matar " has two meanings. M. Mignet supposes the words to mean, " We must be quick and assassinate him before he kills us." He makes Philip suspect Escovedo of intended treason, and resolve to be beforehand with him. But no one would have thought of so interpreting the passage if Escovedo had not in fact been assassinated at a later period. The natural translation would be, " We must despatch him quickly (*i.e.* send him about his business) before he worries us to death ;" and as Escovedo remained, for some months after his arrival, not only unmolested, but transacting business with the King, I cannot infer, with M. Mignet, that Philip had already formed so sanguinary a purpose against him. Unquestionably, however, no good will was felt toward a man who had responded so ill to the confidence which had been placed in him. If Philip could have conveniently punished him without irritating his brother, he would gladly have read him a sharp lesson, and the irritation was likely to be increased as the consequences of his misdoings developed them-selves. The especial uneasiness was on the side of France. In the autumn (1577), three months after Escovedo's arrival, Philip sent a new ambassador there, Juan de Vargas Mexia, to inquire particularly into what was passing between his brother and the Duke of Guise. Mexia ascertained that the correspondence was real, and that secret agents were going to and fro be-tween them, though to what purpose he could not tell. The suspicious feature was the complete silence on the subject both of Don John and his secretary. Escovedo's manners were abrupt and arbitrary. In January Philip received a letter from him, which he described happily as *descosido*, loose, unstitched, visionary. He handed it to Perez, that he might see how "sanguinary" it was.

Don John, at the reopening of the war, had begun with a success. He had defeated the Prince of Orange at Gemblours. He wrote passionately for reinforcements. The victory had to be followed up, and all would be won. He demanded money—money and Escovedo. Philip, unhappily, had won victories before in the Low Countries, and knew better what to expect from them. His own more temperate policy had been thwarted and ruined, and it was but too natural that he should hold his brother's wild adviser as responsible. If he sent him back, it would be only to throw fuel on the fire. Don John, and the Pope, and the Guises would set all Europe in confusion. Escovedo was no fool. He could not be kept waiting at Madrid with dilatory excuses. To imprison him, or bring him to trial, might drive Don John at once into some dangerous course. It would lead to investigations and the publication of State secrets which ought not to be revealed.

There was a theory much in favor at the Spanish court, that criminals who had forfeited their lives, or persons whose lives were for any reason inconsistent with public safety, might, when the facts were certain, and when an open prosecution would be inconvenient, be removed privately by orders of the Council of State. So Don Carlos had been disposed of ; so the Flemish envoy at Simancas. Spain was not the only country where in extreme cases such proceedings were held permissible. Elizabeth would have been grateful to Sir Amyas Paulet if he would have relieved her of the Queen of Scots. In

Italy, in France, in Scotland, a stab with a dagger was an expedient adopted in emergencies, with no great care to ascertain that it was deserved. Spain and England were rather in advance of other nations than behind them; and in Spain, heartily loyal as it was, the public had begun to doubt whether these secret executions ought to be continued.

A zealous court preacher had maintained, in a sermon at which Philip was present, that kings had absolute power over the lives and fortunes of their subjects. The Inquisition, of all courts in the world, took up the question. The preacher was obliged to retract his proposition in the same pulpit, and to confess that kings had no more power over their subjects than divine and human law allowed them. The old view, however, held its ground in spite of the Holy Office, and was professed in its extreme form by no less a person than the King's spiritual adviser, the same Diego de Chaves who was mentioned at the opening of our story. Don Diego's opinion was this : " So far as I understand the law," he said, " a secular prince who for sufficient cause can take his subjects' lives from them by course of law can also do it without course of law when the evidence of the guilt is clear. Form and order are not essentials in such sense that they cannot be dispensed with ; and if the prince has sufficient reasons for proceeding irregularly, the vassal who by his command puts to death another vassal is doing no more than his duty. He is bound to assume the cause to be adequate. The presumption in all cases is that the prince has reason for what he does."

This doctrine was still held by Philip ; and the difficulty with Escovedo was precisely of the kind where the application of it was convenient. Escovedo's guilt might be assumed. He was a confidential minister who had disobeyed his orders, and had caused a great public calamity, involving the renewal of a civil war. If allowed to live, he would still be dangerous. To bring him to an account openly would be dangerous also. Philip directed Antonio Perez to consult the Marques de los Velez. The opinion of the marquis was decided, that Escovedo should be killed; yet that the King must not appear to have directed his execution, lest Don John should be exasperated. Some scheme should be contrived by which it could appear that he had been sacrificed to private revenge. A Government must have been singularly helpless which could have recourse to such expedients. But so it was. For the act itself De los Velez had so little hesitation that, " with the Sacrament in his mouth," he was ready to assert the necessity of it. The best method, he thought, would be to give Escovedo " something to eat " from which he should not recover.

There was nothing in such a proposal to disturb Philip's ignoble conscientiousness. He sincerely believed that by consenting he was discharging a public duty, and with no more personal resentment than if he had been signing a warrant for an ordinary execution. It has never been suggested that Philip had any private malice against Escovedo, or had any motive beyond what was afterward alleged. Why Antonio Perez should have encouraged him, why he should himself have so readily undertaken a treacherous office, is another question on which speculation has been busy. He had been Escovedo's personal friend. They had grown up as boys together in the family of Ruy Gomez. They had been transferred together to the King's service. They had never differed politically until Escovedo had become

Don John's secretary, and they had corresponded afterward on terms of the closest intimacy. It is true that Perez had been the strongest advocate for a policy of peace, and Escovedo for war ; but an antagonism of opinion scarcely explains the readiness with which one Secretary of State undertook to murder another. And it has been assumed as a matter of course that Perez must have had some private motives of his own.

Before entering into these dark regions I will describe briefly what actually happened. The " something to eat " was administered as De los Velez recommended. Perez took into his confidence his own master of the household, Diego Martinez ; he told him that the King and council considered Escovedo's life to be dangerous to the peace of Europe, and that Escovedo must be secretly made away with. To satisfy Martinez's scruples he showed him a letter in the King's hand. Enriquez, a page, was also admitted into the mystery. An apothecary was found far away in Aragon who could mix a potion, and Escovedo was invited to dinner. Two or three experiments were tried with imperfect success. The unlucky wretch became very ill after swallowing a dish of cream with some white powder in it ; but he had not taken enough. He suspected foul play, and afterward dined alone in his apartments in the palace. A page in the palace kitchen was bribed to put a larger dose into a plate which was sent up to him. Escovedo discovered the poison, and an innocent slave girl who had dressed the dish was strangled in the Plaza at Madrid.

The fate of this poor creature, so piteous because so utterly undeserved, passed as a mere incident ; Perez scarcely gave a second thought to it, and the King's conscience could not descend to a kitchen wench. But poison, it was clear, could not be depended on ; and

steel was a surer method. Escovedo's habits were
watched. He was out much after dark, and returned
late to his apartments. Bravoes were brought up by
the exertions of Diego Martinez from remote parts of
the Peninsula. Easter had come, and Perez, to be out
of the way, went for the Holy Week to Alcala de Henares.
On the night of Easter Monday, March 31, 1578, Don
John's secretary was run through the body in a public
street, and was killed on the spot.

Madrid was an orderly city, and open assassinations
were unusual. A person, himself of so much consequence,
and the notorious favorite of a prince who was the idol
of the people, could not be found lying dead without a
considerable stir being caused by it. The police were
out like hornets. The gates were guarded, and no one
was allowed to pass. The hotels and lodging-houses
were called on for a list of their guests. The assassins
were out of reach, for they were secreted in Perez's
own house, and no clue could be found ; yet suspicion
at once and instinctively pointed to Perez as the instiga-
tor, and his absence at Alcala was not enough to clear
him. His wife, Juana Coello, called to condole with
Escovedo's widow. The widow had not forgotten the
dinners and the illness which followed, and the detected
attempts at poison. She said significantly she feared
the blow had been aimed by a friend's hand. Perez
hurried back to the capital, pretending to be horrified.
He saw Escovedo's son. He told the alcalde of the court
that Escovedo had many enemies ; there were rumors
of a love affair in Flanders ; Escovedo, he knew, had
lately received a message, bidding him beware of some
jealous Fleming. Perhaps he overacted his part. The
alcalde and the alcalde's son, Garcia de Arce, cross-ques-
tioned him unpleasantly. The King was out at the

Escurial, where, of course, reports reached him from the
magistrates; but he was anxious for particulars. On
April 3, three days after the murder, Perez wrote to him,
and a copy of the letter survives, with Philip's marginal
remarks upon it. Perez told him what had passed with
the alcalde, and mentioned what he had said about the
love affair. Philip noted, "This was very right." Garcia
de Arce had asked Perez whether there had been a
quarrel between him and Escovedo, implying that he
had heard something to that effect from Escovedo's
wife. Philip observed, "There will be danger from that
woman." "The alcalde," Perez said, "had discovered
that strange things had been going on during the winter
in Escovedo's house; mysterious visitors, night expeditions none knew where, and secret boxes of papers, and
keys of other people's houses." Philip, who evidently
looked on himself as a careful, well-intentioned prince,
who had disposed of a public enemy in a skilful manner, thought more of Escovedo's plots than of awkward
consequences from his murder. He remarked that these
keys and visits had a bad complexion; the alcalde must
look more closely into that matter, and search it to the
bottom. Perez was uncomfortable about his bravoes,
whom he knew not how to dispose of. He had thought
of sending them away with despatches as Government
couriers; but it seemed too dangerous. He recommended Philip to put the inquiry into the alcalde's
hands exclusively, and to forbid any other person to
meddle with it. Philip prudently observed that to interfere with the investigation would provoke suspicion.
He would communicate with the alcalde, and would do
what he could. The bravoes must be kept for the present where they were, and Perez meanwhile might come
out to the Escurial to see him. Finally, to quiet Perez's

8

evident alarm, he said: "If Escovedo's widow desires to speak with me, I cannot refuse to see her; but do not fear that you will be unsupported. I am with you, and will not fail you in anything that may be expedient or necessary. Assure yourself of this. You know it well."

There is no doubt at all that in the last extremity, and if Perez's life was in danger, Philip intended honestly to tell the truth.

Strong, however, as suspicion was, suspicion was not proof; and proof against Perez there was none. He had been many miles from Madrid when the murder was committed. His servants, Diego Martinez and Enriquez, knew that they had been acting by the King's authority. They had everything to gain by keeping counsel, and might be in serious danger if they betrayed their secret. The bravoes slipped away after a week or two, when the vigilance had relaxed. Each of them had a bag of doubloons with a commission as *alferez* (ensign in the army, unattached). They dispersed to Italy, to Central Europe, to all the winds. Every trace was thus swept out which could connect Perez with the murder. The excitement died gradually away, and the affair seemed to be forgotten.

But poisoned wounds will not heal, though they be skinned over. The sore was to break out again, and the story to assume a form which has given it a place among the *causes célèbres* of the world.

Brilliant writers of history are subject to one general temptation—they desire to give their narrative dramatic completeness. The drama, if it is to have flavor, must revolve upon personal motives, and history must follow on the same lines. Sovereigns and statesmen who have been charged with the fortunes of nations, are assumed, where their actions require explanation, to have been influenced by no other passions than those which govern private individuals in their own more limited spheres. When a woman's name appears as connected with such high persons, the connection is always assumed to have been of one peculiar kind. To ask for evidence or look for other explanations is taken as a sign of simplicity or of ignorance of human nature.

The legend now stereotyped in European tradition is that the wife of Ruy Gomez, the Princess of Eboli, was the mistress of Philip the Second, and that the Princess of Eboli preferred Antonio Perez to the King. Escovedo, it is said, discovered the intrigue and threatened to reveal it. Perez, in consequence, calumniated Escovedo to Philip. Philip allowed him to be murdered, but discovered afterward that he had been the dupe of a treacherous minister and a bad woman, and regarded Perez thenceforward with implacable hatred.

Now, before going further, I have to observe that the eleven years during which Philip is assumed to have been occupied with these emotions and the effort to give effect to them, were the busiest in the whole of his long, laborious reign. They were the years in which he annexed Portugal. They were the years of Parma's administration of the Netherlands. They were the years of preparation for the Armada. There was the civil war in France to be watched and guided. There were Naples and Sicily to be ruled, and the Turks to be held in check in the Mediterranean. There were the ambassadors' despatches from foreign courts. There was a close, constant, and elaborate correspondence to be maintained with the Pope. There were the reports of the Inquisition to be received and studied. There were English, Scotch, and Irish Catholic conspiracies to be kept in hand. There was the great new empire across the Atlantic, and Drake and Hawkins, and the English corsairs. There were the various Councils of State for the internal administration at home, and in every one of these departments Philip not only interfered, but exercised the most unrelaxing supervision. Whether he did his work well or ill is not to the purpose ; mind and body were incessantly engaged upon it. Minutes of council, tens of thousands of ciphered despatches with rough drafts of as many ciphered answers to them, survive to witness to the industry of a sovereign who permitted nothing to be done without his knowledge in all his enormous dominions. There is scarcely one of these documents which is not annotated in his hand, and often elaborately ; and students who, like myself, have toiled through these mountains of papers, have cursed the writing, the worst perhaps that ever was seen, but have had to confess, when the meaning was arrived at, that the meaning was a real and often a wise one. The poor King did patiently endeavor to understand the subjects before him, and to resolve upon them with the best efforts of his limited ability ; while if the working hours of every day had been doubled, and thus doubled had been devoted all to duty, they would still seem insufficient for the business which he demonstrably got through.

That a mind so occupied should have had leisure to trouble itself with " jealousies " and " mistresses," or indeed to give more than a passing thought to the Escovedo affair at all after the public dangers from him had ceased, is to me not easily conceivable, for the simple reason that there was no time for it. The King was occupied all but exclusively with other matters. The murder was an angry spot which would not heal ; he had fallen into a scrape, and his behavior was singular ; but it can be more easily explained by clumsy efforts to extricate himself than by a romance of which nine-tenths is conjecture, and the tenth remaining inconsistent with admitted facts.

It is, however, true that the Princess of Eboli was soon supposed to have been connected in some way with Escovedo's assassination. The widow of Escovedo knew that high words had passed between her husband and Antonio Perez, in which the name of the Princess had been mentioned. Perez had been more successful in life than his companion officials, and had borne himself in his prosperity with less moderation than prudence would have recommended. One of these, a priest named Matteo Vasquez, and himself one of Philip's secretaries, disliked Perez, and was also employed in some law-suit against the Princess. He sought out Escovedo's family and learned what they had to tell. He was busy all the summer and the winter following pushing his inquiries, and thought at last that he had made a notable discovery. In December, nine months after the murder, he wrote and circulated an anonymous *pasquil*, full of scandalous reflections on Perez and the lady, while simultaneously Escovedo's widow and her son directly charged Perez with the crime, adding that it had been committed to gratify the Princess of Eboli. Perez carried the *pasquil* to Philip—a daring act on his part, if he knew himself to be the King's successful rival. Philip again assured him, both by word and writing, that he need not be uneasy, that no harm should befall him ; but Perez knew his master well ; he knew his unwillingness that his own share in the matter should be made public, and he observed that Philip seemed not displeased that Vasquez and the Escovedos should be running on a false scent.

It is time, therefore, to say a few words about this fa-

mous lady; to tell who she was, and how she came to
be concerned in a matter which appeared to be wholly
political.

Doña Aña, widow of Ruy Gomez, Prince of Eboli,
was the only child of Don Diego Hurtado, chief of the
great house of Mendoza. There were many Mendozas in
the Spanish peerage. Don Diego's was the eldest branch.
On her father's death a part, but not all, of the inher-
itance descended to the daughter. She was Princess of
Eboli as her husband's widow. Her eldest son, a youth
of twenty or thereabouts, was Duke of Pastraña and
Prince of Melito. She had five younger children. One
of them, a daughter, was married to Alonzo the Good,
Duke of Medina Sidonia, known to history as the admiral of the Armada. Family disputes seem to have
arisen about Don Diego's succession. Some suit was
pending between her and other members of the family.
The Princess was detaining money, jewels, and other
possessions, to which her relatives laid claim ; and the
quarrel was further complicated by the political lean-
ings of the young Prince of Melito, who had deserted
the old party of his father, Ruy Gomez, and had gone
over to the Duke of Alva.

The Princess herself was now thirty-eight years old.
She had lost one eye, and was otherwise not beautiful ;
but she was energetic, imperious, with considerable
talents, and able, if she pleased, to be fascinating. That
she had been Philip's mistress was an Italian scandal ;
nothing had then been heard of it in Spain ; but Perez
gave mysterious hints that the King would have been
more intimate with her if she had encouraged him.
Any way, she had lost Philip's favor. Visitors at the
Eboli palace were frowned upon at the Escurial ; the
world said that the King was irritated at the rejection

of his advances,* and that "wishes unsatisfied were more exasperating than a thousand offences."

This was perhaps but court gossip; but, whether fact or legend, it is certain on the other hand that the relations between the Princess and Antonio Perez were intimate and even affectionate. He had been her husband's adopted son. The Princess professed to believe that Ruy Gomez was his real father, and to her Perez's devotion was unconcealed and unbounded. He describes in an enigmatic letter the position in which he stood toward her. M. Mignet says that there can be no doubt of his meaning, and rushes to a preconceived conclusion. The letter is intentionally obscure, the press is uncorrected, and the text in parts is hopeless. But he alludes to the suggestion that he was the Princess's lover only to fling it from him with disgust. His love was for his own wife, whose attachment to him is the finest feature in the whole of this distracted story. The Princess of Eboli he worshipped as a being beyond his sphere. He spoke of her as "a jewel enamelled in the rarest graces of nature and fortune." To her husband he owed all that he had become, and he repaid his debt by helping his widow in her difficulties. He made her large advances of money, he collected her rents from Italy; she in turn made him handsome presents; but that either with the King or with Perez the Princess had any personal intrigue is a romantic imagination like the legend of Don Carlos and his stepmother.†

* "Por vivir el Rey offendido de la antigua y continua duracion de la entereza de la Princesa de Eboly haciendole menosprecio."—*Relacion de Antonio Perez.*

† There is no evidence for it except what is supposed to lie in the letter of Antonio Perez "à un Gran Personage," which formed part of his public defence. What that letter means it is impossible to say, or even what it was intended to suggest. Perez says that the King dis-

It was but natural, under the circumstances, that the Mendoza family should bear no love to Perez, because in the feuds which had arisen he was taking the Princess's side. The Prince of Melito had threatened to run him through the body. The Marques de Fabara and the Conde de Cifuentes called one day on the Princess, and were kept waiting because she was closeted with the Secretary. Both of them thought that such a fellow was not fit to live. Escovedo, it came out, had taken the opposite side to Perez. He, too, had been brought up by Ruy Gomez, and claimed a right to interfere in defence of his old master's honor. He had disapproved of the acquaintance; he had said that it must and should be put an end to ; and he had spoken to the Princess with so rude a tongue, that she called him a foul-mouthed villain.

A quarrel of this kind explains the ease with which Perez consented to kill Escovedo. We know no actual good of Perez, and there would have been nothing surprising if, out of revenge, he really had misled the King into thinking Escovedo more guilty than he was. But the attempt to prove it broke down ; Philip had been influenced by Don John's and Escovedo's own despatches, which had been deciphered by another hand ; and never to the last felt certain that his secretary had in this matter deceived him. Some personal resentment there was, and the Princess was in some way the occasion of it, but in fact Philip's conduct requires no secret passion to make it intelligible. He did not doubt, at least at first, that he had done right, but he was unwilling to admit

approved of the intimacy between himself and the Princess, and that there was a mystery connected with this. But a mystery was not necessarily a love affair, nor does it follow that there was a mystery because such a person as Perez wished to make himself interesting by hinting at one.

the truth. He had to maintain his respectability, and, therefore, would not try to prevent the Escovedos and their friends from prosecuting their complaints, while he was not ill-pleased that their suspicions should run wide of himself, and fasten in a quarter where he knew that there was nothing to be discovered. It was just the course which small, commonplace cunning would naturally pursue. The Marques de los Velez could not understand it; he did not like the look of things, and applied for the governorship of Peru; Perez offered to retire from the public service and satisfy his enemies thus; but the King refused to accept Perez's resignation; he said that he could not spare him; he reiterated, on the word of a gentleman, "that he would never forsake him, and that Perez knew his word could be depended on."

More and more loudly Matteo Vasquez and the Escovedos demanded a trial. The King could not directly refuse. Perez himself advised acquiescence; the actual assassins, he said, were beyond reach of discovery; there was no evidence; he was ready to face the prosecution; the name of the Princess need not be mentioned. Philip, however, had a conscience above perjury; he was not ashamed to admit what he had done, if it was known only to discreet persons who could be safely trusted. The case was to be heard before the High Court of Castile. The King sent for Don Antonio de Pazos, who was then President, told him everything, and asked his advice. The President thought that the prosecution must be silenced; he informed young Escovedo that if he insisted on justice he should have it, but he was accusing persons of high rank in the State; his charge, if he failed to make it good, would recoil on himself; and he assured him on the word of a priest that Perez and the Princess were as innocent as himself. With Matteo Vasquez the President was more peremptory. Vasquez, he said, was no relation of Escovedo's; his interference, especially as he was a priest, was gratuitous and unbecoming; on the facts he was mistaken altogether. The Escovedos yielded and promised to go no further; Vasquez was obstinate, and persisted. Public curiosity had been excited; it was felt instinctively that the King was in the secret, and there was now a widespread desire to know what that secret was. Vasquez hated Perez and the Princess also, and made himself the representative of the popular anxiety.

Philip had been contented that opinion should run in a false direction; and he had hoped to prevent too close an inquiry by his confidence with the President. He had failed, and he had seemed to wish in consequence to silence Vasquez, and, if possible, to reconcile him with the Princess, whom he had calumniated. But now the difficulty was on her side. She, the greatest lady in Spain after the Queen, had been insulted and slandered; it was not for her to leave a cloud upon her name by stooping to take the hand of her accuser. The Cardinal Archbishop of Toledo was sent to reason with her, but the Archbishop was too much of her own opinion to make an impression on her indignation. She had already a long catalogue of grievances, and this last insult was too much. She wrote Philip a letter, which she showed to Perez, and Perez preserved it.

"Señor :—Your Majesty has commanded the Cardinal of Toledo to speak with me in the matter of Antonio Perez. Matteo Vasquez and his friends have said openly that all who enter my house lose your favor. They have stated also that

Antonio Perez killed Escovedo on my account ; that he was under so many obligations to my family, that he would do whatever I asked him. They have published abroad these speeches ; and I require your Majesty, as a king and a gentleman, to take such notice of this conduct as the world shall hear of. If your Majesty declines, if the honor of my house is to be sacrificed, as our property has been sacrificed, if this is to be the reward of the long and faithful services of my ancestors, be it so. I have discharged my conscience ; self-respect forbids me to say more.

" I write to your Majesty in resentment at the offences which I have received, and I write in confidence, supposing myself to be addressing a gentleman.

" The President presses me about a letter which I wrote to your Majesty, touching bribes taken by —— (word omitted). I am charged with having said something of the Duke of ——. My character suffers from these tokens of your Majesty's good-will. Though justice is on my side, my suit is before a tainted tribunal ; I shall lose it and be put out of possession. When I ask the President why he acts thus toward me, he says that your Majesty will have it so. Melchior de Herrera (?) allows that I am right ; but he swears me to this and that, and pretends that it is your pleasure. You have sent him a memorial from Don Inigo.* Why am I to be twice memorialized ? It is important to me to withdraw the security under which I and my children are bound for Don Inigo. He has broken his obligations, and may leave Valladolid. Antonio de Padilla confesses that it is so ; but your Majesty forbids him to interfere. If this is true, I may as well abandon my suit, and my children too. This is the natural conclusion from the position which you assume toward me. When I reflect what my husband's merits were, such treatment would make me lose my senses did I not need them all to guard myself from this Moorish cur (Matteo Vasquez) whom your Majesty keeps in your service. I demand that neither I nor any of mine may be placed in that man's power."

* Inigo de Mendoza, Marquis of Almenara.

I have given this letter, though it strays far beyond
our immediate subject, because it shows how imperfectly
the circumstances are known to us which surround the
story; and how idle it is for us to indulge imagination
beyond what is written.   Long avenues of questions lie
open before us, which must remain forever unanswered,
yet in the answer to which alone can lie a complete explanation of the relations between the Princess of Eboli
and the King of Spain.

Submit to be reconciled with the "Moorish cur" it
was plain she would not.   He had circulated slanders
against her in the court, and she insisted that he should
withdraw them.*   Perez was obstinate, too, for his

* This article had been written, and was partly in type, before I had
seen the interesting work, lately published, on the Princess of Eboli,
by Don Gaspar Moro.   Although the documents discovered by Don
Gaspar have added largely to our knowledge of the secret history of the
Princess, I have found it unnecessary to withdraw or alter any opinion
which I had formed.   I have had the pleasure of finding my own con-
jectures for the most part confirmed and converted into certainties by
evidence not open to dispute.   Don Gaspar has disproved conclusively
the imagined *liaison* between the Princess and Philip the Second.   He
continues to believe that improper relations existed between her and
Antonio Perez; but as he alleges nothing fresh in proof of it beyond
what was already known, I look on this as no more than part of the
old legend which has continued to adhere to Don Gaspar with no more
authority for it than tradition.   The passionate love which existed between Perez and his own wife is inconsistent with a belief, at least on
her part, that any such relation had been formed.   Be this as it may,
however, Don Gaspar has proved that the jealousy of which Perez
speaks, as having governed Philip's conduct, was no jealousy of the
preference of Perez to himself by the Princess, but a jealousy of the influence of a woman, with whom he was on the worst possible terms,
over his own secretary.   Don Gaspar has found and printed more than
a hundred letters of Matteo Vasquez, whose connection with the Escovedo prosecution was so close, and had hitherto been so unintelligible.
The Crown was in some way interested in the great lawsuits which the
Princess was carrying on.   In all that related to her Matteo Vasquez
was as deep in Philip's confidence as Antonio Perez in the wider world
of politics.   His relations with each of them were carefully concealed

honor was touched. The Archbishop of Toledo and the King's special preacher, Fray Hernando de Castillo, stood by them, and the quarrel had gone into a new form. Philip's position was a ridiculous one. If Vasquez persisted in prosecuting Perez before a judge who was acquainted with the truth, it was scarcely possible that the truth would be unrevealed. Secretary Vasquez is a dark figure. The letter of the Princess shows that Philip was secretly employing this man in various matters in which she supposed herself to be wronged, and there were reasons for his conduct at which, with our imperfect knowledge, it is idle to guess. Consulting no one but his confessor, the King gave orders for the arrest both of Perez and of the Princess and on July 29, 1579, they were ordered into separate confinement. The lady's relations, it is likely, required no explana-

from the other. Perez might know that Matteo Vasquez was employed by his master against the Princess; but Matteo Vasquez never guessed that his master had ordered Perez to assassinate Escovedo : and thus Philip himself, by his passion for secrecy, and for what he regarded as skilful management, had entangled his two secretaries in a furious antagonism. Perez had no knowledge how far Philip had engaged himself in the Eboli litigation. To him Matteo Vasquez appeared to have thrown himself gratuitously into the quarrel. The King was irritated at Perez for unconsciously thwarting him by taking up the Princess's cause. Matteo who, evidently from his letters, hated the Princess, had almost succeeded in dragging into light his master's complicity with Escovedo's murder, by his innocent belief that Perez and the Princess were the guilty parties, and that the cause of the murder was resentment at the part which Escovedo had taken in attempting to separate the Princess from Perez. Not a hint, not a suggestion of any love-scandal appears in the whole of the correspondence. Some great question was at issue, the very nature of which cannot now be accurately made out, on which the court was divided, and which was enveloped in a network of intrigue—the King sitting in the middle of it, playing the part of Providence with the best intentions, with extremely limited ability, and with the most unfortunate results—for he affected especially to imitate Providence in the secrecy of its methods ; and secrecy is only safe to a judgment which cannot err.

tions, but for form's sake Philip offered them. The same night he wrote to the Duke of Infantado and to Medina Sidonia. A dispute had arisen, he said, between his two secretaries, Antonio Perez and Matteo Vasquez, with which the Princess was concerned. She had complained to him unreasonably, and his confessor had vainly endeavored to persuade her to be reconciled to Vasquez. She had been committed, therefore, to the fortress of Pinto, and he had thought it right to give them immediate information. The resentment of the Duke of Infantado was not likely to be deep; Medina Sidonia replied coolly that so wise a sovereign had doubtless good reason for his actions. He was himself laid up with gout, and the pain was in his mind as well as in his body. He trusted that his Majesty would be gracious to the Princess, and that the grace would be even more marked than the punishment.

The Archbishop of Toledo called the next morning on Juana de Coello, Perez's wife. He told her from the King that she was not to be alarmed. Her husband's life was in no danger, nor his honor either. The imprisonment was a mere matter of precaution to prevent other mischiefs.

The Princess now drops out of the scene. Philip informed her that if she would undertake to hold no more communication with Perez, she would be received to favor, and might return to the court. She replied that if Perez ever wrote to her or sent her a message, the King should know of it. But this was not sufficient. After a brief confinement she was allowed to retire to her castle at Pastraña, and there without further disturbance she remained to the end of her life.

Meanwhile, if Philip's object had been to stop the prosecution for Escovedo's murder, and to divert suspicion from himself, both purposes had been attained. Matteo Vasquez must have been satisfied, for his name was never mentioned again. Popular opinion had accused Perez of having committed the murder at the Princess's instigation. Their simultaneous arrest led to a general belief that the suspicion was not unfounded. If the King had made a second confidant of Vasquez, and had concerted the details of the comedy with him, the result, at least for a time, did credit to his ingenuity. Perez's fault, whatever it had been, was not to appear unpardonable. He was left four months in charge of the alcalde at the court. He was treated with kindness, and even distinction, and was permitted to have his children with him. In the November following he became unwell, and was permitted further to return to his own house, though still as a prisoner. Next he was required to sign a bond of *pleytohomenage*, by which he and Matteo Vasquez engaged as king's vassals not to injure each other. The guard was then removed. He recovered his freedom and resumed his duties as secretary to the Council of State, though no longer as confidential secretary to the King. The whole matter seemed to have been thus wound up, and public interest was soon directed on worthier objects. The death of Don Sebastian in Africa had left vacant the Portuguese throne. Philip took possession of the succession as the nearest heir. The Duke of Alva with a few skilful movements disposed of the pretender. Philip went to Lisbon to be installed as sovereign, and in the glory of this grand achievement Escovedo's assassination might have gone the way of other scandals.

But, as Perez said, " it was a thing which had no beginning and could have no end." A cloud still hung over him, and his slightest movements were watched.

The Princess of Eboli sent him presents from Pastraña. It was immediately reported to Philip. He had many friends, the Archbishop of Toledo, and "grandees" of highest rank. They came often to see him, but he was forbidden to return their visits. Philip evidently chose that a sinister suspicion should still remain attached to him. Antonio de Pazos, the President of Castile, knew the whole story, for the King had told him. Juana de Coello complained to him of her husband's treatment, and insisted that his reputation ought to be cleared. The President was of the same opinion, and so informed the King. "If Antonio Perez has committed a crime," he said, "give him a formal trial and hang him. If he is innocent, let him go on his good behavior, and if he offends again, punish him."

The King answered: "If the matter were of a kind which would allow a judicial process, it should have been ordered from the first day. You must tell the woman to be quiet ; no change is possible at present."

"Time," Philip used to say, "cures all evils. Time and I never fail." And so he went on trusting to time when time could not help him.

Perez had friends, but he had enemies also. Matteo Vasquez had withdrawn, but others had taken his place, and Philip's ambiguities encouraged them. Among these were the powerful Mendozas. Perez had managed the Princess's money affairs. He had jewels in his charge and other things also which they conceived to belong to them. His habits were luxurious, and remained so in spite of his semi-disgrace. His palace, his plate, his furniture, his equipments, and entertainments were the most splendid in Madrid. He gambled also ; perhaps he won, perhaps he lost ; in either case it was a reproach. How, men asked, could Antonio Perez support such a vast expenditure? and the answer suggested was, of course, corruption or malversation. He had six thousand ducats a year from his offices; but the Archbishop of Seville, a friendly witness, said that he must be spending fifteen or twenty thousand. The King was advised to order an inquiry into the accounts of all the public offices, and of Perez's, of course, among them. A "lion's mouth," like that of Venice, was opened for secret information, and was not long in want of sustenance. Accusations poured in as venomous as hatred could distil. Rodrigo Vasquez de Arce,* who afterward became President of the High Court, conducted the investigation of them, and the result was not favorable to Perez. Undoubtedly he had received sums of money from all parts of the empire to expedite business, just as Bacon did in England, and as high officials everywhere were then in the habit of doing. They looked on such things as recognized perquisites so long as nothing was said about them; but gratuities were formally prohibited, and, when exposed, were incapable of defence.

On the report being presented, Philip allowed Perez to be prosecuted for corrupt practices, and it was then that, at a venture, he was accused further of having altered ciphered despatches.

No one knew better than Philip that, under the arrangements of his cabinet, the alteration of despatches without his own knowledge was impossible. Perez wrote to Philip to remonstrate. "He could not answer such a charge," he said, "without producing his papers," and among them the King's own notes upon Escovedo's death. The confessor was sent to see these papers, and, having read them, could only recommend his master

* It does not appear whether he was a relation of Matteo Vasquez.

9

to let the charge fall. As to corrupt practices, he advised Perez to make no defence, and assured him that he should not be condemned in the value of a pair of gloves. The sentence went beyond the pair of gloves. Perez was suspended from his office for ten years. He was to suffer two years' imprisonment, and was to pay besides thirty thousand ducats, half to the Crown and half to the family of the Princess of Eboli, as property belonging to them which he had unlawfully appropriated.

This judgment was delivered on January 23, 1585. It was not published; nor is it certain how much of it was enforced. But there were reasons why, at that moment, the sentence of imprisonment was convenient. The Escovedo business was bursting up again. Enriquez, the page who had assisted at the murder, had let fall incautious speeches. The President, Rodrigo Vasquez, took the subject into the scope of his inquiries. He sent for Enriquez and examined him. On his evidence Diego Martinez was arrested also. If these two could be induced to tell the truth, the proofs against Perez would be complete. He might produce his papers, but in a close court the judges might refuse to receive or look at them to save the King's credit; and Perez would certainly be executed. The King was just then going down to Aragon for the opening of the Cortes. In Aragon trials were public, with equal justice between king and subject. Perez, himself an Aragonese, if left free might follow the King thither, and put himself under the protection of the laws of the Province. There certainly, if not in Madrid, his exculpation would be heard. It was therefore determined that he should be at once arrested, and a guard was sent to his house to take him.

Perez from first to last had an honest friend at the court, Cardinal Quiroga, Archbishop of Toledo. The

Archbishop saw, or feared, that Perez was about to be sacrificed, and his sense of equity, though he was Grand Inquisitor, was outraged. He recommended Perez to take sanctuary. He would then be a prisoner of the Church, and his case would be heard in the Holy Office. The Inquisition had already denounced Philip's method of removing doubtful subjects. It would stand by Perez now and prevent a scandalous crime.

Perez took the Cardinal's advice and fled to the nearest church. But the Crown officials were determined to have him, and the sanctuary was not respected. The church door was burst in ; he was torn out of his hiding-place, and carried off again to a State prison. His property was sequestrated, his papers were seized, and the Nuncio, when he protested, was threatened with dismissal. Henry the Eighth himself could not have been more peremptory in his contempt of sacred privileges than the ministers of the Most Catholic King. The documents were at once examined. The secret correspondence was found to have been abstracted. Juana de Coello was supposed to have it ; and, to extort it from her, she and her children were carried off also, and confined in the same castle with her husband. It was true that she had some part of the private papers, and threats of torture could not wring them from her till she had ascertained that those of more special consequence were not among them. She found someone who would take a note to her husband. Being without ink she wrote it with her blood. The answer came back that she might deliver the papers without fear, the Escovedo notes being secured elsewhere. She mentioned where the boxes would be found. The King's confessor himself came to her to receive the keys. He, too, had some sense remaining of right and wrong, and he told her that if Perez was troubled any further, he would himself go "como un loco," like a madman, into the Plaza, and proclaim the truth to all the world.

The boxes being surrendered, Juana de Coello and the children were sent home, there being no longer occasion for keeping them. As the confessor was going off, she could not help telling him that there were still a few papers reserved. The King, when he came to look, must have discovered that this was fatally true. All else was in its place, even to the most secret ciphered correspondence; but the fifty or sixty especial letters, which he knew himself to have written, about Escovedo, and knew also that Perez had preserved—these were not to be discovered. That, if he had got possession of these letters, Philip would have allowed Perez to be tried and executed, is not certain; but it may have been well for him that he was not exposed to the temptation. As matters stood, the judges might refuse to admit the letters, and might pass sentence on the evidence. But Juana de Coello could carry the damning records into Aragon, or across the frontier, and publish them; and all Europe would cry out "Shame!" Nor was the Church idle. The Church authorities, with the Pope behind them, demanded that Perez should be restored to sanctuary. Worried, impatient, cursing the day that he had ever blundered into so detestable a quagmire, the King again paused. Once more the prison doors were opened; once more Perez was brought back to Madrid, and lodged in a handsome house with his family. Evidently the unfortunate King was at his wits' end, and could not determine what course to choose. Perez went to church for mass. The great people came as before to show him countenance. He himself addressed many letters to the King, which were carefully read, if not answered. The Archbishop of Toledo, in particular, was confident that all would be well. The attitude of the Church alone, he said, would suffice to protect Perez. The President, Rodrigo, would have gone on gladly with the trial, but obstacles were continually arising. Some one asked him what was to be done. "How can I tell you?" he replied. "One day the King says go on, the next he says hold back. There is a mystery which I cannot make out."

Fourteen months thus drifted away. At the end of them the King could hold out no longer. There was still but a single witness, for Diego Martinez had so far continued stanch. He might confess, perhaps, if he was tortured, but torture could not be used without the King's permission. Philip wrote to Perez telling him generally that he might rely on his protection, but without saying what steps he was prepared to take. Perez was brought to trial at last before President Rodrigo. He stood upon his innocence, denied that he had murdered Escovedo, and denied all knowledge of the matter. Enriquez gave his evidence with correctness; but Diego Martinez, who was confronted with him, said he was a liar, and his story a fabrication. Conviction on such terms was not to be had. Perez's papers were handed to President Rodrigo to be examined. He searched them through, but found nothing to the purpose. Perez, after all, would probably have been acquitted but for the intervention of a "Deus ex machinâ," Philip himself, who interposed in a manner the most unlooked for. This is the most extraordinary feature in the whole extraordinary story. Philip, it might have been thought, would have welcomed Perez's acquittal as the happiest escape from his embarrassments; but it seems that his conscience was really disturbed at the success of deliberate perjury. Just as it became clear that the prosecution had failed, and that Perez, whether guilty or not, could not be pronounced guilty without a violation of the laws, Philip's confessor, as if from himself, but of course with his master's sanction, wrote to him to say that although he had killed Escovedo, he had a complete defence for it. When the truth was known, his character would be cleared ; he advised him, therefore, to make a complete confession, and at once say that he had acted by the King's order.

This was written on September 3, the year after the defeat of the Armada. Through all that famous enterprise, from its first conception to the final catastrophe, this mean business had simmered on, and was at last at boiling point.

Well as Perez knew his master, he was not prepared for this last move. What could it mean ? The King had promised to stand by him. But if he confessed, his guilt would be clear. He might say what he pleased, but the judges might hang him notwithstanding. There was Diego Martinez, too, to be thought of. He would be hanged, at any rate. So long as the proof was deficient, confession would be insanity. The King, besides, had positively ordered that the motives for the murder were not to be introduced.

In this tone he replied to Diego de Chaves ; but the confessor stood to his opinion. Evidently he had consulted Philip again.

" The plain course for you," he answered, " is to say directly that you had the King's orders for Escovedo's death. You need not enter on the reasons. You ought not to make a false oath in a court of justice ; and if you have done so already you ought not to persevere in it. Where there has been no fault there can be no punishment, and confession will only show the innocence of yourself and your accomplice. When the truth is out, the wound will heal, and his Majesty will have given the Escovedo family the justice which they demand. If they persist after this, they can be silenced or banished. Only, once more, the causes which led the King to act as he did are not to be mentioned."

M. Mignet considers that these letters were written to tempt Perez to a confession, in order that he might be destroyed. The judges would ask for proof, and, having lost his papers, he would be unable to produce it. The answer is simple. Both Philip and the confessor were aware that the compromising letters were still in possession of either Perez or his wife. Perez, who was not troubled about perjury, thought it safer to risk an uncertainty than to act as the confessor advised. To confess was to place his life in the judges' hands. He could feel no certainty that the King's orders would be held a sufficient authority. Philip's conduct had been strange from the beginning, and kings' consciences are not like the consciences of private individuals. They may profess to wish one thing, while their duty as sovereigns requires another. There was another alternative ; the Escovedos, who were now the only prosecutors, might agree to a compromise. Perez proposed it to the confessor ; the confessor permitted Perez to try, if the King was not to be a party to the transaction ; overtures were made and were successful. The Escovedo family consented to withdraw their suit on receiving twenty thousand ducats.

This seemed like the end ; and if there had been nothing more in Escovedo's death than an ordinary murder, the compensation would have been held sufficient, and the end would have really come. But behind the private wrong there was a great question at issue, whether the sovereign had or had not a right to make away with his subjects when he believed them criminal, because for reasons of State it was inexpedient to bring them to trial. Though Castile had no longer constitutional rights like Aragon, a high-minded people (as the Castilians were) had a regard for their own security. The doctrine had been condemned by the Holy Office, and the judges can have liked it as little.

The opportunity of bringing the matter to a point was not to be lost. The President, Rodrigo, wrote to Philip that his reputation was at stake. The prosecution had been dropped, but the world was convinced, notwithstanding, that the murder had been committed by his order. It concerned his honor that Perez should explain why that order had been given. He begged the King to send him an instruction in the following terms: " Tell Antonio Perez, in my name, that as he knows the causes for which I commanded him to kill Escovedo, I desire him to declare what those causes were."

M. Mignet adheres to his opinion that Perez was to be betrayed; that being without his papers, he must fail to prove what he was required to reveal, and could then be executed as a slanderer and an assassin. It would be difficult for him and perhaps impossible to recall satisfactorily a condition of things which was now buried under the incidents of twelve eventful years. But there is no occasion to suspect Philip of such deliberate treachery. The stages through which his mind had passed can easily be traced. He never doubted the righteousness of Escovedo's execution; but he had been afraid to irritate his brother, and had therefore wished his own part in it to be concealed. Therefore, when Perez was first suspected, he had not come forward to protect him ; and therefore also he had connived at the direction of the suspicion on the Princess of Eboli. A long time had passed away, Don John was gone, the aspect of Europe had changed. He had no longer the same reluctance to admit that he had ordered the murder; but he had bidden Perez be silent about the causes, because though sufficient for his own conscience, it would be hard, when circumstances were so much altered, to make them intelligible to others. The Spaniards of 1590, smarting under the destruction of the Armada, might well have thought if Don John and the Duke of Guise had tried the "enterprise" together, when the Queen of Scots was alive, so many of their homes would not then have been desolate.

But public opinion was excited. The compromise of the prosecution seemed to imply that there was something disgraceful behind. A secret half revealed is generally more dangerous than the truth ; and thus, when called on by the judges to direct Perez to make a full confession, the King felt that it was better to consent.

This explanation seems sufficient, without looking for sinister motives. The order was written, and Perez was required to obey.

It might have been thought that he would have seen in such an order the easiest escape from his troubles. To speak was to be acquitted (at least morally) of a worse crime than of having been a too faithful servant. But it is likely that he did feel it would be difficult for him to make out a satisfactory case. He could produce the King's instructions, and could describe the motive in general terms. But State reasons for irregular actions are always looked askance at, and loyal subjects are inclined to excuse their sovereigns at the expense of their advisers. Perez might naturally fear that he would be accused of having misled the King, perhaps through malice. This view was taken of the case by the Archbishop of Toledo. "Señor," he said to the confessor when he heard of this fresh command, "either I am mad or this whole affair is mad. If the King bade Perez kill Escovedo, why does he ask for the causes? The King knew them at the time. Perez was not Escovedo's judge. He placed before the King certain despatches. The King directed a course to be taken upon them, and Perez obeyed. Now after twelve years, without his papers, with so many persons gone who could have given evidence, he is asked for explanations. Give him back his papers, bring back five hundred persons now dead out of their graves, and even then he will not be able to do it."

The Archbishop protested, the Nuncio protested. Juana de Coello and Perez's children wept and clamored; but President Rodrigo, with the King's orders in his hand, persisted that Perez should speak. Three times successively, in the course of a month, he was brought into court, and he remained stubborn. He says that he would not confess, because the King had personally ordered him to be silent, and that a written form could not supersede an immediate direction, without a private intimation that it was to be obeyed. This is evidently an insufficient explanation. He must have felt that if he detailed the causes for the murder he admitted the fact; and that if he admitted the fact he might be sacrificed.

But the King was determined that the whole truth should be told at last, and that, as he could not tell it himself, it should be told by Perez. After a month's resistance, the question was applied in earnest. Perez was tortured. He broke down under the pain, and told all. It was then that Doña Juana appealed to God against Diego de Chaves in the Dominican chapel. It was then

that Doña Gregoria dared President Rodrigo in his hall.
What the King or the judges had intended to do next is
mere conjecture. Diego Martinez, when his master had
spoken, confessed also. He was not punished, and Perez
perhaps would not have been punished either. The
judges might have been contented with the exposure.
But Perez did not care to tempt fortune or Philip's
humors further. His wife was allowed to visit him in
prison. He escaped disguised in her clothes. Horses
were waiting, he rode for his life to Aragon, and the
next day was safe beyond the frontier.

So ends the first part of the tragi-comedy. The next
opened on another stage and with wider issues.

The Fueros or "Liberties" of Aragon were the only
surviving remnant of the free institutions of the Peninsula. At the beginning of the sixteenth century, the
two Castiles, Valencia, Granada, and Aragon had their
separate administrations and their separate legislatures.
The great cities had their municipal corporations, while
Portugal, till within ten years, had been an independent
kingdom. One by one they had been absorbed. Aragon
remained still free, but with a freedom which had been
found inconvenient at Madrid, and was unvalued by the
most powerful of the Aragonese nobles themselves. The
tendency of the age was toward centralization, and the
tenure of the Fueros had been growing yearly more pre-
carious. Isabella had been impatient for a revolt which
would give her an excuse for extinguishing them. The
Duke of Alva more lately, on some provocation, said
that with three or four thousand of his old soldiers he
would make the King's authority supreme. Such as it
was, however, the Constitution still subsisted, being supported chiefly by the populace of the towns, who, as
long as noise and clamor were sufficient, were the en-

thusiastic champions of their national privileges. A
council for the administration of the province sat at Madrid, but its powers were limited to advice. The Cortes
met annually at Saragossa to vote the taxes, but the King
could neither prorogue nor dissolve them without their
own consent. A Committee of the Cortes carried on the
Government, and in the intervals of the sessions remained
in office. The Aragonese had their own laws, their own
judges, their own police, their own prisons, and no
"alien" armed force was permitted within their boundaries. The Grand Justiciary, the highest executive officer, was nominated by the King, but could not be deprived of office by him. A Royal Commissioner resided
in Saragossa, to observe and to report, to act in cases to
which the Crown was a party, perhaps irregularly to dis-
tribute favors and influence opinion. But this was the
limit of his interference. The Commissioner in the year
1590 was Inigo de Mendoza, Marques of Almenara, the
cousin and the chief antagonist of the Princess of Eboli.

Such was Aragon when Antonio Perez sought an asy-
lum in the land of his fathers. He professed to have
been tortured till his limbs were disabled, but he was
able to ride without resting till he had crossed the frontier
and had reached Calatayud. He made no effort, perhaps
he was too weak, to go further, and he took refuge in a
Dominican convent. Within ten hours of his arrival an
express came in from Madrid to a private gentleman,
Don Manuel Zapata, with orders to take him, dead or
alive, and send him back to his master. Perez says that
when his flight was known at the Court, there was general
satisfaction. "Uncle Martin," the palace jester, said to
Philip the next morning : " Sir, all the world rejoices at
the escape of Antonio Perez ; he cannot be very wicked ;
you should rejoice too." Philip did not rejoice at all.

He had put himself in the power of one of his subjects, and he did not choose to remain any longer in so degrading a position. When he had been himself willing to submit his conduct to a judicial inquiry, Perez, who had less to fear if he had been acting uprightly, had shown so much unwillingness that possibly Philip may have now doubted whether Escovedo's conduct had after all been properly represented to him. Perez had fled, carrying the compromising documents along with him; he was probably on his way to France, to delight Philip's enemies with the sight of them, and with the tale of his own wrongs.

Anticipating pursuit, Perez had sent a friend, Gil de Mesa, to the Grand Justiciary, to signify his arrival, and to put himself under the protection of the law. Meanwhile, the town mob at Calatayud rose in his defence, and when Don Manuel arrived at the monastery he found the priests and students in arms to protect their sanctuary. Fifty soldiers arrived immediately after from Saragossa. The orders of the Justiciary were to bring Perez at once to the national prison of the Manifestacion, where he was to be detained till the King could be communicated with. The King's reply was an order to the Marques of Almenara to prosecute him immediately in the Court of Aragon on three charges.

1. For having caused the death of Escovedo, falsely pretending the King's authority.

2. For having betrayed secrets of State and tampered with ciphered despatches.

3. For having fled from justice when his conduct was being judicially inquired into.

If Perez had been wholly innocent he would have felt that he had at last an opportunity of setting himself clear in the face of the world. The court would be open,

the trial public, and his defence could neither be gar-
bled nor suppressed. His reluctance was as vehement
as ever, and was not concealed by his affectation of a
desire to spare his master. From Calatayud, and from
Saragossa afterward, he wrote letter upon letter both to
Philip and to Diego de Chaves, protesting his loyalty,
entreating to be left in quiet with his wife and children ;
indicating that he had the means of defending himself,
but hoping that he might not be forced to use them.
These letters being left unanswered, he took into his
confidence a distinguished Aragonese ecclesiastic, the
Prior of Gotor. He showed the Prior the mysterious
papers which he had brought with him, with Philip's
notes upon them, and desired him to go at once to
Madrid and demand an audience of Philip. "His
Majesty," Perez said in his instructions to the Prior,
"must know that I possess these documents. They
contain confidential secrets affecting others besides Escovedo ; let his Majesty judge whether it is desirable that
evidences should be produced in court which touch the
reputation of distinguished persons, which will create a
scandal throughout Europe, and will reflect on the prudence and piety of his Majesty himself. Though the
confessor has taken most of my papers from me, Providence has been pleased that I should retain these, and
these will suffice for my defence. If brought to trial I
shall certainly be acquitted ; but I prefer to save the
King's reputation ; my case is now notorious, and it will
not be wise to challenge the world's opinion. I have
been shorn like a lamb for eleven years, and I have held
my peace. My blood has been shed. I have been tortured in a dungeon, and I have remained faithful. In
eight or ten days I must give in my answer. Some
people tell me that I ought rather to lose my head than

speak; but if I am driven to it the truth must be told."

The Prior went. Philip saw him more than once, and heard what he had to say. There could be no doubt that Perez had the compromising letters, for the Prior had seen them. Yet Philip's courage did not fail him. After Perez's flight the Court of Castile had given judgment against him in default. He was to be dragged through the streets and hanged. His head was to be cut off and exposed, and all his property was to be confiscated. The answer to the mission of the Prior of Gotor was the publication of his sentence.

Perez, thus driven to bay, took up the challenge. He drew a memorial containing his own account of the causes of Escovedo's murder. He attached it to such notes as sufficed to prove the King's complicity, reserving others in case of future necessity; and this was publicly presented as his reply to the Marques of Almenara. The King had probably expected that the judges of Aragon would not lightly accept so grave a charge against their sovereign; that they would respect the sentence of the better informed Court of Castile, and would understand that there was something behind which was left unexplained. But Aragon was excited, and chose to show its independence. After the admission of the memorial Don Inigo sent word to the King, that if no further evidence were produced, Perez would certainly be acquitted. The King believed that he had other resources at his disposition by which complete defeat could be avoided, and at the last moment directed that the case before the Grand Justiciary should be abandoned. "If," said Philip, " it was possible to reply with the same publicity which Perez has given to his defence, his guilt would be proved, and he would be condemned. Throughout this whole affair I have considered only the public good. The long imprisonment of Perez, the entire course which the cause has taken, has had no other object. Abusing my clemency, and afraid of the issue, he so defends himself that to answer him I must publish secrets which ought not to be revealed, and involve persons whose reputation is of more consequence than the punishment of a single offender. Therefore, I shall go no further with the prosecution in the Court of Aragon. I declare Perez to have sinned worse than ever vassal sinned before against his sovereign — both in time, form, and circumstance ; and I desire this my declaration to be entered with my notice of withdrawal. Truth, which I have always maintained, must suffer no injury. And I reserve such rights as appertain, or may appertain to me, of bringing the offender to account for his crimes in any other manner."

The "other manner" was through the Court of Enquesta. In the Constitution of Aragon, a special reservation excluded from protection the King's servants and officials. Over these the law of the province had no more authority than the King was pleased to allow—and the King under this clause claimed to have Perez surrendered to himself. The local lawyers, however, interpreted "servants" to mean only servants in Aragon and engaged in the affairs in Aragon, not persons belonging to other countries or other provinces. Aragonese, who accepted Crown employment, undertook it with their eyes open and at their own risk, and might be supposed to have consented to their exemption ; but such a case as that of Perez had not been contemplated when the clause in the Constitution was allowed. But the King had one more resource. Though acquitted, the prisoner was still detained, as if the authórities were unsatisfied of his real innocence. Perez had grown impatient, and, in his loose, vain way, had babbled to his companions in the Manifestacion, and his language had been so extravagant that it had been noted down and forwarded to the court. He had threatened to fly to France or Holland, when he would make the King repent of his treatment of him. He had compared himself to Marius, who had been driven into exile and had returned to the consulship. He said that he would raise a revolt in Castile ; he would bring in Henry the Fourth ; he would make Aragon into a Free Republic like Venice. He spoke of Philip as another Pharaoh. He had ventured into more dangerous ground, and had called into question the mysteries of the faith. Some of these rash expressions had been noted down in writing, with the solemn reflections on them of the King's confessor. The impatient wretch had said that "if God the Father allowed the King to behave so disloyally to him he would take God the Father by the nose." The confessor observes, " This proposition is blasphemous, scandalous, offensive to pious ears, and savoring of the heresy of the Vadiani, who affirmed that God was corporeal and had human members. Nor was it an excuse to say that Christ, being made man, had a nose, since the words were spoken of the First Person."

Again, Perez had said, " God is asleep in this affair of mine. If He works no miracle for me, it will go near to destroy the faith."

" This proposition," the confessor noted, " is scandalous. The prisoner has been accused of the greatest enormities ; he has been tried by course of law and condemned to death, and he speaks as if he was without fault."

10

Worse still. Perez had gone on, " God sleeps ! God
sleeps ! God is an idle tale ; there cannot be a God ! "

The confessor observes, " This proposition is heretical,
as if God had no care for human things, when the Bible
and the Church affirm that He does care. To say that
there cannot be a God *is* heresy, for though it be said in
doubt, yet doubt is not allowed in matters of faith ; we
must believe without doubt."

Lastly, Perez had said, " If things pass thus, I cannot
believe in God."

The confessor notes, " This is blasphemous, scandalous,
and offensive, and savors of heresy also."

The confessor's ears had no doubt been outraged.
Many a poor sinner had gone to the stake for less audacious utterances. For nine months after the failure
with the Enquesta, Perez remained in the Manifestacion,
pouring out these wild outcries. At the end of them an
order came from the Holy Office at Madrid to the three
Inquisitors at Saragossa to take possession of his person
and remove him to their own prison in the old Moorish
palace of the Aljaferia.

The Inquisitor-General of Spain was his old friend,
the Archbishop of Toledo. In Madrid the Inquisition
had been well disposed toward him, and once he had
thrown himself on its protection. Had he now submitted voluntarily, he would probably have been safe from
serious injury, and an impartial decision would have
been arrived at. The Inquisition, be it remembered,
was no slave of the Crown, and, though a cruel guardian
of orthodoxy, would not have looked too narrowly at the
fretful words of a man whom the Archbishop believed
to have been ill used. The judges of Aragon were by
this time satisfied that Perez was not entirely the martyr
which he pretended to be, and that the King had some-

thing to say for himself. Philip, who appears to Protestant Europe a monster of injustice, was in Spain respected and esteemed. The Grand Justiciary did not wish to quarrel with the Crown in a case so doubtful, still less to quarrel with the Holy Office, and was preparing quietly to comply. But Perez would not have it so, and preferred to trust to popular jealousy. A mob is always ready to listen when it is told that Liberty is in danger. A story was circulated in Saragossa that the Marques of Almenara had bribed the prisoners in the Manifestacion to send in a false account of Perez's language, that the Inquisition was claiming a right which did not belong to it, that the Fueros were being betrayed, and that the Aragonese were to be made slaves of the Castilians. Symptoms showed themselves of an intended rising, and the Justiciary and Don Iñigo, after a night's conference, agreed that Perez should be removed at once and without notice to the Inquisition prison. At noon on May 24, 1591, he was quietly placed in a carriage at the Manifestacion Gate. A knot of young men tried to stop the horses, and clamored for the Constitution; but they were told that it was *cosa de fey*, an affair of religion, and that they must mind their own business. The carriage reached the Aljaferia without interruption, and Perez was in the Inquisitors' hands. But on the instant Saragossa was in arms. The alarm bell boomed out. The market-place swarmed with a furious multitude shouting "Fueros, Fueros! Libertad! Libertad!" Their plans had been already laid. Half the mob went to attack the Aljaferia, the others to the house of Philip's representative, the Marques of Almenara. He, too, it is likely, had remembered that Perez was the friend of the Princess of Eboli, and had thrown himself into the quarrel with some degree of personal animosity. He

was now to expiate his eagerness. He was urged to
fly. The Mendozas, he answered, never fled. The palace
door was dashed in. The Justiciary, who had hurried
to protect him, was thrown down and trampled on. Don
Inigo was seized, dragged out, and borne away among
cries of "Muera, muera!—Kill him, kill him!" Stripped
naked, his clothes torn off, his arms almost forced out
of their sockets, struck and pelted with stones, he was at
last rescued by a party of police, who carried him into
the city prison. There, a fortnight after, he died of his
injuries, so ending his lawsuit with the widow of Ruy
Gomez.

The Inquisitors at the Aljaferia had a near escape of
the same fate. The walls were strong and the gates
massive. But the fierce people brought fagots in cart-
loads, and raised a pile which would have reduced the
palace and all in it to dust and ashes. The Inquisitors,
they said, had burned others; they should now burn
themselves unless Perez was instantly released. The
Inquisitors would have held out, but the Archbishop of
Saragossa, Almenara's brother, insisted that they must
yield. Perez, four hours only after they had seized him,
was given back to his friends, and borne away in triumph.

But the mob had risen for the rights of Aragon, and
not, after all, for a prisoner of whose innocence even
they were unconvinced. Perez imagined himself a
national hero. He had expected that the Cortez would
take up his case, that he would be allowed to present
himself at the bar, and detail the story of his wrongs in
Philip's own presence. The leaders of the people had
formed a cooler estimate of his merits. They contented
themselves with taking him back to the Manifestacion.
The officials of the province went up to Madrid, to deliberate with the court what was next to be done.

For Perez personally there was no enthusiasm. If the Inquisition would acknowledge the Fueros, the sensible people of Saragossa were ready to surrender him. The Inquisition made the necessary concessions, and Perez's own supporters now advised him to submit unreservedly. But this he did not dare to do ; he tried to escape from the Manifestacion and failed. He appealed again to the mob. Broad sheets were printed and circulated declaring that the officials were betraying the Fueros, and though the chiefs of the first insurrection had withdrawn, the multitude could still be wrought upon. Unfortunately for Aragon, the Grand Justiciary, Don Juan de Lanuza, a wise and prudent man, suddenly died. Had he lived a few weeks longer he might have saved his country, but it was not so to be. The nomination of his successor belonged to the King, but the office had by custom become hereditary in the Lanuza family ; Don Juan's son, a generous, hot-headed youth, claimed to act without waiting for the King's sanction, and, fatally for himself, was ruled or influenced by his uncle, Don Martin, who was Perez's most intimate ally. The officials had returned from the court. The Council of Saragossa had decided that Perez should be restored to the Holy Office. The removal was to be effected on the following morning, September 24 ; but when the morning came the mob were out again. The Manifestacion was broken open, the council-room was set on fire, and Perez was again released. It was understood, however, that he was not to remain any longer at Saragossa to be a future occasion of quarrel. He was escorted a league out of the city on the road to the Pyrenees, and he was made to know that if he returned he would not be protected. He did return ; he pretended that the roads were unsafe, but he came back in secret, and in the closest disguise, and lay concealed in Don Martin's house till it could be seen how the King would act.

Constitutional governments which cannot govern are near their end. When the intelligent and the educated part of the population are superseded by the mob, they cannot continue zealous for forms of freedom which to them are slavery. The mob has usurped the power ; if it can defend its actions successfully, it makes good the authority which it has seized ; if it fails, the blame is with itself. The Aragon executive had protected Perez on his arrival in the province, they had given him the means of making an open defence, and, so far as their own council could decide in his cause, they had pronounced him acquitted. But there were charges against him which could not be openly pleaded, and his innocence was not so clear that it would be right as yet to risk a civil war in a case so ambiguous. The judges considered that enough had been done. The mob and the young Justiciary thought otherwise, and with them the responsibility rested.

Philip was in no hurry. Ten thousand men were collected quietly on the frontier under Don Alonzo de Vargas. The sentiments of the principal persons were sounded, and it was ascertained that from those who could offer serious resistance there was none to be anticipated. Liberty had lost its attractions when it meant the protection of criminals by the town rabble. That the mob had shaken themselves clear of Perez made little difference to Philip, for they had taken him by force out of prison. The middle-class citizens, who still prized their Constitution, believed, on the other hand, or at least some of them believed, that the King had no longer an excuse for interfering with them.

Philip so far respected their alarm that before he ordered the advance of the troops he sent out a proclamation that the Constitution would not be disturbed ; and possibly, if there had been no opposition, he would have found his course less clear. But the more eager spirits could not be restrained ; the nobles held aloof ; the young Justiciary, however, was ardent and enthusiastic —he was compromised besides, for he had taken office without waiting for the King's permission. The invasion was an open breach of the Fueros. He called the citizens of Saragossa to arms, and sent appeals for help to Barcelona and the other towns.

There was no response—a sufficient proof either that the province was indifferent, or that the cause was regarded as a bad one. Lanuza let out a tattered multitude of shopkeepers and workmen to meet the Castilians ; but, though brave enough in a city insurrection, they had no stomach for fighting with a disciplined force. They turned and scattered without a blow, and Alonzo de Vargas entered Saragossa November 12, 1591.

The modern doctrine, that political offences are virtues in disguise, was not yet the creed even of the most advanced philosophers. The Saragossa rabble had resisted the lawful authorities of the province. They had stormed a prison ; they had murdered the King's representative ; fatalest of all, they had taken arms for liberty, and had wanted courage to fight for it. The Justiciary was executed, and fifteen or twenty other persons. The attack on the Aljaferia was an act of sacrilege, and the wrongs of the Inquisition were avenged more severely. A hundred and twenty-three of the most prominent of the mob were arrested. Of these, seventy-nine were burnt in the market-place. The ceremony began at eight in the morning ; it closed at night, when

there was no light but from the blazing fagots; the
last figure that was consumed was the effigy of Antonio
Perez, the original cause of the catastrophe. The punishment being concluded, the Constitution was abolished.
The armed resistance was held to have dispensed with
Philip's promises, and the Fueros of Aragon were at an
end.

Perez himself escaped on the night on which the Castilians entered, and made his way through the Pyrenees
to Pau. He published a narrative of his sufferings—that
is, his own version of them, with the further incriminating
documents which the Protestant world at once received
with greedy acclamations. Much of what he said was
probably true; much might have worn another complexion if the other side had been told. But Philip never
condescended to reply. Perez was taken up by Henry
IV., pensioned, trusted, and employed so long as the war
with Spain continued. He was sent into England. He
was received by Elizabeth, entertained by Essex, and
admitted into acquaintance by Francis Bacon—not with
the approval of Bacon's mother, who disliked him from
the first. He was plausible; he was polished; he was
acute. He had been so long intimately acquainted with
Spanish secrets, that his information was always useful
and often of the highest value. But he was untrue at
the heart. Even his own *Relacion* is in many points inconsistent with itself, and betrays the inward hollowness;
while his estimate of his own merits went beyond what
his most foolish friends could believe or acknowledge.
Gradually he was seen through both in Paris and London. When peace came he was thrown aside, and sank
into neglect and poverty. He attempted often, but
always fruitlessly, to obtain his pardon from Philip
III., and eventually died miserably in a Paris lodging,

a worn-out old man of seventy-two, on November 3, 1611.

So ends the story of a man who, if his personal merits alone were concerned, might have been left forgotten among the unnumbered millions who have played their chequered parts on the stage of the world. Circumstances, and the great religious revolution of the sixteenth century, converted Philip in the eyes of half Europe into a malignant demon. The darkest interpretations were thrown upon every unexplained action which he committed ; and Antonio Perez became the hero of a romance fitter for a third-rate theatre than the pages of accredited history. The imaginative features of it have now disappeared, but there remains an instructive picture of Philip's real character. He said that he had been guided throughout by no motive save concern for the public welfare, and there is no reason to suppose that he was saying anything except what he believed to be true ; yet he so acted as to invite suspicion in every step which he took.

Escovedo, as his conduct was represented by Perry, deserved to be punished, perhaps to be punished severely. To prosecute him publicly would have been doubtless inconvenient ; and Philip, without giving him an opportunity of defending himself, undertook the part of a secret providence, and allowed him to be struck in the dark without explaining his reasons. Providence does not permit vain mortals, even though they be Catholic kings, to usurp a jurisdiction which is reserved for itself. It punished Philip by throwing him into the power of an unscrupulous intriguer, who had, perhaps, in some measure really misled him on the extent of Escovedo's faults.

He tried to extricate himself, but he was entangled in

the net which his own hands had woven ; and, when Perez refused to assist him, and preferred to keep him struggling at his mercy, he was driven to measures which could be represented to the world as a base persecution of the instrument of his own crimes. Thus, out of an unwise ambition to exercise the attributes of omniscience, the poor King laid himself open to groundless accusations, and the worst motives which could be supposed to have actuated him were those which found easiest credit.

But the legend of the loves of Philip II. and the Princess of Eboli was not of Spanish growth. The *Relacion* of Perez was read in the Peninsula, but it did not shake the confidence with which Philip was regarded by his subjects. The Fueros of Aragon perished, but they perished only because constitutional liberties which degenerate into anarchy are already ripe for an end.

SAINT TERESA *

Reprinted from the Quarterly Review.

On the western slope of the Guadarrama Mountains, midway between Medina del Campo and the Escurial, stands the ancient town of Avila. From the windows of the railway carriage can be seen the massive walls and flanking towers, raised in the eleventh century in the first heat of the Spanish crusade. The fortifications themselves tell the story of their origin. The garrison of Avila were soldiers of Christ, and the cathedral was built into the bastions, in the front line of defence, as an emblem of the genius of the age. Time has scarcely touched the solid masonry. Ruy Diaz and his contemporaries have vanished into legend; but these silent monuments of the old Castilian character survive to remind us what manner of men the builders of them were. Revolutions on revolutions overflow the Spanish peninsula, condemn the peasantry to poverty, and the soil to barrenness; but they have not in these later times unearthed in the process a single man like those whose names are part of European history. They have produced military adventurers, and orators like Castelar, of " transcendent eloquence ;" but no Cid, no Grand Captain, no Alva, not even a Cortez or a Pizarro. The Pro-

* 1. *Acta S. Teresiæ a Jesu, Carmelitarum strictioris Observantiæ parentis.* Illustrata a Josepho Vandermoere, Societatis Jesu Presbytero Theologo. Bruxellis, 1845. 2. *Obras de Santa Teresa de J.sus.* Barcelona, 1844.

gresista of our age has a long ascent before him if he is to rise to the old level.

The situation of Avila is extremely picturesque, standing in the midst of gray granite sierras, covered with pine forests, and intersected with clear mountain rivulets. It is now thinly populated, and, like most towns in Spain, has fallen into decay and neglect; but the large solid mansions, the cathedral, the churches, the public buildings, the many convents and monasteries, though mostly gone to waste and ruin, show that once it was full of busy, active life, of men and women playing their parts there in the general drama of their country.

In the Spain of Ferdinand and Isabella there were two peculiarities; first, that there was no recognized capital, for the provinces which formed the monarchy were still imperfectly cemented; and secondly, that the nobles and gentry, the señores and the hidalgos, had their chief residences in the towns, and not on their estates. The causes and consequences of this practice of theirs it would be interesting to trace, were the present the occasion for it, but of the fact itself there is no doubt at all. Of feudal châteaux and manor-houses, so numerous in France and England, there were not many in any part of Spain, and very few in the Castiles. The landed aristocracy congregated within the walls of the provincial cities. Their palaces are still to be seen in grand and gaunt neglect, with their splendid staircases, their quadrangles, their columned verandas, the coats of arms carved over the portals. In the cities also were the learned professions : the lawyers, the doctors, the secular clergy, the religious orders. The Court moved from place to place, and there was no central focus to draw away men of superior rank or superior talents from their local homes. The communications were difficult; the roads were horse-tracks; the rivers, save where some enterprising municipality had built a bridge, were crossed only by fords and pontoons. Thus each important town was the heart of a separate district, a complete epitome of Spanish life, with all its varied circles. An aristocracy was in each, proud and exclusive. A religious world was in each; a world of art and literature, of commerce and adventure. Every family had some member pushing his fortunes in the army or in the New Hemisphere. The minds of men were in full activity. They were enterprising and daring. Their manners were polished, and their habits splendid; for into Spain first had poured the fruits of the discoveries of Columbus, and the stream of gold was continually growing with fresh conquests. Perhaps nowhere on the earth was there a finer average of distinguished and cultivated society than in the Provincial Castilian cities, as it is described in Cervantes's novels. The Castilians were a nation of gentlemen, high bred, courteous, chivalrous. In arms they had no rivals. In art and literature Italy alone was in advance of them, and Italy led by no great interval; while the finest characteristics were to be met with equally in every part of the country.

They were a sincere people too, Catholic in belief, and earnestly meaning what they professed. In the presence of the Moors, Christianity had retained its mediæval features. Of Christianity itself they knew no form, and could conceive of none, save that for which they had fought against the Moslem; and the cause of the Church was the cause of patriotism. Therefore, when the Reformation began in Germany, the Spaniard naturally regarded its adherents as the old enemy in another dress. An Italian priest could mutter at the altar,

" Bread thou art, and bread thou wilt remain." No such monster could have been found in the Spanish Peninsula. Leo X. was said to have called Christianity a profitable fable. To the subjects of Isabella it was a truth, which devils only could deny.

The Northern nations revolted from the Church in the name of liberty. The Spaniards loved liberty, but it was the liberty of their country, for which they had been fighting for centuries against the Infidel. As aristocrats, they were instinctively on the side of authority. United among themselves, they believed in the union of Christendom; and they threw themselves into the struggle against heresy with the same enthusiasm with which they contended with the Crescent in the Mediterranean. They sent their chivalry to the Low Countries as if to a crusade. Two Spaniards, Ignatius Loyola and Francis Xavier, created the spiritual army of the Jesuits. While some were engaged with the enemy abroad, the finer spirits among them undertook the task of setting in order their own house at home. They, too, required a Reformation, if they were to be fit champions of a Holy Cause; and the instrument was a woman, with as few natural advantages as Ignatius himself, distinguished only in representing, as he did, the vigorous instincts of the Spanish character.

The Church of Rome, it has been said, does not, like the Church of England, drive her enthusiasts into rebellion, but preserves and wisely employs them. She may employ them wisely while they are alive, but when they are dead she decks them out in paint and tinsel, to be worshipped as divinities. Their history becomes a legend. They are surrounded with an envelope of lies. Teresa of Avila has fared no better than other saints in the calendar. She has been the favorite idol of modern Spain, and she deserved more modest treatment.

The idolatry may merit all that Mr. Ford has said about it, but the account which he has given of the lady herself is so wide of the original, that it is not even a caricature. Ford, doubtless, did not like Catholic saints, and the absurdities told about them disgusted him; but the materials lay before him for a real portrait of Teresa, had he cared to examine them; and it is a pity that he did not, for no one could have done better justice to his subject.

Teresa de Cepeda was born at Avila on March 28, 1515 —the time, according to her biographer, "when Luther was secreting the poison which he vomited out two years later." . . . She was one of a large family, eleven children in all, eight sons and three daughters. Her father, Don Alfonso, was twice married. Teresa's mother was the second wife, Beatrice de Ahumada, a beautiful, imaginative woman, whom bad health confined chiefly to a sofa. The Cepedas were of honorable descent; Don Alfonso was a gentleman of leisure and moderate fortune. He spent his time, when not engaged with works of charity, in reading Spanish literature—chiefly Church history and lives of the saints. His library, if the Barber and Curate had sat upon it, would have been sifted as ruthlessly as the shelves of the Ingenious Knight of La Mancha, for half of it was composed of books of Knight Errantry—the same volumes probably which those stern Inquisitors condemned to the flames. These books were devoured as eagerly by the delicate Beatrice as the graver pages by her husband, and her example was naturally imitated by her children. They sat up at nights in their nursery over Rolando and Don Belianis and Amadis of Gaul. Teresa composed odes to imaginary cavaliers,

who figured in adventures of which she was herself the
heroine. They had to conceal their tastes from their
father, who would not have approved of them. He was
a very good man, exceptionally good. He treated his
servants as if they were his sons and daughters. He was
never heard to swear, or to speak ill of anyone. He was
the constant friend of the Avila poor. If too indulgent,
he had sense and information, and when he discerned
what was going on, he diverted Teresa's tastes in a safer
direction. By nature, she says, she was the least religious of her family, but her imagination was impressible,
and she delighted in all forms of human heroism. She
early forgot her knights, and devoted herself to martyrs ;
and here, being concrete and practical, she thought she
would turn her new enthusiasm to account. If to be in
heaven was to be eternally happy, and martyrs went to
heaven straight, without passing through Purgatory, she
concluded that she could do nothing more prudent than
become a martyr herself. When she was seven years old,
she and her little brother Antonio actually started off to
go to the Moors, who they expected would kill them.
The children had reached the bridge on the stream which
runs through the town, when an uncle met them and
brought them back. As they could not be martyrs, they
thought, as next best, that they would be hermits. They
gave away their pocket-money to beggars. They made
themselves cells in the garden. Teresa's ambition grew.
When other girls came to see her, they played at nunne-
ries, when she was perhaps herself the abbess. Amid
these fancies her childish years passed away. She does
not seem to have had much regular teaching. Nothing
is said about it ; and when she grew up she had difficulty in reading her Latin Breviary.

The Knight Errantry books, however, had left their

traces. Her mother died while she was still very young, and she was much affected. But natural children do not long continue miserable. As she passed into girlhood, her glass told her that she was pretty, and she was pleased to hear it. She was moderately tall, well shaped, with a fine complexion, round brilliant black eyes, black hair, crisp and curly, good teeth, and firmly chiselled lips and nose. So fair a figure deserved that pains should be taken with it. She was particular about her dress ; she liked perfumes ; her small dainty hands were kept scrupulously white. Cousins, male and female, went and came ; and there were small flirtations with the boys, and with the girls not very wise confidences. One girl cousin there was especially, whom the mother, while she lived, would not allow to visit at the house, and whom an elder sister would still have kept at a distance had she been able. But Teresa was wilful, and chose this especial young lady as her principal companion. There were also silly servants, too ready to encourage folly, and Teresa says that at this time nothing but regard for her honor kept her clear of serious scrapes.

Don Alfonso grew uneasy ; the elder sister married and went away ; so, feeling unequal himself to the task of managing a difficult subject, he sent Teresa to be educated in an Augustinian convent in the town. Neither her father nor she had any thoughts of her adopting a religious life. He never wished it at any time. She did not wish it then, and had undefined notions of marrying as her sister had done. The convent to her was merely a school, where there were many other girls of her own age, nor did she wholly like the life there. She made friends among the elder nuns, especially with one, a simple, pious woman, who slept in the same room with her. But the younger sisters were restless. They had

11

acquaintances in the town, and were occupied with other things besides religious vows. Within the convent itself all was not as it should have been. The vicar of the Order had the whole spiritual management both of the nuns and of their pupils. No one but himself might hear their confessions, and the prioress could not interfere with him, since by his position he was her superior. Teresa does not hint that there was anything positively wrong, but when she came to lay down rules in later years for the regulation of her own houses, she refers to her recollections of what went on in language curiously frank :

" The confessor in a convent," she says, " ought not to be the vicar or the visitor. He may take a special interest in some sister. The Prioress will be unable to prevent him from talking to her, and a thousand mischiefs may follow. . . . The sisters should have no intercourse with the confessor except at the confessional. . . . The very existence of our institutions depends on preventing *these black devotees* from destroying the spouses of Christ. The devil enters that way unperceived." *

The vicar confessor encouraged Teresa in her views for marriage, but her fancies and her friendship were suddenly broken off by an attack of illness. She required change of air ; she was sent on a visit to her sister ; and on her way home she spent a few days with an uncle, a man of secluded and saintly habits, who afterward withdrew into a monastery. The uncle advised his niece to take the same step that he was himself meditating ; and

* " Va nos todo nuestro Ser, en quitar la ocasion para que no haya estos negros devotos destruidores de las esposas de Christo, que es menester pensar siempre en lo peor que puede suceder, para quitar esta ocasion, que se entra sin sentirlo por aqui el demonio."—*Cartas de la Santa Madre*, vol. vi. p. 232.

she discussed the question with herself in the same
spirit with which she had designed throwing herself
among the Moors. She reflected that convent discipline
might be painful, but it could not be as painful as Purgatory, while if she remained in the world she might
come to something worse than Purgatory. She read
St. Jerome's Epistles ; she then consulted her father,
and was distressed to meet with strong objections. Don
Alfonso was attached to his children, and Teresa was his
especial favorite. The utmost that she could obtain was
a permission to do as she pleased after his own death.
But "a vocation" was held to dispense with duties to
parents. She made up her own mind, and, like Luther,
she decided to act for herself, and to take a step which,
when once accomplished, could not be recalled. One
morning she left her home with her brother, and applied
for admission at the Carmelite Convent of the Incarnation. She was then eighteen. She had been disappointed with the Augustinians ; but the Carmelites had
a reputation for superior holiness, and she threw herself among them with the passionate enthusiasm of an
ardent girl, who believed that she was securing her
peace in this world, and happiness in the next. Again
she was to be undeceived. The Order of Mount Car-
mel had been founded by Albert, Patriarch of Jerusalem,
in the second Crusade. The rule had been austere—
austere as the rule of the Carthusians—with strict seclusion, silence, solitude, the plainest dress, the most
ascetic diet. But by the beginning of the sixteenth
century time and custom had relaxed the primitive
severity, and Carmelite convents had become a part of
general society ; the nuns within the cloisters living and
occupying themselves in a manner not very different
from their friends outside, with whom they were in con-

stant communication.   Austerity was still possible, but
it was not insisted on, and was a sign of presumption
and singularity.   In the "incarnation" there were a
hundred and ninety sisters, and the discipline among
them was scarcely more than a name.   They went in and
out as they pleased ; they received visits and returned
them ; they could be absent from the cloister for months
at a time.   Catholics accuse Protestants of having
libelled the monastic life of Europe as it existed before
the Reformation.   Luther himself has said nothing
harsher of it than the saint of Avila.   She followed the
stream, she said ; she abandoned herself to vanity and
amusement, and neither custom nor the authority of her
superiors laid the slightest check upon her.   She had as
much liberty as she liked to ask for, and liberty in a
convent meant free opportunities of evil.   She does not
assert that there was gross licentiousness ; but she does
assert that to "ill-disposed women" convent life "was
rather a road to hell than an aid to weakness ;" and
that "parents would do better to marry their daughters honestly than to place them in relaxed houses of
religion :"

"The girls themselves," she says, "are not so much to
blame, for they do no worse than they see other sdo.   They
enter convents to serve the Lord and escape the dangers of
the world, and they are flung into ten worlds all together,
with youth, sensuality, and the devil tempting them to evil.
. . . In the same house are two roads, one leading to
virtue and piety, another leading *away* from virtue and piety ;
and the road of religion is so little travelled, that a sister who
wishes to follow it has more to fear from her companions
than from all the devils.   She finds it easier far to make in-
timacies with the devil's instruments than to seek friendship with God."

How dangerous this lax temper might have been to herself Teresa tells us in an instructive incident. Her health was never strong, and the convent had disagreed with her. She was sick every morning, and could touch no food till noon. She often fainted, and there were symptoms of heart disorder. Nor was she happy in herself. She had tried to be good, and had only made enemies by her efforts. She found herself rebuked for small offences of which she was wholly innocent. She lived much alone, and the sisters thought she was discontented. Her father became alarmed for her, and again sent her away into the country, with a single nun for a companion. At the place where she went to reside there was an attractive priest, a man of intellect and culture. Teresa was fond of cultivated men. She took the priest for her confessor, and found him more and more agreeable. He flattered her conscience by telling her that she could never wish to do wrong. He said it was his own case also, and they became extremely intimate. She was informed after a time that this charmingly innocent person had been living for some years with a female companion, while he continued to say mass as if nothing were the matter. She was at first incredulous. She made inquiries, but the scandal was notorious. Everyone was aware of it, but the offender had influence, and it was unsafe to interfere with him. Even so, however, Teresa would not abandon her friend, and looked for excuses for him. The woman, she found, had given him an amulet, and while he wore it he was under a spell. He told her this himself, and her interest was now increased by pity and anxiety. She admits that she was unwise, that she ought at once to have ended the acquaintance. She preferred to endeavor to save a perishing soul. She was but twenty ; she was very beautiful ;

she spoke to the attractive sinner of God ; and of course to a lesson from such lips he was delighted to listen. She perceived the cause, but was not discouraged. She pressed him to give her the amulet, and equally of course he consented. She threw it into the river, and he at once broke off his guilty connection, and devoted himself to spiritual communion with herself. She flattered herself that he was penitent, though it was equally clear that he was in love with her ; and he abandoned himself to his affection with the less reserve, because she says he had confidence in her virtue, and supposed that he could do so without danger. The danger was as great as it usually is under such circumstances. They had " opportunities of sin," she said, and though she believed that they would not have fallen mortally, she admits that they might have gone seriously wrong if they had not kept God before their eyes. The priest died a year after, and, as Teresa observes naïvely, was delivered from further temptation. She long retained some tenderness for him ; twenty years later, when she wrote the story, she expressed a conviction that he was saved ; but the experience must have helped her to the opinion, which she afterward so strongly insisted on, that confessors were the most unsafe of friends.

After this adventure, which she relates with perfect simplicity, she returned to the convent. Her health was not improved. She was still constantly sick ; she had paroxysms of pain ; her nervous system was shattered, and the physicians were afraid of madness. In this state she remained for three years. At the end of them it occurred to her to pray for help to San Josef. From some cause she became comparatively better ; and to San Josef she supposed that she owed her recovery. " God," she says, " has allowed other saints to help us on some occasions ; my experience of this glorious saint is that he helps us in all : as if the Lord would teach us that, as he was subject to San Josef on earth, and San Josef was called his father though only his guardian, so San Josef, though in heaven, has still authority with him."

The illness had become less acute ; but, as the pain of body grew less, Teresa became conscious of spiritual maladies that were left uncured. " She loved God with half her mind, but she loved the world with the other." Her prayers troubled her, she says, for she could not fix her mind on them. Meditation was yet more difficult. " She had a slow intellect and a torpid imagination." She required a book to help her, for the right reflections and emotions would not occur to herself ; other thoughts persisted in intruding themselves ; and at length, being, as she was, a veracious woman, she abandoned prayer altogether. Among all her faults, she says she was never a hypocrite, and prayer when it was no more than a form of words seemed an indecent mockery.

Her confessor, when she explained her troubles, only thought her morbid. In the convent she was regarded as exceptionally strict, and wide as was the general liberty, with her every rule was dispensed with. She spent her time in the society of Avila with more enjoyment than she was herself aware of, and when a pious old nun told her that she was causing scandal, she would not understand it, and was only angry.

" Unless God had brought me to the earth," she says, " I should most assuredly have gone at last to hell. I had many friends to help me to fall, while, as to rising again, I was utterly alone. My confessor did nothing for me. For twenty years I was tossed about on a stormy sea in a wretched condition, for if I had small content in the world, in God I had no pleasure. There were months, once there was an entire year, when I was careful not to offend ; but of all those years eighteen were years of battle. At prayer time I watched for the clock to strike the end of the hour. To go to the oratory was a vexation to me, and prayer itself a constant effort."

Such was Teresa's conventual experience, as described by herself. She began her noviciate in 1534. The twenty years, therefore, extended to 1554, the year in which Philip went to England to be married to our Queen Mary. She was then nearly forty, and her efforts so far in the direction of religion had consisted rather in helping others (which she says she was always eager to do) than in framing any steady resolutions for herself. Her conversion, as it is called, her first attempt to think with real seriousness, was occasioned by the death of her father. She had watched by him in his last illness. She saw his spirit take flight, and heard the assurance of his Dominican confessor that it had gone straight to heaven. She had been deeply attached to him. She woke up out of her irresolutions, and determined to use the rest of her life to better purpose than the beginning.

She was not a person to do anything by halves. She thought of Mary Magdalene. She read the " Confessions " of St. Augustine, and saw an image there of her own state of mind. One day, as she was entering the oratory, she was struck by the sight of an image which had been brought thither for an approaching festival. It was a wounded Christ, the statue colored with the painful realism which suited the Spanish taste, the blood streaming over the face from the thorns, and running

from the side and the hands and feet. Protestants and
Catholics experience an identical emotion when the
meaning of Christianity is brought home to them.
Each poor sinner recognizes, as by a flash of lightning,
that these tortures were endured for him or her—that
he or she was actually present in the Saviour's mind
when he was suffering on the cross. The thought when
it comes is overpowering. Teresa felt as if her heart
were wrenched in two. She fell in tears at the feet of
the figure. She did not seek for sentimental emotions.
She surrendered herself wholly and forever to the Being whose form was fastened on her soul, and from that
moment every worldly feeling was gone, never to return.
Her spiritual life had begun. She explains the condition in which she found herself by an image familiar to
everyone who has seen the environs of a Spanish village.
She apologizes for its simplicity, but it is as true and
pregnant as a Gospel parable.

"A man is directed to make a garden in a bad soil overrun
with sour grasses. The lord of the land roots out the weeds,
sows seeds, and plants herbs and fruit-trees. The gardener
must then care for them and water them, that they may thrive
and blossom, and that 'the Lord' may find pleasure in his
garden and come to visit it. There are four ways in which
the watering may be done. There is water which is drawn
wearily by hand from the well. There is water drawn by the
ox-wheel, more abundantly and with lighter labor. There
is water brought in from the river, which will saturate the
whole ground ; and, last and best, there is rain from heaven.
Four sorts of prayer correspond to these. The first is a
weary effort with small returns ; the well may run dry ; the
gardener then must weep. The second is internal prayer and
meditation upon God ; the trees will then show leaves and
flower-buds. The third is love of God. The virtues then
become vigorous. We converse with God face to face. The

flowers open and give out fragrance. The fourth kind cannot be described in words. Then there is no more toil, and the seasons no longer change ; flowers are always blowing, and fruit ripens perennially. The soul enjoys undoubting certitude ; the faculties work without effort and without consciousness ; the heart loves and does not know that it loves ; the mind perceives yet does not know that it perceives. If the butterfly pauses to say to itself how prettily it is flying, the shining wings fall off, and it drops and dies. The life of the spirit is not our life, but the life of God within us."

This is very beautiful. It is the same, in fact, as what Bishop Butler says, in less ornamented prose, of the formation of moral habits. We first learn to do right with effort. The habit grows till it pervades the nature, and afterward we act as we ought spontaneously, with no more consciousness than animals have, which do what they do by instinct.

But we are now on the edge of the abnormal features of Teresa's history, and before I enter on the subject I must explain briefly how I myself regard the aberrations which will have to be related. All physicians, all psychologists of reputation, agree that besides sleeping and waking there are other conditions—trances, ecstasies, catalepsies, and such like—into which the body is liable to fall ; and, as in sleep images present themselves more vivid than can be called up by waking memory or waking fancy, so in these exceptional states of the system peculiar phenomena appear, which are none the less real because fools or impostors have built extravagant theories upon them. The muscles sometimes become rigid, the senses become unnaturally susceptible. The dreaming power is extraordinarily intensified, and visions are seen (we say " seen " for want of a more scientific expression) palpable as sense itself. Such conditions are

usually brought about by ordinary causes. Perhaps
they may be created artificially. They are not supernatural, for they have an exact analogy in the universal
experience of sleep. They are considered supernatural
only because they are exceptional, and the objects perceived are always supplied out of the stores with which
memory is furnished. Teresa's health was peculiar.
For twenty years she had been liable to violent nervous
attacks—those, too, an imperfectly understood form of
disorder. She was full-blooded, constantly sick, constantly subject to fainting fits and weakness of the heart.
Her intellect and moral sense, on the other hand, were
remarkably strong. She was not given to idle imaginations. She was true and simple, was never known to
tell a lie or act one. But her mental constitution was
unusual. Objects that interested her, she says, never
ran into words, but fastened themselves as pictures
upon her brain. Meadows, trees, and rivers, effects of
sky, all materials of landscape beauty, gave her intense
emotions, but emotions which she was unable to describe. She was a painter, but without the faculty of
conveying her impressions to canvas. She perceived
with extreme vividness, but the perception ended in itself. If she wanted phrases she had to look for them
in books, and what she found in books did not satisfy
her because it did not correspond to her own experience.

This was her general temperament, on which powerful religious emotion was now to work. The figure of
Christ had first awakened her. The shock threw her
into a trance. The trances repeated themselves when-
ever she was unusually agitated. Such a person would
inevitably see "visions," which she would be unable to
distinguish from reality; and if she believed herself

subject to demoniac or angelic visitations, she was not
on that account either weak or dishonest.

In the life of everyone who has really tried to make a
worthy use of existence, there is always a point—a point
never afterward forgotten—when the road has ceased to
be downhill, and the climb upward has commenced.
There has been some accident perhaps ; or someone has
died, or one has been disappointed in something on
which the heart had been fixed, or some earnest words
have arrested attention ; at any rate, some seed has
fallen into a soil prepared to receive it. This is called
in religious language conversion ; the turning away
from sin and folly to duty and righteousness. Beginnings are always hard. Persons who have hitherto acted
in one particular way, and suddenly change to another
way, are naturally suspected of having unworthy personal motives. They have lived so far for themselves.
They cannot be credited at once with having ceased to
live for themselves. They must still be selfish. They
must have some indirect object in view.

Teresa in her convent had resolved to be thenceforward a good woman, and to use to better purpose the
means which the Church offered to her. She found at
once that she was misunderstood and disliked. She
wished to be peculiar, it was said ; she wished to be
thought a saint ; she was setting herself up to be better
than other people. Her trances and fits of unconsciousness were attributed to the most obvious cause. She
was said to be "possessed" by a devil. She had been
humbled in her own eyes ; and she herself thought that
perhaps it was a devil. She could not tell, and her
spiritual adviser could not tell any better. The Jesuits
were then rising into fame. Francisco Borgia, ex-Duke
of Gandia, had joined them, and had been made Pro-

vincial General for Spain. He came to Avila, heard of
Teresa, and took charge of her case. He put her under a course of discipline. He told her to flog herself
with a whip of nettles, to wear a hair cloth plaited with
broken wires, the points of which would tear her skin.
Had her understanding been less robust, he would have
driven her mad ; as it was, he only intensified her nervous agitation. He bade her meditate daily on the details of Christ's passion. One day, while thus occupied,
she became unconscious ; her limbs stiffened, and she
heard a voice say, " Thou shalt no more converse with
men, but with angels." After this the fits always returned when she was at prayers. She saw no distinct
form, but she felt that Christ was close to her. She told
her confessor what she had experienced. He asked how
she knew that it was Christ. She could not explain. A
few days after, she was able to tell him that she had
actually seen Christ. She had seen Him, she said (without being aware that she was explaining from whence
the figure had been derived), exactly as He was painted
rising from the sepulchre. The story went abroad. The
ill-natured sisters made spiteful remarks ; the wisest
shook their heads. Teresa had not been noted for
special holiness in the many years that she had been
among them. Others, much more like saints than she,
had never seen anything wonderful ; why should God
select her to visit with such special favor? They were
more clear than ever that she was possessed. She was
preached at from the pulpit ; she was prayed for in
chapel as bewitched. She could not tell how to behave :
if she was silent about her visions, it was deceit ; if she
spoke of them, it was vanity. She preserved her balance
in this strange trial remarkably well. Her confessor had
been warned against her, and was as hard as the rest.

She continued to tell him whatever she supposed herself to see and hear, and absolutely submitted to his judgment. He confidently assured her it was the devil, and directed her when Christ appeared next to make the sign of the cross and point her thumb at Him. God would then deliver her. She obeyed, though with infinite pain. Christ's figure, whoever made it, ought, she thought, to be reverenced ; and to point her thumb was to mock like the Jews. As her trances recurred always at her devotions, she was next forbidden to pray. Under these trials Christ himself interposed to comfort her. He told her that she was right in obeying her confessor, though the confessor was mistaken. The inhibition to pray, He said, was tyranny, and, in fact, it was not long maintained. The apparitions grew more frequent and more vivid. One day the cross attached to her rosary was snatched out of her hands, and when it was given back to her it was set with jewels more brilliant than diamonds. A voice said that she would always see it so, though to others it would seem as before. She had often an acute pain in her side ; she fancied once that an angel came to her with a lance tipped with fire, which he struck into her heart. In after years, when she became legendary, it was gravely declared that the heart had been examined, and had been found actually pierced. A large drawing of it forms the frontispiece of the biography provided for the use of pious Catholics.

This condition continued for several years, and became the talk of Avila. Some held to the possession theory ; others said it was imposture ; others, especially as there was no further harm in poor Teresa, began to fancy that perhaps the visions were real. She herself knew not what to think. Excellent people were satisfied that she was under a delusion, and the

excellent people, she thought, might very likely be
right, for the apparitions were not all of a consoling
kind. She had seen Christ and the angels, but also
she had seen the devil. "Once," she says, "the devil
appeared to me in the oratory ; he spoke to me ; his
face was awful, and his body was of flame without
smoke. He said that I had escaped him for the present, but he would have me yet. I made the sign of the
cross ; he went, but returned ; I threw holy water at
him, and then he vanished." At another time she was
taken into hell ; the entrance was by a gloomy passage,
at the end of which was a pool of putrid water alive
with writhing snakes. She fancied that she was thrust
into a hole in a wall where she could neither sit nor lie,
and in that position was tortured with cramps. Other
horrors she witnessed, but did not herself experience :
she was shown only what would have been her own
condition if she had not been rescued.

One act she records, exceedingly characteristic. Avila
was not wholly unbelieving. Afflicted persons sometimes came to her for advice. Among the rest a priest
came, who was living in mortal sin, miserable, yet unable to confess in the proper form, and so made fast in
the bonds of Satan. Teresa prayed for him ; and then
he managed to confess, and for a time did not sin any
more ; but he told Teresa that the devil tortured him
dreadfully, and he could not bear it. She then prayed
that the tortures might be laid on her, and that the
priest might be spared. For a month after the devil
was allowed to work his will upon her. He would sit
upon her breviary when she was reading, and her cell
would fill with legions of imps.

An understanding of less than unusual strength
would have broken down under so severe a trial. Teresa

knew nothing of the natural capacities of a disordered
animal system. She had been taught theologically that
angels and devils were everywhere busy, and it was inevitable that she should regard herself as under a pre-
ternatural dispensation of some kind ; but, as long as
she was uncertain of what kind, she kept her judgment undisturbed, and she thought and reasoned on
the common subjects of the day like a superior person of ordinary faculty.

Society at Avila, as throughout Spain, was stormily
agitated at the advance of the Reformation. From Germany it was passing to the Low Countries and into
France. England, after a short-lived recovery, had
relapsed into heresy, and dreadful stories were told of
religious houses suppressed, and monks and nuns breaking their vows and defying heaven by marrying. Antichrist was triumphing, and millions of souls were
rushing headlong into the pit. Other millions too of
ignorant Indians, missionaries told her, were perishing
also for want of vigor in the Church to save them.
Teresa, since she had seen hell, had a very real horror
of it. Torment without end ! What heart could bear
the thought of it ? To rescue any single soul from so
terrible a fate, she felt ready herself to die a thousand
deaths ; but what could one poor woman do at such a
time—a single unit in a Spanish country town ? Something was wrong when such catastrophes could happen.
What the wrong was she thought she saw within the
limits of her own experience. The religious orders
were the Church's regular soldiers. Their manual was
their rule ; their weapons were penance, prayer, and
self-denial ; and as long as they were diligent in the
use of them, God's favor was secured, and evil could
not prevail. But the rules had been neglected, penance

laughed at, and prayer become half-hearted. Cloister discipline had been accommodated to the manners of a more enlightened age.

> " Hôc fonte derivata clades
> In patriam populumque fluxit."

Here was the secret of the great revolt from the Church, in the opinion of Teresa, and it was at least part of the truth ; for the cynical profligacy of the religious houses had provoked Germany and England more than any other cause. Teresa herself had learned how little convent life in Spain could assist a soul in search of perfection. At the Incarnation she could not keep her vows if she wished to keep them ; for the cloister gates were open, and the most earnest desire for seclusion could not insure it. Friends who wanted a nun to visit them had only to apply to the provincial, and the provincial would give a dispensation, not as a permission, but as a mandate which was not to be disobeyed.

Puzzled with what she found, Teresa had studied the ancient rule of the Carmelite Order before it was relaxed by Eugenius the Fourth. If a house could be founded where that rule could be again kept, she considered, how much easier her own burden would be ; how much better God would be served ; and then, perhaps, the Church would regain her strength. No improvement could be looked for in the Convent of the Incarnation itself. Two hundred women, accustomed to indulgences which a Pope had sanctioned, were not likely to be induced to submit again to severities. She talked of her scheme with her friends in the town. The difficulties seemed enormous ; she had no money to begin with, and her friends had little. If this obstacle could be overcome, she had another and a worse before her; she could do nothing without the consent of the provincial, and for such a consent she knew that it would be idle to ask. She was thinking the matter over one day after communion, when she fell into her usual trance. "The Lord" appeared and told her that her design was to be carried out. A house was to be founded and was to be dedicated to her old patron, San Josef. It would become a star which would shine over the earth. She was to tell her confessor what He had said, and to require him to make no opposition.

The apparition was a natural creation of her own previous musings, but it fell in so completely with her wishes that she would not and could not doubt. It appeared again and again. She wrote an account of it by her confessor's orders, and it was submitted to the provincial and the bishop. If they hesitated, it was but for a moment; they naturally consulted Teresa's prioress, and at once the tempest was let loose. "This then," exclaimed the incensed mother and the rest of the sisterhood, "this is the meaning of the visions we have heard so much of. Sister Teresa thinks herself too good for us. We are not holy enough for her. Pretty presumption! Let her keep the rule as it stands before she talks of mending it." From the convent the disturbance passed to the town. The Spaniards had no love for novelties; they believed in use, and wont, and the quiet maintenance of established things. They looked on ecstasies and trances as signs rather of insanity than sanctity; they thought that people should do their duty in the state of life to which they had been called, and duty was hard enough without artificial additions. Teresa's relations told the provincial she was out of her mind. Some thought a prison would be the best place for her, others hinted at the Inquisition and a possible trial for witchcraft. Her confessor called her scheme a woman's nonsense, and insisted that she should think no more of it.

She went for refuge to her Master. The Lord told her that she was not to be disturbed ; good things were always opposed when first suggested ; she must wait quietly, and all would go well. Though Avila seemed unanimous in its condemnation, there were two priests there of some consequence—one a Dominican, the other a Franciscan—who were more on a level with the times. They saw that something might be made of Teresa, and they wrote to their friends in Rome about her. Her Jesuit confessor held to his own opinion, but a new rector came to the college at Avila, with whom they also communicated. The rector, after a conversation with her, removed the confessor and appointed another. The provincial remained obstinate, but the bishop, Alvarez de Mendoza, was privately encouraging. Teresa was made to feel that she was not deserted, and, with a new spiritual director to comfort her, she took up her project again.

She was in a difficulty, for she was bound by her vows to obey the provincial ; he had already refused his permission, and she dared not apply to him again. But she probably knew that an appeal had been made to the Pope, and, pending the results of this, she thought that she might begin her preparations. She had to be secret —almost deceitful, and might have doubted if she was keeping within even the letter of her duty if her visions had been less inspiriting. A widow friend in the town bought a house as if for her own private occupation. Alterations were wanted to make it suitable for a small convent, and Teresa had no money to pay for them ; but San Josef told her to engage workmen, and that the money should be found ; and in fact at that moment a remittance came unexpectedly from a brother in Lima. She was afraid of the Carmelite authorities. The house, Christ told her, should be under the bishop, and not under the Order ; she was herself to be the superior, and she saw herself robed for office by San Josef and the Virgin in person.

Careful as she was, she still feared that the provincial would hear what she was doing, and would send her an inhibition, to which, if it came, she had resolved to submit. It became expedient for her to leave Avila till the answer from Rome could arrive. At that moment, most conveniently, Doña Aloysia de la Cerda, a sister of the Duke of Medina Celi, wrote to the provincial to say that she wished Teresa to pay her a visit at her house at Toledo. Doña Aloysia was a great lady, whose requests were commands. The order came to her to go, and she was informed by the usual channel that the invitation had been divinely arranged. She was absent for six months, and became acquainted with the nature and habits of Spanish grandees. Doña Aloysia treated her with high distinction ; she met other great people, and was impressed with their breeding and manners. But the splendor was disagreeable. She observed shrewdly, that between persons of rank and their attendants there was a distance which forbade familiarity ; if one servant was treated with confidence, the others were jealous ; she was herself an object of ill-will through Doña Aloysia's friendship ; and she concluded that it was a popular error to speak of "Lords and Ladies ;" for the high friends whom she had made were slaves in a thousand ways. Her chief comfort at

Toledo was the Jesuit College, where she studied at leisure the details of monastic rule. Her visit was unexpectedly ended by a letter from her provincial. The feeling in the Incarnation convent had suddenly changed ; a party had formed in her favor, who wished to choose her as prioress. The provincial, who disliked her as much as ever, desired Doña Aloysia privately to prevent her from going home ; but "a vision" told her that she had prayed for a cross, and a cross she should have. She concluded that it was to be the threatened promotion, and after a stormy scene with her hostess she went her way.

She was mistaken about the cross. On reaching Avila, she found that she had not been elected, but that the bull had arrived privately from Rome for her new convent. The Pope had placed it under the bishop, as "the Lord" had foretold, and the bishop had undertaken the charge. The secret had been profoundly kept ; the house was ready, and nothing remained but to take possession of it. It was to be a house of "Descalzos" (Barefoots), the name by which the reformed Order was in future to be known in opposition to the Relaxed, the Calzados. The sisters were not to be literally "shoeless ;" "a barefoot," as Teresa said, "makes a bad beast of burden." They were to wear sandals of rope, and, for the rest, they were to be confined to the cloister strictly, to eat no meat, to sleep on straw, to fast on reduced allowance from September till Easter ; they were to do needlework for the benefit of the poor, and they were to live on alms without regular endowment. Teresa had been careful for their health ; the hardships would not be greater than those borne without complaint by ordinary Spanish peasants. The dress was to be of thick undyed woollen cloth, with no

ornament but cleanliness. Dirt, which most saints regarded as a sign of holiness, Teresa always hated. The
number of sisters was to be thirteen ; more, she thought,
could not live together consistently with discipline.

Notwithstanding the Pope's bull, difficulty was anticipated. If the purpose was known, the Carmelites would
find means of preventing the dreaded innovation ; an accomplished fact, however, would probably be allowed to
stand. Teresa selected four poor women as the first to
take the habit, and quietly introduced them into the
house. She had gone out on leave from her own cloister,
as if to attend a sick relative, and was thus unobserved.
On August 24, 1562, ten years exactly before the massa-
cre of St. Bartholomew, the sacrament was brought into
the tiny chapel of San Josef's, a bell was hung, mass was
said, and the new Order had begun to exist.

Teresa was still bound by her vows to her convent.
When the ceremony was over, she returned to the Incarnation, half frightened at what she had done. She had
stirred a hornets' nest, as she was immediately to find.
The devil attacked her first ; he told her that she had
broken obedience, she had acted without the provincial's
leave, and had not asked for it because she knew it
would be refused ; her nuns would starve ; she herself
would soon tire of a wretched life in such a wretched
place, and would pine for her lost comforts. She lay
down to rest, but was soon roused by a storm. The
townspeople were the first to discover what had happened. It was easy to foresee the anger of the Carmelites ; why the townspeople should have been angry is
less obvious. Perhaps they objected to the establishment of a colony of professed beggars among them ; perhaps they were led by the chiefs of the other religious
Orders. A riot broke out ; the prioress sent for Teresa ;

the provincial arrived, hot and indignant. She was rebuked, admonished, informed that she had given scandal, and required to make instant submission before the
assembled convent. The Alcalde meanwhile had called
a meeting of the citizens, where the provincials of the
Dominicans, Franciscans, and Augustinians attended. A
resolution was first passed for the instant dissolution of
the new house and the removal of the sacrament ; on
second thoughts, it was decided to refer the matter, being of such high importance, to the Council of State at
Madrid. Teresa had but one friend to go to. "My
Lord," she said, on her knees, "this house is not mine,
it is yours ; all that I could do is done. You must see
to it." She was not to be disappointed.

The bishop prevented immediate violence, and Avila
waited for the action of the Council. The Council was
in no hurry with an answer. Certain persons wrote to
Philip ; Philip referred to the Pope, and there were six
months of suspense, the four poor sisters living as they
could, and Teresa remaining in disgrace. The town
authorities cooled ; they said the house might stand if
anyone would endow it. Afterward, finding that they
were not likely to be supported from Madrid, they were
ready to dispense with endowment. On the arrival of
a fresh bull from Pius the Fifth all remains of opposition
vanished, except among the Carmelites, and the Carmelites found it prudent to suppress their objections. Public opinion veered round ; the foundation was declared
to be a work of God, and Teresa to be His special servant, instead of a restless visionary. The provincial
gave her leave to remove and take charge of her flock.
The luggage which she took with her from the Incarnation was a straw mattress, a patched woollen gown, a
whip, and a hair-cloth shirt ; that was all.

Thus furnished, she entered on the five happiest years of her life. Other sisters joined, bringing small dowries with them, and the number of thirteen was soon filled up. Her girls, she says, were angels, perfect especially in the virtue of obedience. She would try them by orders contradictory or absurd ; they did their best without a question. One sister was told to plant a rotten cucumber in the garden ; she merely asked if it was to be planted upright or lengthways.

The visions were without intermission. She was taken up to heaven and saw her father and mother there. The Virgin gave her a cope, invisible to all eyes but her own, which would protect her from mortal sin. Once at "hours" she had a very curious experience. She fancied that she was a mirror without frame, without dimensions, with Christ shining in the centre of it, and the mirror itself, she knew not how, was in Christ. He told her that when a soul was in mortal sin the glass was clouded, and though He was present it could not reflect Him. With heretics the glass was broken, and could never be repaired.

Heretics and the growth of them still occupied her, and the more keenly as the civil war grew more envenomed in France. They were too strong, she thought, to be overcome by princes and soldiers. In such a contest the spiritual arm only could prevail. In a trance she saw seven Carmelite monks, of the pristine type, reformed like her own sisterhood, with swords in their hands on a battle-field. Their faces were flushed with fighting. The ground was strewn with the slain, and they were smiting still, and the flying enemy were the hosts of Luther and Calvin. These air-drawn pictures, lately called illusions of Satan, were now regarded as communications direct from heaven. They were too important to be lost. Her superior ordered her to write them down, and the result was the singular auto-biography which has hitherto been our guide to her history.

She wrote it unwillingly ; for it is evident that, deeply as these communications had affected her, and definitely as her spiritual advisers had at length assured her of their supernatural origin, she was herself still uncertain of their nature. Many of her visions, she was confident, had been the creation of her own brain. If any had come from another source, she did not regard them as of particular importance, or as symptoms of a high state of grace. This is certain, from a passage on the subject in one of her writings. Hysterical nuns often fancied that they had received revelations, and their confessors were too apt to encourage them. She says :

" Of 'revelations' no account should be made; for though some may be authentic, many are certainly false, and it is foolish to look for one truth amidst a hundred lies. It is dangerous also, for 'revelations' are apt to stray from the right faith, and the right faith is of immeasurably greater consequence. People fancy that to have 'revelations' im-plies exceptional holiness. It implies nothing of the kind. Holiness can be arrived at only by acts of virtue and by keeping the commandments. We women are easily led away by our imagination; we have less strength and less knowl-edge than men have, and cannot keep things in their proper places. Therefore I will not have my sisters read my own books, especially not my autobiography, lest they look for revelations for themselves in fancying that they are imitating me. The best things that I know came to me by obedience, not by revelation. Sisters may have real visions, but they must be taught to make light of them. There is a subtle deceit in these experiences. The devil may lead souls to evil on a spiritual road."

The priest editor of Teresa's works makes an honest observation on this remarkable acknowledgment. " I know not how it is," he says, " but the revelations received by women seem of consequence to men, and those received by men of consequence to women." Though he pretends that he did not know how it was, he knew very well, for he goes on: "It must arise from those accursed sexual inclinations—each sex believes most where it loves most." He should have drawn one more inference—that young men were the worst possible spiritual advisers for young women.

Teresa was not to be left to enjoy her quiet. A single convent had hitherto sufficed for her ambition ; but she had been told that it was to be a star which was to shine over the earth, and at that solitary taper other flames were now to be kindled. The Church of Rome was rallying from its confusion, and was setting its house in order. The clergy were clearing themselves of the scandals which had brought such tremendous consequences on them. The Catholic powers were putting out their strength, and Teresa's energetic spirit would not allow her to rest. The Carmelites themselves now partially recognized her value. The General came to Spain, and visited her at Avila. He reported what he had seen to Philip, and, with Philip's sanction, he sent her powers to found other houses of Descalzos, forbidding the provincials to interfere with her. The champions whom she had seen on the battle-field in a vision had been *brothers* of her reformed Order. The General empowered her to establish institutions of men as well as women, if she could find recruits who were willing. In other respects she was left to herself, and she was to show what a single woman, with no resources but her own internal force, was able to accomplish. She was now fifty-two, with bad health, which was growing worse by age. The leaders of the Church were awake ; princes and statesmen were awake ; but the body of the Spanish people was still unstirred. She had to contend with official pedantry, with the narrow pride of bishops, with the dislike of change, and the jealousies of rival jurisdictions. As to barefoot monks, it was long before she could find a single man in flesh and blood whom she could tempt to join with her.

Her adventures in the fifteen years of her pilgrimage would fill a long volume. We must content ourselves with fragmentary incidents of her wanderings, a few pictures of persons with whom she came in contact, a few glimpses of Peninsular life in the sixteenth century, and the human features of a remarkable person still traceable behind the paint and tinsel of miracle with which her biographers have disfigured Teresa de Cepeda.

Her first enterprise was at Medina del Campo, a large town fifty miles from Avila, on the road to Valladolid, and lately the residence of Isabella's Court. A lady of Medina, of small property, had applied for admission into San Josef's, and could not be received for want of room. She purchased a house, at Teresa's suggestion, which could be turned into a second convent. Difficulties were to be anticipated, of the same kind which had been encountered at Avila, and promptitude and secrecy were again necessary. A house itself was not enough. Medina could not provide the first sisters, and a colony had to be introduced from the parent stock. Teresa set out with two nuns from San Josef's, and four from the Incarnation, of whom two went with sinking hearts. Julian of Avila, the chaplain, was their single male escort and companion. They travelled in a cart, with a picture or two, some candlesticks for the altar—probably of tin, for they were utterly poor—a bell, and the sacrament. To a stranger who met them they must have appeared like a set of strolling mountebanks. In Avila itself they were thought mad, and the bishop had much the same opinion, though he would not interfere. It was hot August weather—the eve of the Feast of the Assumption—and the roads were parched and dusty. On the way they were met by the news that the Augustinians, whose wall adjoined the building which the lady had bought, intended to prevent them from settling there. They went on, nothing daunted, and reached Medina at nightfall. On the road they had been in danger of being arrested as vagrants by the police. Within the gates they were in worse peril; for the next day there was to be a bull-fight; and the bulls were being driven in through the streets. But nothing could stop Teresa. She had resolved to take possession at once, before she could be interrupted, and she went straight to her point. The party arrived at midnight, and never did intending settlers in an American forest look round upon a less promising scene. The courtyard walls were in ruins, the doors were off their hinges, the windows shutterless, the roof fallen in, the single room which would serve for a chapel half open to the air and littered with dirt and rubbish. The group and the surroundings would have made a subject for Murillo—seven poor women and their priest, with the sacrament, for which they were more alarmed than for themselves, the desolate wreck of a place, ghastly in the moonlight, to which they had come expecting to find a home. Four hours of night remained, and then daylight would be on them. Teresa's energy was equal to the occasion. Not a thought was wasted on their accommodation. The sisters were set to clear the

dirt from the chapel. In a garret, the one spot that
was waterproof, were some tapestries and bed-hangings.
These would protect the altar. They had no nails, and
at that hour the shops were closed ; but they picked as
many as they wanted out of the walls. By dawn the
altar was furnished, the bell was hung, mass was said,
and the convent was an instituted fact.

Sleepless and breakfastless, the unfortunate creatures
then looked about them, and their hearts sank at their
prospects. They crept disconsolate into their garret and
sat watching the sacrament through a window, lest rude
hands might injure it. In the evening a Jesuit father
came. Teresa begged him to find lodgings for them till
the house could be put in order ; but the town was full,
and for a week no suitable rooms could be found. Medina, naturally, was excited at the strange invasion, and
was not inclined to be hospitable. At length a charitable
merchant took compassion. An upper floor was provided, where they could live secluded, with a hall for a
chapel. A Señora de Quiroga, a relation perhaps of the
Archbishop of Toledo, undertook the repairs of the convent. The citizens relented and gave alms ; and in two
months the second house of the reformed Descalzos was
safely established.

This was in 1567. In the next year a third convent
was founded at Malaga, with the help of another sister of
the Duke of Medina Celi. From Malaga Teresa was
"sent by the Spirit" to Valladolid, where a young nobleman offered a villa and garden. While she was considering, the youth died ; he had led a wild life, and she
was made to know that he was in purgatory, from which
he was to be released only when the first mass was said
on the ground which he had dedicated. She flew instantly across Spain with her faithful Julian. The villa

did not please her ; for it was outside the town, near
the river, and was reported to be unhealthy. But the
gardens were beautiful. Valladolid, stern and sterile in
winter, grows in spring bright with flowers and musi-
cal with nightingales. Objections melted before the
thought of a soul in penal fire. She took possession ;
the mass was said ; and, as the Host was raised, the
pardoned benefactor appeared in glory at Julian's side
on his way to paradise. Another incident occurred before she left the neighborhood. Heresy had stolen into
Castile : a batch of Lutherans were to be burnt in the
great square at Valladolid ; and she heard that they
meant to die impenitent. That it could be anything but
right to burn human beings for errors of belief could
not occur to her ; but she prayed that the Lord would
turn their hearts, and save their souls, and inflict on her
as much as she could bear of their purgatorial pains.
She supposed that she had been taken at her word—the
heretics recanted at the stake—she herself never after
knew a day without suffering.

Toledo came next. She was invited thither by her
Jesuit friends. She was now famous. On her way she
passed through Madrid. Curious people came about
her, prying and asking questions. " What fine streets
Madrid has ! " was her answer on one such occasion.
She would not stay there. Philip wished to see her,
but she had already flown. She had two sisters with
her to start the colony ; of other property she had four
ducats, two pictures, two straw pallets, and nothing besides. She had gone in faith, and faith as usual works
miracles. Doña Aloysia had not forgiven her desertion,
and from that quarter there was no assistance ; but a
house was obtained by some means, and the sisters and
she, with their possessions, were introduced into it. Of

further provison no care had been taken. It was winter, and they had not firewood enough "to boil a herring." They were without blankets, and shivered with cold ; but they were never more happy, and were almost sorry when fresh recruits came in and brought money and ordinary conveniences.

The recruits were generally of middle rank. "The Lord" had said that he did not want members of high families ; and Teresa's own experience was not calculated to diminish her dislike of such great persons. Ruy Gomez, Prince of Eboli and Duke of Pastraña, was Philip's favorite minister. His wife was the famous Aña de Mendoza, whom history has determined to have been Philip's mistress. I have told the story else-where.* The single evidence for this piece of scandal is the presumption that kings must have had mistresses of some kind. Antonio Perez says that Philip was jealous of his intimacy with her. It is a pity that people will not remember that jealousy has more meanings than one. Perez was Philip's secretary. The Princess was a proud, intriguing, imperious woman, with whom Philip had many difficulties ; and he resented the influence which she was able to use in his cabinet. More absurd story never fastened itself into human annals, none which more signally illustrates the appetite of mankind for garbage. For a short period Teresa was brought in contact with this high lady, and we catch an authentic glimpse of her. She wanted some new excitement, as ladies of rank occasionally do. She proposed to found a nunnery of a distinguished kind. She had heard of the Nun of Avila as one of the wonders of the day, and she sent for her to Pastraña. Teresa had not liked the Princess's letters ; but Ruy Gomez was too

* Vide supra, pp. 118, 119.

great a man to be affronted, and her confessor told her
that she must go. A further inducement was a proposal
held out to her of a house for monks, also of the reformed rule, for which she had been trying hitherto in
vain. The Princess had a young Carmelite about her,
a Father Mariano, who was ready to take charge of it.

Teresa was received at Pastraña with all distinction.
A *casa* was ready to receive sisters, but she found that
the Princess had already chosen a prioress, and that in
fact the convent was to be a religious plaything of a fash-
ionable lady. Three months were wasted in discussion ;
and in the course of them Teresa was questioned about
her history. The Princess had heard of her autobiography, and begged to see it. She was not vain of her
visions, and consented only when the Princess promised
that the book should be read by no one but herself and
her husband. To her extreme disgust she found that it
became the common talk of the household, a subject of
Madrid gossip and of vulgar impertinence. Doña Aña
herself said scornfully that Teresa was but another Magdalen de la Cruz, an hysterical dreamer, who had been
condemned by the Inquisition.

Ruy Gomez had more sense than his wife, and better
feeling. The obnoxious prioress was withdrawn, and
the convent was started on the usual conditions. The
Barefoot Friars became a reality under Father Mariano,
whom Teresa liked perhaps better than he deserved. As
long as Ruy Gomez lived, the Princess did not interfere.
Unfortunately he survived only a few months, and nothing would satisfy Doña Aña in her first grief but that
she must enter the sisterhood herself. She took the
habit, Mariano having provided her with a special dress
of rich materials for the occasion. In leaving the world
she had left behind her neither her pride nor her self-

indulgence. She brought her favorite maid with her. She had a separate suite of rooms, and the other sisters waited upon her as servants. Teresa had gone back to Toledo.* The Princess in her absence quarrelled with the prioress, who had been substituted for the woman whom she had herself chosen ; and finally she left the convent, returned to the castle, and stopped the allowance on which the sisters depended.

Teresa, when she heard what had passed, ordered the removal of the establishment to Segovia. Two years later we find her on the road to Salamanca. It was late in autumn, with heavy snow, the roads almost impassable, and herself suffering from cough and fever. This time she had but one companion, a nun older and scarcely less infirm than herself. "Oh, these journeys!" she exclaims. She was sustained only by the recollection of the many convents which the "Lutherans" had destroyed, and the loss of which she was trying to repair. It was All Saints' Eve when they reached Salamanca. The church-bells were tolling dismally for the departed souls. The Jesuits had promised that she should find a habitation ready, but they found it occupied by students, who at first refused to move. The students were with difficulty ejected. It was a great straggling place, full of garrets and passages, all filthily dirty. The two women entered worn and weary, and locked themselves in. The sister was terrified lest some loose youth might be left hidden in a corner. Teresa found a straw loft, where they laid themselves down, but the sister could not rest, and shivered with alarm.

* The Princess had sent her back in her own carriage. "Pretty saint you, to be travelling in such style as that!" said a fool to her as she drove into Toledo. "Is there no one but this to remind me of my faults?" she said, and she never entered a carriage again.

Teresa asked her what was the matter. "I was thinking," she said, "what would become of you, dear mother,
if I was to die." "Pish," said Teresa, who did not
like nonsense, "it will be time to think of that when it
really happens. Let me go to sleep."

Two houses were founded at Alva with the help of
the Duke and Duchess; and the terrible Ferdinand of
Toledo, just returned from the Low Countries, appears
here with a gentler aspect. Teresa's "Life" was his
favorite study; he would travel many leagues, he said,
only to look upon her. In one of her trances she had
seen the Three Persons of the Trinity. They were
painted in miniature under her direction, and she made
the likenesses exact with her own hand. These pictures
had fallen into the Duchess's hands, and the miniature
of Christ was worn by the Duke when he went on his
expedition into Portugal.

After this Teresa had a rest. In her own town she
was now looked on as a saint, and the sisters of the Incarnation were able to have their way at last and to
elect her prioress. There she was left quiet for three
years. She had much suffering, seemingly from neu-
ralgia, but her spirit was high as ever. Though she
could not introduce her reformed rule, she could insist
on the proper observance of the rule as it stood. She
locked up the locutoria, the parlors where visitors were
received, keeping the keys herself, and allowing no one
to be admitted without her knowledge. A youth who
was in love with one of the nuns, and was not allowed a
sight of her, insisted once on seeing Teresa and remon-
strating. Teresa heard his lamentations, and told him
then that if he came near the house again she would
report him to the King. He found, as he said, "that
there was no jesting with that woman." One curious

anecdote is told of her reign in the Incarnation, which
has the merit of being authentic. Spain was the land
of chivalry ; knights challenged each other to tilt in the
lists ; enthusiastic saints challenged one another to feats
of penance, and some young monks sent a cartel of defiance to Teresa and her convent. Teresa replied for
herself and the sisters, touching humorously the weak-
nesses of each of her own party :

" Sister Anne of Burgos says that if any knight will pray
the Lord to grant her humility, and the prayer is answered,
she will give him all the merits which she may hereafter earn.

" Sister Beatrice Juarez says that she will give to any
knight who will pray the Lord to give her grace to hold her
tongue till she has considered what she has to say, two years
of the merits which she has gained in tending the sick.

" Isabel de la Cruz will give two years' merits to any
knight who will induce the Lord to take away her self-will.

.   .   .   .

" Teresa de Jésus says that, if any knight will resolve
firmly to obey a superior who may be a fool and a glutton,
she will give him on the day on which he forms such a
resolution half her own merits for that day—or, indeed, the
whole of them—for the whole will be very little."

The best satire of Cervantes is not more dainty.

The sisters of the Incarnation would have re-elected
their prioress when the three years were over ; but the
provincial interfered, and she and her cart were soon
again upon the road. She had worse storms waiting
for her than any which she had yet encountered.

At Pastraña, besides Mariano, she had become acquainted with another Carmelite, a Father Gratian,
who had also become a member of the Descalzos. Gratian was then about thirty, an eloquent preacher, ambitious, passionate, eager to rule and not so eager to

obey, and therefore no favorite with his superiors. On Teresa this man was to exert an influence beyond his merits, for his mind was of a lower type than hers. Such importance as he possessed he derived from her regard ; and after her death he sank into insignificance. He still tried to assume consequence, but his pretensions were mortified. In a few years he was stripped of his habit and reduced to a secular priest. He wandered about complaining till he was taken by the Moors, and was set to work in a slave-yard at Tunis. Ransomed at last, he became confessor to the Infanta Isabella in Flanders, and there died. But it was his fate and Teresa's, that before these misfortunes fell upon him he was to play a notable part in connection with her. He had friends in Andalusia, and he persuaded Teresa that she must found a convent at Seville. It was a rash adventure, for her diploma extended only to the Castiles. She set out with six sisters and the inseparable Julian. The weather was hot, the cart was like purgatory, and the roadside posadas, with their windowless garrets at oven heat, were, she said, "like hell." "The beds were as if stuffed with pebbles." Teresa fell into a fever, and her helpless companions could only pray for her. When they were crossing the Guadalquivir in a pontoon the rope broke. The ferryman was thrown down and hurt ; the boat was swept away by the current. They were rescued by a gentleman who had seen the accident from his terrace. Cordova, when they passed through it, was crowded for a fête. The mob, attracted by their strange appearance, "came about them like mad bulls." At Seville, where Gratian professed to have prepared for their reception, they were met by a flat refusal from the archbishop to allow the establishment of an unendowed foundation, and to live on alms only was an essential of their rule. Teresa was forced to submit.

"God," she wrote, "has never permitted any foundation of mine to be set on its feet without a world of worry. I had not heard of the objection till I arrived. I was most unwilling to yield, for in a town so rich as Seville alms could have been collected without the least difficulty. I would have gone back upon the spot, but I was penniless, all my money having been spent upon the way. Neither the sisters nor I possessed anything but the clothes on our backs and the veils which we had worn in the cart. But we could not have a mass without the archbishop's leave, and leave he would not give till we consented."

But sharper consequences were to follow. In over-stepping the boundaries of her province, Teresa had rashly committed herself. From the first the great body of the Carmelites had resented her proceedings. Circumstances and the Pope's protection had hitherto shielded her. But Pius the Fifth was gone. Gregory the Thirteenth reigned in his stead, and a chapter-general of the Carmelite Order held at Piacenza in 1575 obtained an injunction from him prohibiting the further extension of the reformed houses. The foundation of the Seville Convent was treated as an act of defiance. The General ordered its instant suppression. Teresa's other foundations had been hitherto quasi-independent; Father Jerome Tostado was despatched from Italy as commissioner to Spain, to reduce them all under the General's authority; and a new nuncio was appointed for the special purpose of giving Tostado his support. If Philip objected he was to be told that the violation of order had caused a scandal to the whole Church.

Little dreaming of what was before her, Teresa had

been nourishing a secret ambition of recovering the entire Carmelite body to their old austerities. The late nuncio had been a hearty friend to her. She had written to the King to ask that Gratian might be appointed visitor-general of her own houses for the whole peninsula. The King had not only consented to this request, but with the nuncio's request, irregular as it must have seemed, Gratian's jurisdiction was extended to all the Carmelite convents in Spain. Philip could not have taken such a step without Teresa's knowledge, or at least without Gratian's ; and in this perhaps lies the explanation of the agitations in Italy and of Tostado's mission. Evidently things could not continue as they were. Teresa's reforms had been made in the teeth of the chiefs of the Order, and her houses, so far as can be seen, had been as yet under no organized government at all. She might legitimately have asked the nuncio to appoint a visitor to these ; for it was through the Pope's interference that she had established them ; but she was making too bold a venture in grasping at the sovereignty of a vast and powerful foundation, and she very nearly ruined herself. Gratian was refused entrance to the first convent which he attempted to visit. The new briefs arrived from Rome. Teresa received a formal inhibition against founding any more houses. She was ordered to select some one convent and to remain there ; while two prioresses whom she had instituted were removed, and superiors in whom Tostado had confidence were put in their places. Teresa's own writings, on which suspicion had hung since they had been read by the Princess, were submitted to the Inquisition. She herself chose Toledo for a residence, and was kept there under arrest for two years. The Inquisitors could find no heresy in her books ; and, her pen not being under

restriction, she composed while in confinement a history
of her foundations as a continuation of her autobiography. Her correspondence besides was voluminous. She
wrote letters (the handwriting bold, clear, and vigorous
as a man's) to princes and prelates, to her suffering sisters, to her friends among the Jesuits and Dominicans.

The sequel is exceedingly curious. There is a belief
that the administration of the Roman Church is one and
indivisible. In this instance it proved very divisible indeed. The new nuncio and the General of the Carmelites intended to crush Teresa's movement. The King
and the Archbishop of Toledo were determined that she
should be supported. The Spanish Government were
as little inclined as Henry the Eighth to submit to the
dictation of Italian priests ; and when the nuncio began
his operations, Philip at once insisted that he should not
act by himself, but should have four assessors, of whom
the Archbishop of Toledo should be one. It was less
easy to deal with Tostado. Each religious order had its
own separate organization. Teresa had sworn obedience,
and Tostado was her lawful superior. She acted herself
as she had taught others to act, and at first refused
Philip's help in actively resisting him. The nuncio had
described her as "a restless woman, unsettled, disobedient, contumacious, an inventor of new doctrines under
pretence of piety, a breaker of the rule of cloister residence, a despiser of the apostolic precept which forbids
a woman to teach." Restless she had certainly been,
and her respect for residence had been chiefly shown in
her anxiety to enforce it on others—but disobedient she
was not, as she had an opportunity of showing. In
making the change in the government of her houses,
Tostado had found a difficulty at San Josef's, because it
was under the bishop's jurisdiction. The alteration

could not be made without per presence at Avila. He
sent for her from Toledo. She went at his order, she
gave him the necessary assistance, and the house was
reclaimed under his authority.

By this time temper was running high on all sides.
Tostado was not softened by Teresa's acquiescence.
The nuncio was exasperated at the King's interference
with him. He regarded Teresa herself as the cause of
the schism, and refused to forgive her till it was healed.
She was now at Avila. The office of prioress was again
vacant at the Incarnation. The persecution had endeared
her to the sisters, and a clear majority of them were
resolved to re-elect her. Tostado construed their action
into defiance ; he came in person to hold the election ;
he informed the sisters, of whom there were now a
hundred, that he would excommunicate every one of
them who dared to vote for a person of whom he disapproved. The nuns knew that they had the right with
them, for the Council of Trent had decided that the
elections were to be free. Fifty-five of them defied
Tostado's threats and gave their votes for Teresa. As
each sister handed in her paper, Tostado crushed it
under his feet, stamped upon it, cursed her, and boxed
her ears. The minority chose a prioress who was agreeable to him ; he declared this nun duly elected, ordered
Teresa into imprisonment again, and left her supporters
cut off from mass and confession till they submitted.
The brave women would not submit. They refused to
obey the superior who had been forced on them, except
as Teresa's substitute. The theologians of Avila declared unanimously that the excommunication was in-
valid. Tostado was only the more peremptory. He
flogged two of the confessors of the convent, who had
been appointed by the late nuncio, and he sent them

away under a guard. "I wish they were out of the power of these people," Teresa wrote. "I would rather see them in the hands of the Moors."

One violence was followed by another. Father Gratian was next suspended, and withdrew into a hermitage at Pastraña. The nuncio, caring nothing about the assessors, required him to surrender the commission as visitor which he had received from his predecessor. Gratian consulted the Archbishop of Toledo, who told him that he had no more spirit than a fly, and advised him to appeal to Philip. The nuncio, without waiting for an answer, declared Gratian's commission cancelled. He cancelled also Teresa's regulations, and replaced her convents under the old relaxed rule. The Bishop of Avila was of opinion that the nuncio had exceeded his authority and had no right to make such a change. Teresa told Gratian that he would be safe in doing whatever the Bishop advised ; and she recommended an appeal to the Pope and the King for a formal division of the Carmelite Order. Tostado had put himself in the wrong so completely in his treatment of the sisters of the Incarnation, that she overcame her dislike of calling in the secular arm and wrote a detailed account of his actions to Philip. Gratian himself lost his head and was only foolish. One day he wrote to the nuncio and made his submission. The next, he called a chapter of the Descalzos and elected a separate provincial. The nuncio replied by sending Teresa back as a prisoner to Toledo, and Gratian to confinement in a monastery.

But the Spanish temper was now thoroughly roused. Philip and the Archbishop of Toledo had both privately communicated with the Pope on the imprudence of the nuncio's proceedings ; and the King on his own account had forbidden the magistrates everywhere to support either Tostado or his agents. The Duke of Infantado, the proudest of the Spanish grandees, insulted the nuncio at Court ; and the nuncio, when he appealed to Philip for redress, was told coldly that he had brought the insult upon himself. The Pope, in fact, being better informed, and feeling that he would gain little by irritating the Castilians for the sake of the relaxed Carmelites, had repented of having been misled, and was only eager to repair his mistake. Teresa's apprehensions were relieved by a vision. Christ appeared to her, attended by His mother and San Josef. San Josef and the Virgin prayed to Him. Christ said "that the infernal powers had been in league to ruin the Descalzos ; but they had been instituted by himself, and the King in future would be their friend and patron." The Virgin told Teresa that in twenty days her imprisonment would be over. Not her imprisonment only, but the struggle itself was over. The nuncio and Tostado were recalled to Italy. Spain was to keep her "barefoot" nuns and friars. We need not follow the details of the arrangement. It is enough to say that the Carmelites were divided into two bodies, as Teresa had desired. The Descalzos became a new province, and were left free to choose their own officers. We have told the story at so much length, because it illustrates remarkably the internal character of the Spanish Church and the inability of the Italian organization to resist a national impulse.

All was now well, or would have been well, but for mortal infirmity. Gratian went to Rome to settle legal technicalities. Teresa resumed her wandering life of founding convents. Times were changed since her hard fight for San Josef. Town Councils met her now in procession. Te Deums were sung in the churches, and eager crowds waited for her at the roadside inns.

But so far as she herself was concerned, it is a question whether success added to her happiness. So long as an object is unattained, we may clothe it in such ethereal colors as we please; when it is achieved the ideal has become material; it is as good perhaps as what we ought to have expected, but is not what we did expect. Teresa was now sixty-four years old, with health irrevocably broken. Her houses having assumed a respectable legal character, many of them had after all to be endowed, and she was encumbered with business. "The Lord," as she said, continued to help her. When she was opposed in anything, the Lord intimated that He was displeased. If she doubted, He would reply, "*Ego sum*," and her confessor, if not herself, was satisfied. But she had much to do, and disheartening difficulties to overcome. She had been working with human beings for instruments, and human beings will only walk straight when the master's eye is on them. In the preliminary period the separate sisterhoods had been left very much to themselves. Some had grown lax. Some had been extravagantly ascetic. In San Josef, the firstfruits of her travail, the sisters had mutinied for a meat diet. A fixed code of laws had to be enforced, and it was received with murmurs, even by friends on whom she had relied.* She addressed a circular to them all, which was characteristically graceful:

"Now then we are all at peace—Calzados and Descalzados. Each of us may serve God in our own way, and none

* One of the rules referred to prayers for the King, which were to be accompanied by weekly whippings, such as Merlin ordered for the disenchantment of Dulcinea. "Statutum fuit ut perpetuis temporibus una quotidie Missa, preces item continuæ, et una per singulas hebdomadas corporis flagellatio pro Rege Hispaniæ ejusque familiâ in universis conventibus Carmelitarum utriusque sexus excalceatorum Deo offeratur."

can say us nay. Therefore, my brothers and sisters, as He has heard your prayer, do you obey Him with all your hearts. Let it not be said of us as of some Orders, that only the beginnings were creditable. We have begun. Let those who come after us go on from good to better. The devil is always busy looking for means to hurt us; but the struggle will be only for a time; the end will be eternal."

Three years were spent in organization—years of outward honor, but years of suffering—and then the close came. In the autumn of 1581 Gratian had arranged that a convent was to be opened at Burgos. Teresa was to be present in person, and Gratian accompanied her. They seem to have travelled in the old way—a party of eight in a covered cart. The weather was wretched; the floods were out; the roads mere tracks of mud, the inns like Don Quixote's castle. Teresa was shattered with cough; she could eat nothing; the journey was the worst to which she had been exposed. On arriving at Burgos she was taken to a friend's house; a great fire had been lighted, where she was to dry her clothes. The damp and steam brought on fever, and she was unable to leave her bed.

The business part of her visit had been mismanaged. Gratian had been as careless as at Seville, and the same difficulties repeated themselves. The Council of Trent had insisted that all new convents should be endowed. The Archbishop of Burgos stood by the condition, and no endowment had been provided. Teresa was too ill to return to Avila. Month after month passed by. A wet autumn was followed by a wetter winter. Terms were arranged at last with the Archbishop. A building was found which it was thought would answer for the convent, and Teresa removed to it; but it was close to the water-side and half in ruins. The stars shone and

the rain poured through the rents of the roof in the
garret where she lay. The river rose. The lower story
of the house was flooded. The sisters, who watched day
and night by her bed, had to dive into the kitchen for
the soaked crusts of bread for their own food and hers.
The communication with the town being cut off, they
were nearly starved. Friends at last swam across and
brought relief. When the river went back, the ground
floors were deep in stones and gravel.

Sister Anne of St. Bartholomew, who was herself
afterward canonized, tells the rest of the story. When
spring came the weather mended. Teresa was slightly
stronger, and, as her own part of the work at Burgos was
finished, she was able to move, and was taken to Valladolid. But it was only to find herself in fresh trouble.
One of her brothers had left his property to San Josef's.
The relations disputed the will, and an angry lawyer
forced his way into her room and was rude to her. She
was in one of her own houses, where at any rate she
might have looked for kindness. But the prioress had
gone over to her enemies, shown her little love or reverence, and at last bade her "go away and never return."

She went on to Medina. She found the convent in
disorder ; she was naturally displeased, and found fault.
Since the legal establishment of the Descalzos she had
no formal authority, and perhaps she was too imperious. The prioress answered impertinently, and Teresa
was too feeble to contend with her. Twenty years had
passed since that gypsy drive from Avila, the ruined
courtyard, the extemporized altar, and the moonlight
watch of the sacrament. It had ended in this. She
was now a broken old woman, and her own children had
turned against her. She ate nothing. She lay all night

sleepless, and the next morning she left Medina. She
had meant to go to Avila, but she was wanted for some
reason at Alva, and thither, in spite of her extreme weakness, she was obliged to go. She set out before breakfast with one faithful companion. They travelled all day
without food, save a few dried figs. They arrived at night
at a small pueblo, all exhausted, and Teresa fainting;
they tried to buy an egg or two, but eggs were not to be
had at the most extravagant price. Teresa swallowed a
fig, but could touch nothing more. She seemed to be
dying. Sister Anne knelt sobbing at her side. " Do not
cry," she said ; " it is the Lord's will." More dead than
alive, she was carried the next day to Alva. She was just
conscious, but that was all. She lay quietly breathing,
and only seemed uneasy when Sister Anne left her for a
moment. After a few hours she laid her head on Sister
Anne's breast, sighed lightly, and was gone. It was St.
Michael's Day, 1582.

Nothing extraordinary was supposed to have happened at the time. A weak, worn-out woman had died
of sufferings which would have destroyed a stronger
frame. That was all. Common mortals die thus every
day. They are buried ; they are mourned for by those
who had cause to love them ; they are then forgotten,
and the world goes on with its ordinary business. Catholic saints are not left to rest so peacefully, and something has still to be told of the fortunes of Teresa
of Avila. But we must first touch for a moment on
aspects of her character which we have passed over in
the rapid sketch of her life. It is the more necessary
since she has been deified into an idol, and the tenderness, the humor, the truth, and simplicity of her human
nature, have been lost in her diviner glories. Many
volumes of her letters, essays, treatises, memoranda of

various kinds, survive in addition to her biography. With the help of these we can fill in the lines.

She was not learned. She read Latin with difficulty, and knew nothing of any other language except her own. She was a Spaniard to the heart, generous, chivalrous, and brave. In conversation she was quick and bright. Like her father, she was never heard to speak ill of anyone. But she hated lies, hated all manner of insincerity, either in word or action. In youth she had been tried by the usual temptations ; her life had been spotless ; but those whose conduct has been the purest are most conscious of their smaller faults, and she had the worst opinion of her own merits. The rule which she established for her sisterhoods was severe, but it was not enough for her own necessities. She scourged herself habitually, and she wore a peculiarly painful haircloth ; but these were for herself alone, and she did not prescribe them to others. She sent her hair shirt to her brother, but she bade him be careful how he used it. "Obedience," she said, "was better than sacrifice, and health than penance." One of her greatest difficulties was to check the zeal of young people who wished to make saints of themselves by force. A prioress at Malaga had ordered the sisters to strike one another, with a view of teaching them humility. Teresa said it was a suggestion of the devil. "The sisters are not slaves," she wrote ; "mortifications are of no use in themselves ; obedience is the first of virtues, but it is not to be abused." The prioress of Toledo again drew a sharp rebuke upon herself. She had told a sister who had troubled her with some question to go and walk in the garden. The sister went, and walked and walked. She was missed the next morning at matins. She was still walking. Another prioress gave the Penitential Psalms for a gen-

eral discipline, and kept the sisters repeating them at
irregular hours. "The poor things ought to have been
in bed," Teresa wrote. "They do what they are told,
but it is all wrong. Mortification is not a thing of ob-
ligation."

Gratian himself had to be lectured. He had been
inventing new ceremonies. "Sister Antonia," she
wrote, "has brought your orders, and they have scan-
dalized us. Believe me, father, we are well as we
are, and want no unnecessary forms. For charity's
sake, remember this. Insist on the rules, and let that
suffice." Gratian had given injunctions in detail about
dress and food. "Do as you like," she said, "only
do not define what our shoes are to be made of. Say
simply, we may wear shoes, to avoid scruples. You
say our caps are to be of hemp — why not of flax?
As to our eating eggs, or eating preserves on our bread,
leave it to conscience. Too much precision only does
harm."

Her own undergarments, though scrupulously kept
clean, were of horse-cloth. She slept always on a
sack of straw. A biscuit or two, an egg, a few peas
and beans, made her daily food, varied, perhaps, on
feast-days with an egg and a slice of fish, with grapes
or raisins.

Her constant trances were more a trial than a pleasure to her. She writes to her brother : "Buen anda Nuestro Señor. I have been in a sad state for this week
past. The fits have returned. They come on me sometimes in public and I can neither resist nor hide them.
God spare me these exhibitions of myself. I feel half
drunk. Pray for me, for such things do me harm. They
have nothing to do with religion."

Nothing can be wiser than her general directions for

the management of the sisterhoods. To the sisters themselves she says :

"Do not be curious about matters which do not concern
you. Say no evil of anyone but yourself, and do not listen to
any. Never ridicule anyone. Do not contend in words about
things of no consequence. Do not exaggerate. Assert nothing as a fact of which you are not sure. Give no hasty
opinions. Avoid empty tattle. Do not draw comparisons.
Be not singular in food or dress ; and be not loud in your
laughter. Be gentle to others and severe to yourself. Speak
courteously to servants. Do not note other people's faults.
Note your own faults, and their good points. Never boast.
Never make excuses. Never do anything when alone which
you would not do before others."

Her greatest difficulty was with the convent confessors.
Teresa had a poor opinion of men's capacities for understanding women. "We women," she said, "are not so
easily read. Priests may hear our confessions for years
and may know nothing about us. Women cannot describe their faults accurately, and the confessor judges
by what they tell him." She had a particular dislike of
melancholy women who fancied that they had fine sen-
sibilities which were not understood or appreciated. She
found that confessors became foolishly interested in such
women, and confidences came, and spiritual communications of mutual feelings, which were nonsense in themselves and a certain road to mischief. Teresa perhaps
remembered some of her own experiences in her excessive alarm on this point. She insisted that the confessor should have no intercourse with any sister, except
officially, and in the confessional itself. At the direction
of her superiors, she wrote further a paper of general

14

reflections on the visitation of convents, which show the same insight and good sense.

The visitor was the provincial or the provincial's vicar, and his business was to inspect each convent once a year.

"The visitor," she said, "must have no partiality, and, above all, no weakness or sentimentality. A superior must inspire fear. If he allows himself to be treated as an equal, especially by women, his power for good has gone. Once let a woman see that he will pass over her faults out of tenderness, she will become ungovernable. If he is to err, let it be on the side of severity. He visits once only in a twelvemonth, and unless the sisters know that at the end of each they will be called to a sharp reckoning, discipline will be impossible. Prioresses found unfit for office must be removed instantly. They may be saints in their personal conduct, but they may want the qualities essential to a ruler, and the visitor must not hesitate.

"He must look strictly into the accounts. Debt of any kind is fatal. He must see into the work which each sister has done, and how much she has earned by it. This will encourage industry. Each room in the house must be examined, the parlor gratings especially, that no one may enter unobserved. The visitor must be careful, too, with the chaplains, learn to whom each sister confesses, and what degree of communication exists between them. The prioress, as long as she retains office, must always be supported. There can be no peace without authority, and sisters sometimes think they are wiser than their superiors. No respect must be shown for morbid feelings. The visitor must make such women understand that if they do wrong they will be punished, and that he is not to be imposed upon.

"As to the prioress, he must learn first if she has favorites; and he must be careful in this, for it is her duty to consult most with the most discreet of the sisters; but it is the nature of us to overvalue our own selves. When preference is shown, there will be jealousy. The favorite will be sup-

posed to rule the Holy Mother : the rest will think that they
have a right to resist. Sisters who may be far from perfect
themselves will be ready enough to find fault. They will
tell the visitor that the prioress does this and that. He will
be perplexed what to think ; yet he will do infinite harm if
he orders changes which are not needed. His guide must
be the Rule of the Order. If he finds that the prioress
dispenses with the rule on insufficient grounds, thinking this a small thing and that a small thing, he may be sure
that she is doing no good. She holds office to maintain the
rule, not to dispense with it.

" A prioress is obviously unfit who has anything to conceal.
The sisters must be made to tell the truth ; they will not
directly lie, perhaps, but they will often keep back what
ought to be known.

" Prioresses often overload the sisters with prayers and
penances, so as to hurt their health. The sisters are afraid
to complain, lest they be thought wanting in devotion ; nor
ought they to complain, except to the visitor. . . . The
visitor, therefore, must be careful about this. Especially let
him be on his guard against saintly prioresses. The first and
last principle in managing women is to make them feel that
they have a head over them who will not be moved by any
earthly consideration ; that they are to observe their vows,
and will be punished if they break them ; that his visit is
not an annual ceremony, but that he keeps his eye on the
daily life of the whole establishment. Women generally are
honorable and timid ; they will think it wrong sometimes
to report the prioress's faults. He will want all his discretion.

" He should inquire about the singing in the choir ; it
ought not to be loud or ambitious ; fine singing disturbs devotion, and the singers will like to be admired. He should
notice the dresses, too ; if he observe any ornament on a
sister's dress, he should burn it publicly. This will be a
lesson to her. He should make his inspection in the morning, and never stay to dinner, though he be pressed ; he
comes to do business, not to talk. If he does stay, there

must only be a modest entertainment. I know not how to prevent excess in this respect, for our present chief never notices what is put before him—whether it is good or bad, much or little.* I doubt whether he even understands.

"Finally the visitor must be careful how he shows by any outward sign that he has a special regard for the prioress. If he does, the sisters will not tell him what she really is. Each of them knows that she is heard but once, while the prioress has as much time as she likes for explanations and excuses. The prioress may not mean to deceive, but self-love blinds us all. I have been myself taken in repeatedly by mother superiors who were such servants of God that I could not help believing them. After a few days' residence, I have been astonished to find how misled I had been. The devil, having few opportunities of tempting the sisters, attacks the superiors instead. I trust none of them till I have examined with my own eyes."

Shrewder eyes were not perhaps in Spain. "You deceived me in saying she was a woman," wrote one of Teresa's confessors. "She is a bearded man."

To return to her story. She died, as has been said, at Alva, and there was nothing at first to distinguish her departure from that of ordinary persons. She had fought a long battle. She had won the victory; but the dust of the conflict was still flying; detraction was still busy; and honor with the best deserving is seldom immediately bestowed. The air has to clear, the passions to cool, and the spoils of the campaign to be gathered, before either the thing accomplished or the doer's merits can be properly recognized. Teresa's work was finished; but she had enemies who hated her; half friends who were envious and jealous; and a world of

* This was meant as a hint to Gratian, who was much too fond of dining with the sisterhoods. Perhaps much of the rest was also intended for him.

people besides, to say that the work was nothing very wonderful, and that they could have done as well themselves if they had thought it worth while.

It is always thus when persons of genuiue merit first leave the earth. As long as they are alive and active they make their power felt ; and when they are looked back upon from a distance they can be seen towering high above their contemporaries. Their contemporaries, however, less easily admit the difference ; and when the overmastering presence is first removed, and they no longer feel the weight of it, they deny that any difference exists.

Teresa was buried where she died. Spanish tombs are usually longitudinal holes perforated in blocks of masonry. The coffin is introduced ; the opening is walled up ; and a tablet with an inscription indicates and protects the spot. In one of these apertures attached to the Alva convent Teresa was placed. The wooden coffin, hastily nailed together, was covered with quicklime and earth. Massive stones were built in after it, and were faced with solid masonry. There she was left to rest ; to be regarded, as it seemed, with passionate affection by the sisters who survived her, and then to fade into a shadow, and be remembered no more forever. But the love of those sisters was too intense, and their faith too deep. " Calumny," says Sir Arthur Helps, " can make a cloud seem a mountain ; can even make a cloud become a mountain." Love and faith are no less powerful enchanters, and can convert into facts the airy phantoms of the brain. The sisters when they passed her resting-place paused to think of her, and her figure as it came back to them breathed fragrance sweet as violets. Father Gratian, who had been absent from the deathbed, came on a visitation to the convent nine months after. His imagination was as active as that of the sisterhood ; he perceived, not the violet odor only, but a fragrant oil oozing between the stones. The tomb was opened, the lid of the coffin was found broken, and the earth had fallen through. The face was discolored, but the flesh was uncorrupted, and the cause of the odor was at once apparent in the ineffable sweetness which distilled from it. The body was taken out and washed, Gratian cut off the left hand and secured it for himself. Thus mutilated, the body itself was replaced, and Gratian carried off his prize, which instantly worked miracles. The Jesuit Ribera, who was afterward Teresa's biographer, and had been present at the opening, saved part of the earth. He found it "sweet as the bone of St. Lawrence which was preserved at Avila." The story flew from lip to lip. Gratian, zealous for the honor of the reformed branch of the Carmelites, called a chapter, and brought his evidence before it that their founder was a saint. Teresa's communications with the other world at once assumed a more awful aspect. The chapter decided that, as at Avila she was born, as at Avila she was first admitted to converse with Christ, and as there was her first foundation, to Avila her remains must be removed, and be laid in the chapel of San Josef. The sisters at Alva wept, but submitted. They were allowed to keep the remnant of the arm from which Gratian had taken off the hand. Other small portions were furtively abstracted. The rest was solemnly transferred.

This was in 1585, three years after her death. But it was not to be the end. The Alva family had the deepest reverence for Teresa. The Great Duke was gone, but his son who succeeded him, and his brother, the Prince of St. John's, inherited his feelings. They

were absent at the removal, and had not been consulted.
When they heard of it, they held their town to have
been injured and their personal honor to have been outraged. They were powerful. They appealed to Rome,
and were successful. Sixtus the Fifth, in 1586, sent an
order to give them back their precious possession, and
Teresa, who had been a wanderer so long, was sent again
upon her travels. A splendid tomb had been prepared
in the convent chapel at Alva, and the body, brought
back again from Avila, lay in state in the choir before it
was deposited there. The chapel was crowded with
spectators ; the Duke and Duchess were present with a
train of nobles, the Provincial Gratian, and a throng of
dignitaries, lay and ecclesiastic. The features were still
earth-stained, but were otherwise unaltered. The mi-
raculous perfume was overpowering. Ribera contrived
to kiss the sacred foot, and to touch the remaining arm.
He feared to wash his hands afterward, lest he should
wash away the fragrance ; but he found, to his delight,
that no washing affected it. Gratian took another finger
for himself ; a nun in an ecstacy bit out a portion of
skin ; and for this time the obsequies were ended. Yet,
again, there was another disentombment, that Teresa
might be more magnificently coffined, and the General
of the Carmelites came from Italy that he might see
her. This time, the Pope had enjoined that there
should be no more mutilation ; but nothing could re-
strain the hunger of affection. Illustrious persons who
were present, in spite of Pope and decency, required
relics, and were not to be denied. The General distributed portions among the Alva sisterhood. The eye-
witness who describes the scene was made happy by a
single finger-joint. The General himself shocked the
feelings or roused the envy of the bystanders by tearing

out an entire rib. Then it was over, and all that remained of Teresa was left to the worms.

But the last act had still to be performed. Spanish opinion had declared Teresa to be a saint; the Church had to ratify the verdict. Time had first to elapse for the relics to work miracles in sufficient quantity, and promotion to the highest spiritual rank could only be gradual and deliberate. Teresa was admitted to the lower degree of beatification by Paul the Fifth in 1614. She was canonized (*relata inter Deos*) eight years later by Gregory the Fifteenth, in the company of St. Isidore, Ignatius Loyola, Francis Xavier, and Philip Neri. If a life of singular self-devotion in the cause of Catholic Christianity could merit so lofty a distinction, no one will challenge Teresa's claim to it. She had been an admirable woman, and as such deserved to be remembered. But she was to be made into an object of popular worship, and evidence of mere human excellence was not sufficient. A string of miracles were proved to have been worked by her in her lifetime, the witnesses to the facts being duly summoned and examined. Her sad, pathetic death-scene was turned into a phantasmagoria. Old people were brought to swear that the Convent Church had been mysteriously illuminated; Christ and a company of angels had stood at the bedside to receive the parting soul; and the room had been full of white floating figures, presumed to be the eleven thousand virgins. Others said that a white dove had flown out of her mouth when she died, and had vanished through the window, while a dead tree in the garden was found next morning covered with white blossom.

The action of the relics had been still more wonderful. If cut or punctured they bled. They had continued uncorrupted. They were still fragrant. A cripple at Avila had been restored to strength by touching a fragment; a sister at Malaga with three cancers on her breast had been perfectly cured—with much more of the same kind.

Next the solemn doctors examined Teresa's character, her virtues of the first degree, her virtues of the second degree, the essentials of *sanctitas in specie*. Faith, Hope, Charity, love of Christ, were found all satisfactory. Her tears at the death of Pius the Fifth proved her loyalty to the Church. The exceptional features followed, her struggles with the cacodæmon, her stainless chastity, her voluntary poverty, her penance, her whip, her hair-cloth, her obedience, her respect for priests, her daily communion, her endurance of the devil's torments, and, as the crown of the whole, her intercourse with San Josef, the Virgin, and her Son.

Her advocate made a splendid oration to the Pope. The Pope referred judgment to the Cardinals, Archbishops, and Bishops, whose voices were unanimous, and Teresa was declared a member of the already glorified company to whom prayers might lawfully be uttered.

Teresa's image still stands in the Castilian churches. The faithful crowd about her with their offerings, and dream that they leave behind them their aches and pains; but her words were forgotten, and her rules sank again into neglect. The Church of Rome would have done better in keeping alive Teresa's spirit than in converting her into a goddess. Yet the Church of Rome is not peculiarly guilty, and we all do the same thing in our own way. When a great teacher dies who has told us truths which it would be disagreeable to act upon, we write adoring lives of him, we place him in the intellectual pantheon; but we go on as if he had never lived at all. We put up statues to him as if that would do as well, and the prophet who has denounced idols is made an idol himself. Yet good seed scattered broadcast is never wholly wasted. Though dying out in Spain and Italy, the Carmelite Sisterhoods are reviving in Northern Europe, and they owe such life as they now possess to Teresa of Avila. The nuns of Compiègne, who in 1794 fell under the displeasure of Robespierre, were Carmelites of Teresa's order. Vergniaud and his twenty-two companions sang the Marseillaise at the scaffold, the surviving voices keeping up the chorus, as their heads fell one by one till all were gone. Teresa's thirteen sisters at Compiègne sang the "Veni Creator" as the knife of the Convention made an end of them, the prioress singing the last verse alone amid the bodies of her murdered flock.

THE TEMPLARS

I.

I HAVE chosen, I fear, a somewhat remote subject for these lectures,* and the remoteness is not the only objection. I might have gone farther back, and yet been nearer to our modern interests. I might have given you an account, had I known anything about the matter, of the people who lived in the pile-dwellings in the Swiss lakes; or of the old sea-rovers who piled up the kitchen middens on the shores of the Baltic; or I might have gone back to the primeval missing link between us and the apes, the creatures who split the bones which we find in Kent's Cavern, and were the contemporaries of the cave bears and the big cats who then lived in these islands. In talking about any of these, I should have been on a level with modern curiosity. We are all eager to know more about these ancestors of ours, since Darwin has thrown doubts upon our supernatural origin. At any rate, however, I shall not ask you to go so far back with me by a good many thousand years. The military orders of the Middle Ages, if different from ourselves, are but creatures of yesterday in comparison, and there is an interest even of a scientific kind in observing the strangely varied forms which human nature is capable of assuming. Whatever has come out of man lies somewhere in the character of man. Human nature

* These papers were originally lectures delivered at Edinburgh before the Philosophical Institution in 1885.

is said to be always the same; but it is the same only in the sense that the crab-apple and the endless varieties of garden apples are the same. Analyze the elements and you find them to appearance the same. There is some force in the seed (we cannot tell what) which makes one plant a crab and another a fruit-tree. In the man the difference lies in the convictions which he entertains about his origin, his duties, his responsibilities, his powers. With him, too, there is an original vital force which will make each individual something different from his neighbor; but the generic type is formed by his creed. As his belief, so is his character. According to his views of what life is given him for, he becomes a warrior, a saint, a patriot, a rascal, a sensualist, or a comfortable man of business, who keeps his eye on the main chance, and does not go into dreams. And as you look along the ages you see a tendency in masses of men to drift into one or other of these forms.

Carlyle tells of a conversation at which he was once present in this city more than fifty-six years ago. Someone was talking of the mischief which beliefs had produced in the world. "Yes," Carlyle said, "belief has done much evil; but it has done all the good." We do not, we cannot certainly know what we are, or where we are going. But if we believe nobly about ourselves, we have a chance of living nobly. If we believe basely, base we shall certainly become.

In a lecture which I had once the honor of addressing you in this place I spoke of the effect of the Reformation on the Scotch character. I described it as like turning iron into steel. There had been steel enough before among the lairds and barons, but the people had been soft metal; they followed their chiefs, going this way and that way as they were told. After Knox's time they had wills of their own, and we all know what they became. The military Orders about whom I am now to speak grew into a shape at least equally noticeable. Their history is extremely curious. It raises the most intricate questions as to the value of historical evidence. It illustrates both sides of *belief*, the good of it and the evil of it. I speak of Orders, but I shall confine myself to *one*—to the Order of the Templars. There were three great military Orders—the Templars, the Knights Hospitalers, and the Teutonic Knights. Other smaller bodies of the same kind grew up beside them; but it was in the Templars that the idea, if I may call it so, was perfectly realized. To understand them is to understand the whole subject.

Scotch and English people, when they hear of Templars, all think instinctively of Brian de Bois Guilbert. In Sir Brian a Templar stands before us, or seems to stand, in flesh and blood, and beside him stands Scott's other Templar, Sir Giles Amaury, the Grand Master, in "The Talisman." No one can doubt that we have here real men, as distinct as genius could produce. The Germans say that when a genuine character has been brought into being, it matters nothing whether such a figure ever existed in space and time. The creative spirit has brought him forth somehow, and he belongs thenceforward to the category of real existences. *Men*, doubtless, Sir Brian and Sir Giles both *were;* but Scott, like Homer, sometimes slept. They were *men*, but in one important respect, at least, they were not Templars. Rebecca calls Sir Brian a perjured priest. Sir Giles Amaury hears Conrad's confession before he gives him absolution with his dagger. The Templars were not priests; they were laymen as much as kings and barons. They bound themselves by the three monastic vows of poverty, chastity, and obedience. They were, as a religious order, subject to the Pope, and soldiers of the Church. Other orders they had none. They had chaplains affiliated, who said mass for them and absolved them. But these chaplains were separate and subordinate. They could hold no rank in the society. Grand Masters, preceptors, priors, were always lay. They were a new thing in Christendom, as St. Bernard said. The business of priests was to pray. The business of the knights was to pray, too, but only as all other men prayed. Their peculiar work was to fight. Sir Walter was an Episcopalian, but owing, perhaps, to his North British training, he never completely apprehended the great mystery of apostolical succession. To him a monk was a priest. We in this generation, who have learned the awful nature of the difference, must clear our minds of that error, at any rate.

Now for what the Templars were.

A good many of us have probably been in the Temple Church in London. The Templars were famous for the beauty of their churches, and this particular church, now that the old pews have been cleared out, is almost in the condition in which they left it. In the ante-chapel there lie on the floor the figures of nine warriors, represented, not as dead or asleep, but reclining as they might have reclined in life, modelled all of them with the highest contemporary art, figures that have only to rise to their feet to stand before us as they actually were when quick and breathing on earth. The originals of them, if they are rightly named, were not themselves Templars; they were great Barons and Statesmen. But they were associates of the Order, and in dress and appearance doubtless closely resembled them. They are extremely noble figures. Pride is in every line of their features, pride in every undulation of their forms; but it is not base, personal pride. There is the spirit in them of the soldier, the spirit of the saint, the spirit of the feudal ruler, and the spirit of the Catholic Church—as if in them was combined the entire genius of the age, the pride of feudalism, and the pride of the Church, the pride of a soul disdainful of all personal ease or personal ambition.

That they were placed where they are, and that they were allowed to remain there, is at least some indication that the charges on which the Templars were condemned found no belief in England. The monuments of the Pembrokes would never have been allowed to remain in a scene which had been desecrated by unimaginable infamies. What the charges were, and how the Order fell, it will be my business to tell you. I have no cause to defend, or sympathy to tempt me to make out a case one way or the other. The Templars in Europe, if they had been allowed to survive, would have become the Pope's Janissaries, and so far as I have any special leaning in those mediæval quarrels, it is toward the Civil Powers and not toward the Church. I believe that it would have been worse for Europe, and not better, if the Popes had been able to maintain their pretensions. If it had really been made out that there was as much vice in the Templars' houses as there undoubtedly was among the other celibate Orders, there would have been nothing in it to surprise me, and it would have interfered with no theory of mine. So now I will go on with the story.

The Templars grew out of the Crusades—that supreme folly of the Middle Ages, as it is the fashion now to call them. For myself, I no more call the Crusades folly than I call the eruption of a volcano folly, or the French

Revolution folly, or any other bursting up of the lava which lies in nature or in the hearts of mankind. It is the way in which nature is pleased to shape the crust of the earth and to shape human society. Our business with these things is to understand them, not to sit in judgment on them.

In the eleventh century a great wave of religious enthusiasm passed over Christendom. Men had expected that the world would end at the year 1000. When it did not end, and went on as before, instead of growing careless, they grew more devout. The Popes, under the influence of this pious emotion, acquired a universal and practical authority, such as had never before been conceded to them. Religion became the ruling principle of life to an extent which has never perhaps been equalled, save in Protestant countries in the century which succeeded the Reformation. There was then one faith in western Christendom, one Church, and one Pope. The creed, if you please, was alloyed with superstition, but the power of it, so long as the superstition was sincere, was not less on that account, but was greater ; and Christendom became capable of a united action which had not before been possible. In times when religion is alive Christianity is not a history, but a personal experience. Christ himself was supposed to be visibly present on the altar of every church and chapel. His mother, the apostles, and the saints were actively at work round the daily life of everyone. The particular part of the earth where the Saviour had been born and had lived, where the mystery of human redemption had been wrought out, where occurred all the incidents which form the subject of the Gospel story, Nazareth and Capernaum, Bethlehem and Jerusalem, acquired a passionate interest in proportion to the depth of the belief.

People didn't travel in those days for amusement. There was no Mr. Cook to lead them in flocks over the globe, or Murray's Handbooks, or omnibuses making the round of the Pyramids, but they travelled a great deal for their own purposes ; they travelled to scenes of martyrdom and to shrines of saints ; they travelled for the good of their souls. We go ourselves to Stratford-on-Avon, or to Ferney, or to Abbotsford ; some of us go already to Ecclefechan and Craigenputtock, and the stream in that direction will by and by be a large one. Multiply the feeling which sends us to these spots a thousand-fold, and you may then conceive the attractions which the Holy Places in Palestine had for Catholic Christians in the eleventh century. Christ was all which gave the world and their own lives in it any real significance. It was not a ridiculous feeling on their part, but a very beautiful one. Some philosopher after reading the Iliad is said to have asked, " But what does it prove ? " A good many people have asked of what *use* pilgrimages were. It depends on whether we have got souls or not. If we have none, the Iliad is a jumble of nonsense, and the pilgrim's cockle-shell was no better than a fool's cap and bells. But the prevailing opinion for the present is, that we have souls.

From the beginning there had been pilgrimages to the Holy Places. Even after the Saracens had conquered Palestine the caliphs had so far respected Christian piety as to leave the Holy Sepulchre undesecrated and allow pilgrims to go and come unmolested. But the caliphs' empire was now disturbed by the wild tribes from the north behind the Caspian Sea, who had poured down into Syria. New and fiercer bands of Mahometans had possession of Palestine, and just when Europe was under the influence of the most powerful

15

religious emotion, and had become able to combine to give effect to it, the Seljuks, Turcomans, miscellaneous Arabian robbers, became masters of the one spot on earth which was most sacred in the eyes of the western nations, and the pilgrims had no longer access to it.

With a single impulse Christian Europe rose. They rushed blindly at their object, without preparation, without provision, half of them without arms, trusting that as they were on God's service God would provide. Famine, disease, the sword swept them away in multitudes, and multitudes more followed, to die like the rest. The crusades altogether are supposed to have cost six million lives, some say ten; but the end was for a time attained. In the last decade of the eleventh century Godfrey of Bouillon fought his way into Palestine with sixty thousand princes, peers, knights, and their own personal followers. He took Jerusalem. He made a Latin kingdom of it. For eighty-seven years the Holy City was ruled by a Christian sovereign; Palestine was distributed into fiefs, to be held by knights serving under the King of Jerusalem; and Christian Europe believed that it had done its duty. Alas! it had but half done it. The object was to open the Holy Places again to western piety. Jerusalem might be Christian, but the country between Jerusalem and the sea swarmed with bands of roving Bedouins. The pilgrims came loaded with offerings, and fell as a rich prey to robbers at every turn of the road. The crusading knights in their iron coats could meet armies in the field and take towns which could not run away; they could build castles and portion out the districts, and try to rule on the European system; but Europe was not Asia, and they could as little brush away the Saracen banditti as they could brush away the mosquitoes. So it went on year after year, and Jerusalem was hardly more accessible to pious devotees than it had been before the conquest.

At last, in the very spirit and genius of the age, a small company of young French nobles volunteered their services as a pilgrims' guard. It was a time when all great work was done by volunteers. There was already a hospital volunteer service like our own modern Red Cross. The crusaders had suffered miserably from wounds and sickness. A company of Hospitalers had been established with its headquarters at Jerusalem, who grew afterward into the Knights of St. John.

Exactly on the same principle there was formed a fighting company, who undertook to keep the road between Acre and Jerusalem. The originators of it were two young French knights of noble birth, Hugh de Payens and Godfrey of St. Omer. They found seven others ready to join them, all like themselves of high rank, who had won their spurs in the battle-field. They called themselves poor brothers in Christ. They devoted themselves to Christ's service and his mother's. They took vows in the presence of the Patriarch, vows of the usual kind, to cut themselves off from all worldly interests ; the vow of poverty, the vow of chastity, the vow of absolute obedience to the Patriarch, and to the one among them whom they should choose as their head. Thus organized, they took the field as mounted police on the pilgrims' road.

The palace of the Latin kings was on the site of Solomon's Temple. A wing of it was set apart as a pilgrims' home, and as the home and station of their guards. The knights had their suite of rooms, with appointments for their horses and servants, and it was from this that they took their name as Brothers of the Order of the Temple.

The Church of the Holy Sepulchre was their chapel. They had a Gothic hall with lances in rack, and suits of armor hanging on the walls, and long swords and crossbows, and battle-axes—very strange objects in the Temple of Jerusalem, almost as strange as the imaginary Gothic castle in the mountains above Sparta, to which Faust and Mephistopheles transported Helen of Troy.

It was here and thus that the Knight-Templars, who were so soon to fill so large a place in the world, began their existence—nine young gentlemen whose sole object in life was to escort pious souls to the scene of Christ's sufferings and resurrection. So much belief was able to do. Their life was spent in fighting. They had a battle-cry by which to know each other—*Beaucéant,* as we know from "Ivanhoe;" but what Beaucéant meant, no one can tell with certainty. It was, I believe, a cry of the Burgundian peasantry—a sort of link with the old home.

Every prince and baron had his armorial bearings. The Templars had theirs, though again we are astray for a meaning. It was two knights riding on one horse, and has been supposed to indicate their original poverty. But two knights on a single horse would have made but poor work with the light-armed and lightly mounted Bedouins; and we know, besides, that each knight had two or three horses with servants to wait on him and them. Some think it meant brotherly love; some that it was a badge of humility and simplicity. But this is guesswork; the Templars were not clerks, and have left no explanatory records behind them; when they perished, they perished entirely, and scarcely any documents of their own survive to gratify our curiosity. Anyway, it is clear that, though individually vowed to poverty, they were supplied either by the King or out of their own combined resources with everything that was necessary to make their work effective. The only fault among them was that they were too few for the business which they had undertaken.

But enthusiasm was contagious in those days. These Brothers of the Temple made a noise in Europe ; the world talked about them. Popes and bishops sang their praises. Other earnest youths were eager to join. The Order was like a seed thrown into a soil exactly prepared for it. So far there were but nine knights held together by their own wills and their own vows. It was desirable to give them more cohesion and an enduring form. One of the nine was a kinsman of St. Bernard of Clairvaux. At the end of nine years, in 1127, there was to be a great Church Council held at Troyes. Baldwin, King of Jerusalem, sent two of the brethren to Europe to see St. Bernard, to see if possible Pope Honorius, to give an account to the Council of themselves and their doings, and to learn if it would be possible to enlarge their numbers. Evidently King Baldwin thought that if he was to hold Palestine he must have a military force of some kind for constant service. The Crusades were single efforts, exhausting and expensive. The Christian nobles came at their own cost ; they fought gallantly, but if they were not killed they went home after their first campaign. The Holy Land could not be held thus. An organized army, with paid troops, and regimental chests, and a commissariat, was out of harmony with the time. If the enthusiasm of Europe was to take a constant form, it could take effect best in a religious military order, to be sustained in perpetuity as a permanent garrison.

St. Bernard received his visitors with open arms. He

carried them to the Pope. The Pope gave them his blessing, and sent them on to the Council. The Council gave them a Charter, as we may call it, and formed them into an Order of regulars; and at once, from all parts of Europe, hundreds of gallant young men came forward to enter the ranks. The Pope had promised heaven to all who would take the cross against the infidels. Service in person could be commuted in favor of anyone who would give lands to support the Knights of the Holy Brotherhood. The kings took up the cause. Hugh de Payens came back in person; he was received in Paris; he was received in London by our first Henry. Rich manors were settled on the Order in France, in England, in Spain, and in Germany. Priories were founded on each estate, to be as depots to a regiment, where novices could be received and learn their duties, and from which they could be passed on to the Holy Land as their services were required. The huge torrent of crusading enthusiasm was, as it were, confined between banks and made to run in an even channel.

A regular Order required a rule, and St. Bernard drew up a rule for the Knights of the Temple. There was now, he said, to be a war, the like of which had never been seen before; a double war against the whole powers of the devil in the field of battle and in the heart of man. The rule of the Templars had, of course, to be something different from the rules of the Benedictines and Cistercians. They were not humble men of peace, meek recluses whose time was divided between cloister and garden, whose chief duty was to sing masses for the souls of erring mankind. They were soldiers to whom peace was never known, who were to be forever in the field on desperate and dangerous errands. They were men of fiery temper, hot of blood, and hard of hand, whose sinew had to be maintained in as much efficiency as their spirits. They were all nobly born, too ; younger sons of dukes, and counts, and barons. Very curious to look at, for we can see in them what noble blood meant at the time when the aristocracy rose to the command of Europe.

If you please, therefore, we will look at this rule of theirs. It has not come down to us precisely as St. Bernard drew it up. It received additions and alterations as the Order enlarged. In essentials, however, the regulations remained unchanged as they had been at the beginning. St. Bernard was a Cistercian. He followed as far as he could his own pattern. The Templars were to be purely self-governed. The head was called the Grand Master. They chose him themselves, and he was to reside always at the post of danger, in Palestine. Under him were Preceptors—four or five in each of the great nations of Europe. Under them were Priors, the superiors of the different convents of the Order. All these officers were knights, and all laymen. The knights, as I said, took the three monastic vows. They abjured all personal property ; they swore to remain pure ; they swore to obey the orders of their superiors without question, without hesitation, as if it came from God. We need not think this servile. Even in our own days of liberty such obedience is no more than is required of every officer and private in a modern army. Except in battle, their dress was a white cloak, on which a red cross was afterward embroidered ; white signifying chastity. Unless a knight remained chaste he could not see God. He had no lady-love in whose honor he could break a lance in the tournament, he had not even an imaginary Dulcinea, like Don Quixote, or a Gloriana, like

the Paladins of King Arthur's court. The only woman
to whom a Templar might devote himself was the Queen
of Heaven. They were allowed no ornaments ; hair and
dress were to be kept plain and simple. Abundant food
was provided for them, meat and wine and bread and
vegetables. And there is a very curious provision that
they were to eat in pairs, each pair at a single board,
that one knight might keep watch over the other, and
see that he ate his dinner properly, and did not fast.
To fast it seems was a temptation, to eat and drink a
penance.

Besides the general servants of the house, each knight
had a special attendant of his own. The knight was
forbidden to speak sharply to him, and was specially
forbidden to strike him.

Religious duties were strictly prescribed, but were
modified by good sense. The knights, as a rule, were
to attend the regular chapel services ; but if they had
been out on duty at night they were let off matins, and
might say their prayers in bed. If they had done anything wrong or foolish they were to confess to the
Grand Master or head of the house ; if it was a breach
of discipline the head of the house set them a penance ;
if it was a sin they were sent to a priest, who at first was
a secular outside the order. They had little leisure ;
their chief occupation was war. When not in the field
they had their arms and horses to look after, which they
were allowed to buy for themselves, charging the account to the house.

Except by leave of the superior, they were to hold no
correspondence with anyone in the outer world, not
even with mothers, sisters, or brothers. No brother of
the Order might walk about alone, or, when in a town,
go into the streets, unless with leave asked and given.

Fighting men had hot blood, and hot blood required to be restrained. Even an angry word spoken by one to another was instantly punished, and so was all light talk, especially when it turned on the other sex. If a brother of the Temple wanted to converse it must be on serious or, at least, rational subjects. The most innocent amusements were considered trifling, and were not to be encouraged. A Templar was not to hunt, or hawk, or shoot, still less to play idle games. One exception only was made ; it is a very noticeable one, and had not escaped Sir Walter. In Syria and Palestine there were still wild beasts, as there had been in David's time. St. Bernard could not permit his Templars to hunt deer or net partridges ; he did, however, by special statute, allow them to hunt lions. And, mind, those were not days of repeating rifles and explosive bullets : it was man and lion face to face, with spear and knife against teeth and claws. The lion no doubt in St. Bernard's mind was a type of the adversary ; to hunt the lion was to hunt Satan. None the less, just as he had taken care that they should eat and drink enough, and not emaciate themselves like intending saints, so he would have them men at all points, and give them sport, too, so long as it was dangerous, and needed courage.

We have travelled far since those days. The taste for sport still survives among us, and along with it at bottom there is, I dare say, in our young aristocrats, as firm a temper and as high a spirit as in those young pupils of the Abbot of Clairvaux, were there any modern abbots who could give their lives a meaning and a purpose suited to our own times. I heard the other day of a very fine young fellow, who in the twelfth century might have been spearing lions and escorting pilgrims among the Templars, performing the extraordinary exploit of shooting fifty brace of grouse in twenty-five minutes on some moor in Yorkshire ; and the feat was considered so memorable that a granite column was erected on the spot to commemorate it. Some modern St. Bernard seems to me to be desperately needed.

I will mention one more point in the rule of the Templars. It was customary in those days when men of rank were taken in battle to hold them to ransom, the price of redemption being measured by their wealth. The Templars had no personal wealth ; and the wealth of the Order was to be spent in God's service, not in man's. If a Templar was taken by the Saracens no ransom was to be paid for him ; he was to be left to his fate. His fate invariably was to be offered the alternative of the Koran or the sword ; and there is scarcely a recorded instance in which a Templar saved his life by abandoning his faith.

I have said enough about these rules to show what sort of people the Templars were at the time when they began their career as a regular Order. Their numbers increased with extraordinary rapidity. A special branch was established in Aragon, where they could fight the Moors without leaving Europe. Hugh de Payens took three hundred knights back with him to Palestine, and if they wanted fighting he gave them enough of it. In every battle the Templars were in the front. Five years after nearly every one of the three hundred had been killed. Popes and bishops glorified them as martyrs, and the ranks filled faster than death could empty them. They were the passion and the admiration of the whole Christian world.

II.

As time went on, and the first enthusiasm passed
away, the Templars became a political and spiritual
force in the European system.   The Grand Master took
rank among the peers in the councils of princes, and
in ordinary times he had the command of the military defence of Palestine.   The kingdom of Jerusalem
was never the stablest of monarchies ; but even the
Saracens were sometimes exhausted.   There were intervals of truce, intervals of peace ; negotiations and
treaties had to pass between the Christian and the Moslem powers.   The conduct of these negotiations fell to
the Templars, and between them and the Saracens there
grew up some kind of acquaintance.   Having their home
in the East they got to know the Eastern character.   It
was alleged afterward that in this way their faith became corrupted.   Scott has taken this view in his character of Sir Brian.   Whether it was so or not I shall
consider by and by.   Nothing to their discredit can be
concluded from the fact of the intercourse, because it
was inevitable.   Nor was any suspicion of the kind ever
breathed till the eve of their fall.   All that appears for
certain is that, being soldiers, they became statesmen
also, and the general experience is that soldiers make
very good statesmen.   Only this is to be observed, that
they became more closely connected with the Popes,
and the Popes with them.   For the first thirty years
they were subject to the Patriarchs of Jerusalem, while
secular priests, under the patriarchs' authority, heard
their confessions and said mass for them.   As a reward
for their services the Popes relieved them from the patri-

archs' jurisdiction, and took them specially to themselves. In their houses and on their domains in Europe they were exempted from all authority except that of Rome. No bishop anywhere was allowed to interfere with them. Instead of secular priests they were permitted to have special chaplains, ordained by bishops, but subject, after their introduction, to the rule of the Temple only. They were entirely isolated from all the other regulars. No brother of the Temple might leave it and become a Benedictine ; and the more separate they became the ampler the privileges which the Popes seemed delighted to heap upon them. Many thousands of them by this time were spread over France, and England, and Spain. Their lands were released from tithe ; no priest or bishop's officer could levy tax or rate on a Templar's manor, while the Templars on their side might take the tithe which the priests looked on as their own. No prelate, no prince even, might put a Templar on his oath, or call on him for any feudal service. Popular as they had been at the beginning, the extraordinary favor with which the Popes honored them began to be looked on with jealousy and resentment. And they had another privilege, peculiarly irritating to the bishops, and even to the Benedictines and Cistercians, who thought that if conferred on one Order it should have been conferred on all. Those who are acquainted with the state of Europe in the twelfth and thirteenth centuries know generally what an interdict meant. When any country or province was under an interdict the churches were closed, the church services were suspended ; the young could not get married, the sick could not be absolved, the dead could not be buried in consecrated ground, but lay in ditches like dogs ; human life stood suspended as if under a horrible curse.

You may think so frightful a sentence was only issued on extraordinary occasions. On the contrary, it was the bishops' universal weapon, the instrument of their power, the unfailing fountain of their revenue, for an interdict once issued was not easily raised till every person in the province had bled for it. When bishops and nobles quarrelled, when archbishops quarrelled with bishops, or quarrelled with their flocks, they launched their interdicts like thunderbolts, striking whole districts without discrimination. To the astonishment and rage of these great persons the manors of the Templars were made a land of Goshen, which the plague could not touch. Nor was this all. Wherever any Templar went on business of the order the interdict was suspended, the church-bells rang out, the sacraments were dispensed to the flocks, the bodies of the dead could be laid peacefully in hallowed graves. It was even believed, so bitter was the animosity, that individuals who were excommunicated were allowed to confess and receive absolution in the Templars' chapels.

Thus protected, thus curtained round with exemptions and securities, it is not to be wondered at that if the rival clergy looked askance at the Templars, they came to think considerably of themselves. They were dangerous from their military strength; they owed allegiance to no earthly power, secular or spiritual, except the Pope's. To the Popes they owed their position, and in those long conflicts between the See of Rome and the kings and emperors, they repaid the Papacy by standing by it in all its quarrels. Princes feared them, bishops hated them for their independence, the clergy envied their liberties. They cared little; they were rich, they were strong; their persons were sacred. Being regarded so doubtfully, it is very remarkable that for the two centuries during which they were in their vigor, and down to the moment of their fall, you rarely find anywhere in the contemporary monastic writers any moral scandals reported of them. Giraldus Cambrensis and others are never weary of drawing pictures of the gluttony and sensuality in the monasteries. Abbots and priors, if you can believe what is told by chroniclers and satirists, were wrapped often in the seven deadly sins, and bishops were not much better. But there is a curious silence about the Templars. They are credited invariably with desperate courage in the field. They are hardly ever, that I remember, accused of being false to their vows, and, undoubtedly, if there had been notorious ground for scandal we should have heard enough of it. For we do hear complaints of them of another kind, complaints of them as laymen encroaching on churchmen's functions, and of their overbearing ways. Now and then they were rebuked, even by the Popes, for overstraining their privileges. Very generally, indeed, you find remarks upon their haughty bearing. They had the double loftiness in them of churchmen and warriors, loftiness too great when single, when double past endurance. You see it in all their actions, you see it in the lines of those recumbent figures in the Temple Church, lines fashioned by the habitual tone of their thoughts, and perpetuated in stone by the artist who had seen and known them.

King Richard (our Cœur de Lion) being sick once was attended by a French priest. The father spoke to him especially of three questionable daughters that he had, called Avarice, Sensuality, and Pride. Richard said, " I have disposed of those three you speak of. I have given my avarice to the Cistercians ; I have given my sensuality——" It is a well-known story, but the authors differ

on the recipient of this quality. Some say to the Black
Friars, some to the bishops, some to the clergy. I fear
the variety implies that it fitted with each of them ; but
all agree on the last, that he gave his pride to the Templars.

Proud they were, but with the pride of soldiers.
Always on the testimony of their worst enemies, where-
ever there was fighting to be done with the infidel the
Templars were in the thickest of it. No man ever knew
a Templar a coward. Again and again in Palestine,
when their ranks were thin and the Saracens hemmed
them round in thousands, the Templars stood till the
last man of them fell on the field, or fell afterward for
his faith if carried off a wounded prisoner. Such fighting was rarely or never seen among the bravest men that
ever lived.

In 1187, when Saladin destroyed the Christian army
near the Lake of Gennesareth, and when the wood of the
true cross which they had with them fell into Saladin's
hands, the Grand Master of the day and a number of
knights were taken prisoners. Saladin admired their
daring. He would have made them princes of his own
empire if they would have changed their creed ; they all
refused, and were all slain.

Yet the kings did not like them : they were always too
true to the Popes. The Templars were a thorn in the
side of Cœur de Lion. They were a thorn in the side of
the great Frederick the Second of Germany. I need not
go through the details of their history. The kingdom
of Jerusalem lasted but eighty-seven years ; Saladin then
took the Holy City, and the Templars built themselves a
great feudal castle near Acre, where they continued to
protect the pilgrims. Pilgrims' Castle was the name of
it—a palatial fortress like old Windsor, vast, stern, and

splendid. Here henceforth were the headquarters of the order. Here the Grand Master held his chapters and ruled as a sovereign; hither came the fresh draughts of knights from the European preceptories. Rich as they were, the austere severity of their habits never seems to have been relaxed. Their wealth was all expended upon the wars; they were powerful, but they stood apart from all other men, loved by few and feared by all. They had no personal ties; they had no national ties; their nation was the Catholic Church; their chief was the Holy Father, and his enemies were theirs. They were in France, in England, in Scotland, in Spain, but they were not French, or English, or Scots, or Spaniards. They rarely mixed in any national struggles, and only when the Pope's interests were concerned—as, for instance, when they supported the legate, Pandulf, against King John. From the nature of the case, therefore, they could take no root in the national life anywhere. They were maintained only by the surviving enthusiasm for the Crusades, and the unquestioned constancy with which they upheld the Cross against the Crescent. Yet even in Palestine they were watched with jealousy. They knew the country. From long experience they knew the Arab nature; and they had become prudent. If left to themselves, they would have made peace with the Soldans; they could have secured the neutralization of Jerusalem, and a peaceful access to it for the pilgrims. But when they advised anything of this kind they were accused of treacherous correspondence with the enemy, and had to wipe the charge out by fresh acts of desperate gallantry. They would have saved the army of St. Louis in Egypt in the last fatal Crusade, but their advice was not taken. They were suspected of bad faith. Sir William of Sonnac, the Great Master, when he

could not be listened to in the council of war (one of
his eyes had been dashed out in battle the day before,
and the socket was still bleeding), cried out: "Beaucéant to the front! The army is lost. Beaucéant and
death!" He and all his comrades fell sword in hand.

Surely those Templars were an extraordinary form of
human beings. Loved they could not be; they were
anomalous, suited only to an anomalous state of things,
yet some way admirable too; for, whatever else they
were, they could never have entered such an institution
for their own pleasure. Dangers were gathering about
them toward the end of the thirteenth century. Their
lands were sometimes plundered, and the law was
slow to help them. Bishops, in spite of Rome and its
orders, now and then excommunicated individual Templars, and a Pope had to issue another angry bull to protect them. Kings began to think that they were too
rich and to covet some of their treasures. Our Henry
the Third told the Grand Preceptor of England that
they had been indulged too much, and that he must
have money out of them. The Templars answered coldly
that the King spoke as one that was not wise, and that
the attempt might cost him his throne. It was their
own existence that was in peril, not the Crown's, if they
had known the truth of their position.

The meaning of them was as a garrison for Palestine.
Their strength was the service which they were rendering
in the cause of the Crusades; and the Crusades and all
that they had accomplished were now coming to an end.

The campaign of St. Louis in Egypt was the last serious effort. After the defeat of St. Louis on the Nile, the
Crusading spirit died away. The fortresses which the
Christians held in the Holy Land fell one by one, and at
last, after two hundred years of fighting, nothing was

16

left of their conquests except the town of Acre and the
country for a few miles round. The management of the
defence rested on the Templars. The European princes
had professed to maintain a garrison in Acre independent of them, but in 1289 the Templars had to report
that the garrison were a mere company of vagabonds, ill
fed and unpaid, and a universal nuisance. There had
been a peace of several years with the Saracens, but the
Acre soldiers plundered the country indiscriminately.
The Saracens could get no redress. They declared
war again, and this time they meant to rally all their
strength and drive the Christians finally out. They
came down on Acre with 150,000 men. The Grand
Master took the command of the miserable troops there,
but against such a force he could do nothing. Pilgrims'
Castle was evacuated and destroyed; Acre was taken by
storm; out of his own five hundred Templars only ten
escaped; the garrison was destroyed, and the Holy Land
from one end to the other was once more in the hands
of the successors of Mahomet. The ten surviving Templars, with a few of the Hospitalers, escaped to Cyprus,
which our Richard had taken one hundred years before.
They chose a new Grand Master, Jacques de Molay, who
was to prove their last. They refilled their ranks; they
had saved their treasury, and they renewed the war in
Syria. But it was the feeble flicker of a dying flame.
The mission of the Templars in the East was over. They
held their vast estates for a purpose which was no longer a reality, and it became a question what was to be
done with them.

In Europe they were still strong and formidable, and
to one of the great parties into which Europe was divided
they could still be extremely serviceable. The Popes and
the great powers of Europe had not yet settled their

long differences. The successor of St. Peter still pretended to wield both the swords of the Apostle. Boniface
the Eighth was as firm a champion of the pretensions
of the Roman See to universal sovereignty as the boldest
of his predecessors. As the military orders were no
longer required in Palestine, Boniface perhaps conceived
that they could be employed no better than as soldiers
of the Church at home. He proposed, as Innocent the
Third had proposed before, to unite the three military
orders—Templars, Hospitalers, and the Teutonic Knights
—into a single body. Could he succeed, he might then
keep them in his own hand, to bring princes to order,
who, like Frederick the Second of Germany, were not
afraid of excommunication.

It was a daring scheme, and worthy of the head which
designed it. If carried out, it might have changed the
face of Europe. The smaller orders must have been
absorbed in the stronger, and the new organization
would have been simply the Templars enlarged. The
Holy See could count with certainty on their allegiance.
Like the Jesuits, they had renounced all natural ties ;
they had no nation but the Church, and, like the Jesuits
also, they had been trained in habits of unquestioning
obedience. Their exceptional privileges were a retaining
fee. They could keep these privileges only by the Pope's
favor and in virtue of the fear which the Pope still inspired in the bishops and clergy of the National Churches.
No temptation could be offered which could induce them
to waver in their dependence, and it is quite possible
that if the Popes could have secured to themselves the
service of so strong an arm the theocratic despotism
of the Gregories and the Innocents might have been
fixed for some centuries longer on the kingdoms of
Western Christendom.

Whether such a despotism would have been good for mankind is another question. If the Popes were infallibly wise, or infallibly good, or if they were wiser and better than the civil authorities; if, under their rule, with the Templars to help them, the poor man would have found more justice and the wrongdoer have been made to smart more surely for his sins, I, for one, am not so much in love with liberty but that I could have wished the Popes better success than they found. We ought to welcome, all of us, the rule and authority of those who have more knowledge of what is right and good than ourselves.

If it was so ; but the " if " is the difficulty. We cannot be sure of this supreme excellence of the Popes—at least some of us cannot. The intellectual revolt was only beginning, but wherever Albigenses or other speculative people were thinking for themselves, the Popes had betaken themselves already to sword and fagot. As to morals, princes might be wilful and ambitious, and barons harsh, and law courts venal ; but prelates, too, could be overbearing, and the Church courts were no purer than the civil courts. Every mediæval chronicler, every monastic annalist is forever declaiming at the avarice and rapacity of Rome.

If the Popes had reason for wishing to keep the military orders for their Janissaries, the French and English kings and the German Emperor might reasonably enough regard such an arrangement with alarm.

I have the greatest admiration for the poor brothers of the Temple. The fate which overtook them was as undeserved as it was cruel. But Nature, or Providence, or the tendencies of things, do as a fact sweep away obstacles which stand in the way of human development. Institutions may long survive their usefulness ; but they are taken away when they become actively mischievous. One could only wish that the process of taking them away was not so often tainted with a violent injustice which binds us to the necessity of their removal.

Their proper work was gone. If work was to be found for them in the future it was to be as the armed hand of the Papacy. But the Hildebrand theory of things was near its close also. The struggle between the Popes and the temporal princes was to end in a compromise. The Popes were to have the shadow, or the spiritual supremacy ; the civil powers were to have the substance, and thus for such a body as the Templars there was no place left. The kings in Europe intended to be sovereign, each in his own dominions. The Templars were, or might be, in the way. They had vast revenues, which, now that the war in the East was over, they would be free to use for other aims and ambitions. The national bishops and clergy resented their arrogance, and were jealous of their immunities. In some way or other the kings would find it necessary to suppress them. But it was no easy task. They were brave, they were noble. As soldiers they were the best organized in Europe. They were careless of death, and as long as they had the Popes at their back it was quite certain that they would not fall without a struggle, while the Popes could not in honor consent to the abolition of an order whose only crime was too great fidelity to the Holy See. It was accomplished by making the Templars the victims of an extraordinary accusation, which was intended to render them odious to mankind, and the story is one of the most curious in mediæval history.

As a rule I think it unwise to attempt to go behind the legal verdicts of distant ages. As a rule, those who have been convicted of great crimes were probably guilty of them. Men have different ways of arriving at truth, but it is generally truth which they aim at, and so many circumstances are known to contemporaries of which posterity is absolutely ignorant, that it argues some presumption in posterity when it reviews confidently contemporary judgments. But the process of the Templars was peculiar. It was considered violent even in a violent age. The details are preserved almost to the smallest particulars, and are worth examining, if only as a picture of the manners of the time.

The French king at that time was Philip le Bel— Philip the Beautiful—one of the most remarkable sovereigns that France ever had. His daughter we know of as Edward the Second's queen—*She Wolf*, as the poet Gray calls her. The parent wolf was born in 1268. He became king at sixteen. He fell early into wars with England and Burgundy, extended his frontiers, drilled into subjection his own vassals. He then quarrelled, on the old grounds of the Papal pretensions, with Pope Boniface the Eighth. He had required a subsidy from his clergy. The Pope forbade them to pay. Philip answered with calling the Pope a fool, changing your "Holiness" into your "fatuity." Boniface excommunicated Philip. Philip burnt the bull as boldly as Luther burnt Pope Leo's. He denounced Boniface as a heretic, made war upon him, and took him prisoner. The poor Pope died three days after, it was said of rage and mortification. Philip had been swift; Napoleon was not quicker in his movements. The Templars had supplied Boniface with money. They had not time to help him with arms. Boniface's successor, Benedict the Tenth, made peace on Philip's own terms. The French clergy were made to give him all that he wanted. The

Templars appealed to their privileges ; but they, too, had to submit under protest. The King was master of the situation, and meant to make the most of his victory. Benedict the Tenth reigned only for a year. The majority in the College of Cardinals was French. They chose after him the French Archbishop of Bordeaux, who was to reside in France, and could be made to do the King's bidding. Archbishop Bertrand became Pope at the beginning of 1305, under the name of Clement the Fifth.

So much for the position, which I have merely sketched in outline.

The Templars had no suspicion of their danger, and that no hint of it reached them is a proof how few friends they could have had. In outward respect they stood high as ever. No scandal had been breathed against them. Their churches were the admiration of Europe. Faithful as they were to their salt, they had never so much as dreamed that the master whom they had served so loyally could betray them. What could they have to fear? And yet it got abroad somehow that the King would be well pleased if evidence could be found of the Templars' misconduct, and when evidence is wanted, especially if it will be well paid for, sooner or later it will be forthcoming.

In the Temple, as in other bodies, there were black sheep. Knights or servants of the order now and then broke the rules, and had to be punished, and, if incorrigible, to be expelled. At the accession of Clement the Fifth there were two knights thus degraded, in prison, at Toulouse ; one of them, Esquin von Florian, who had been prior of Montfaucon, and the other with the unusual name of Noffodei. These men, after their expulsion, had been engaged in some conspiracy at Paris, and were under sentence of death. They informed the governor of the jail that they could possess the King of a secret which would be worth another realm to him, and that if their lives were spared they would reveal it. They were sent up to the court; Philip examined them himself, and they made the following singular statement :

1. Every Templar on his admission to the order swore to defend it for his life long, in all causes, just or unjust, without exception.

2. The chiefs of the order corresponded with the Saracens, and were more like Mahometans than Christians. The Novices were required to spit upon the cross, and trample on it, and deny Christ.

3. Anyone suspected of intending to betray the secrets of the order was murdered and secretly buried.

4. The Templars despised the sacraments. They worshipped idols and were heretics.

5. They committed unnatural crimes. Their houses were nests of vice and profligacy.

6. They betrayed the Holy Land, and lived without fear of God.

These were the chief articles of a long list. There were many others ; such as incest, worship of the devil under various forms, etc.

It is certainly strange that if the Templars were so horribly depraved no whisper of their enormities should hitherto have gone abroad. It is strange that, as the secrets of the order were necessarily known to all its members, they should have ventured to expel misdemeanants who could so easily betray them. If they killed everyone that they suspected of letting out their mysteries, it is strange that they should have allowed the knights to confess to secular priests outside the

order, as it is certain that in the absence of their own
chaplains they habitually did.

The King took down the depositions, and, without
going into the particulars of them, wrote privately to
the Pope. On August 24, 1305—the dates are important—the Pope replied that it was a singular story.
The King's letter was so positive, however, and the persons who had brought the letter to him were so positive,
also, that he supposed the charges must be true. It
seemed, however, that some rumor of the matter had by
this time reached the Templars themselves. The Pope
added that the Grand Master and the preceptors had
also written to him, alluding to the accusations, and
begging him to examine into them. This he would do,
and would inform the King of the result.

The inquiry so conducted would have been fair
enough, but for some reason it did not suit Philip's purpose. He sent the Pope the depositions themselves.
The Pope made no further move. The whole matter
was allowed to drop for a year ; and the next thing which
we find is a confidential and affectionate letter from
the Pope to the Grand Master, who was in Cyprus, written in the following summer. Not a word was said by
him about the accusations. The Pope seemed to have
forgotten them. He merely told the Grand Master
that he wished to consult him about various subjects of
great consequence—the condition of the East, the prospects of the Crusades, and the general state of Christendom. He therefore begged De Molay to come to
him in France as soon as he could, and to bring with
him such of the knights as he had most dependence on.

De Molay clearly had no suspicion. He was under
the impression that the headquarters of the Templars
were to be transferred from Cyprus to France. They

had a grand palace in Paris. The site of it still bears the old name, and the palace itself was the prison of the royal family in the Revolution. Thither came De Molay, bringing with him the chest, or chests of the order —twelve mules' load of gold and silver. The King received him with the proper courtesies. There was no sign of displeasure. The treasure was put away in the Templars' vaults. The Pope was at Poitiers. De Molay and the preceptors went to him, and had a long friendly conversation with him. The projected union of the military orders was certainly the subject of part of it, and De Molay was less cordial on the subject than perhaps Clement wished. This was at the end of 1306, nearly two years after the two knights had told their story. All was outwardly smooth. The winter went by. In the spring there were once more rumors in the air which made De Molay uneasy. In April, 1307, he went again to the Pope, taking the four French preceptors with him, and spoke very earnestly about it. The Pope listened with apparent satisfaction, and dismissed them as if perfectly assured that the accusations were baseless.

Again one asks, Was all this treachery?—was it a plan agreed upon between the Pope and the King to put the Templars off their guard, to seize the treasure, and get into their power the persons of the Grand Master and the leading knights? That certainly was the effect. Such a plot, supposing it real, might be defended if the charges against the Templars were true. They were a formidable body. Had they been alarmed, and had their chief been at large, they could perhaps have set the King at defiance. At least they could not have been suppressed without desperate bloodshed. But all turns on the truth of the charges, or on the King's sincere belief in them.

Even kings and popes are seldom deliberately and consciously wicked. But, like other men, they have a power of convincing themselves of what they wish to believe. The Pope was afraid of Philip, and wished to please him. The Templars had really become an anomaly. They were a danger to the State. Philip might legitimately wish to bring the order to an end. From a wish to end them to a conviction of their crimes the step would be short in a politic ruler's mind. Politics are a corrupting trade.

Anyway, the Templars were lulled into absolute security. They were spread all over France in their various houses. At the beginning of October this same year, 1307, the King sent a secret instruction round the provinces for their universal and simultaneous arrest. Not a whisper was allowed to reach them. They had lived in friendless and haughty isolation. They had relied on the Pope, and the Pope had failed them. The only support which never fails—some legitimate place among the useful agencies of the time—this was wanting.

III.

At the break of day on October 13, 1307, the Templars were surprised in their beds, carried off to the provincial prisons of the different bishops, and flung into dungeons. More willing jailers they could not have had. They had long defied the bishops, and the bishops' turn was come. They took on themselves the responsibility of the King's action. Such prelates as were in Paris, with the heads of the University and the abbots and priors of the religious houses, assembled two days after in the Templars' Hall. They drew up an Act of Accusation, in which the knights were described as ravening wolves, idolaters, perjurers, and guilty of the vilest crimes. They asserted, to meet the inevitable incredulity, that the Grand Master and the preceptors had confessed their guilt. The Templars belonged to Europe, not to France alone. Philip sent circulars to Edward the Second of England, to Germany, to the Kings of Aragon, Portugal, and Castile, telling his story, and inviting them to follow his example. His letter was read in England with astonishment. A great council was called at Westminster. Edward with his peers and prelates replied that the charges were incredible. The Templars were men of unstained honor. The Pope must examine into the matter. He would take no action till the Pope had decided. He sent his own protest to his brother princes.

The Pope—the poor, infallible Pope—was in straits; he had not been consulted before the arrest; he could not refuse an inquiry; yet, perhaps, he knew too well how an honest inquiry would terminate. The King and the bishops had begun the work, and they had no choice but to go through with it. Before the Pope could proceed the bishops might prepare their case. It was winter. The Templars had been flung into cold, damp dungeons, ill-fed and ill-clothed. In the first month they had begun to die of mere hardship. They were informed of the charges against them; they were told that denial was useless, that the Grand Master and preceptors had confessed, and wished them all to confess. They were promised rewards and liberty if they obeyed; imprisonment and torture if they were obstinate. After some weeks of this, to bring them into a proper frame of mind, the bishops issued commissions to examine them.

And I must now beg you to attend. What I am about to tell you is strict fact ; as well authenticated as any historical facts can be. Belief, or the credulity of noble-ness, had created the Templars. Belief, the ugly side of it, the credulity of hatred, was now to destroy them. Universal confession would alone satisfy the world's suspi-cions, and confession the King and his prelates were re-solved to have. Wasted with hunger and cold, the knights were brought one by one before the bishops' judges. The depositions of the two approvers were formed into interrogatories. Did the knights, on their admission to the order, spit on the cross? Did they deny Christ? Did they receive a dispensation to commit unnatural of-fences ? Did they worship idols ? A paper was read to them professing to be the Grand Master's confession ; and to these questions they were required to answer yes or no. A few said yes, and were rewarded and dismissed. By far the greater number said that the charges were lies ; they said they did not believe that the Grand Master had confessed ; if he had, he had lied in his throat. And now what happened to the men who an-swered thus? They were stripped naked, their hands were tied behind their backs ; a rope was fastened to their wrists, the other end of which was slung over a beam, and they were dragged up and down till they were senseless, or till they acknowledged what the bish-ops wanted. If this failed, their feet were fixed in a frame like the old English stocks, rubbed with oil, and held to the fire till the toes, or even the feet themselves, dropped off. Or the iron boot was used, or the thumb-screws, or another unnamable and indescribably painful devilry. Thirty-six of them died under these tortures in Paris alone. The rest so treated said anything which the bishops required. They protested afterward that their confessions, as they were called, had been wrung out of them by pain only. They were returned to their dungeons, to be examined again when the Pope pleased. But having confessed to heresy, they were told that, if they withdrew their confessions afterward, they would be treated as relapsed heretics, and would be burnt at the stake. Such was then the Church's law ; and it was no idle threat.

I am not telling you a romance. These scenes did actually occur all over France ; and it was by this means that the evidence was got together under which the Templars were condemned. But we are only at the first stage of the story.

The confessions were published to the world, and the world, not knowing how they had been obtained, supposed that they must be true. The Pope knew better ; he remonstrated ; he said that the Templars were not subject to the bishops, who were going beyond their power. The King accused him of trying to shield the Templars' guilt ; the bishops, he said, were doing nothing but their duty, and the Faculty of Theology at Paris declared that no privilege could shelter heresy. The conduct of the Grand Master and the four preceptors is a mystery. They were evidently bewildered, disheartened, shocked, and terrified, and confessions alleged to have been made by them were certainly taken down and published. It appears, also, that in January, 1308, three months after the arrest, they were brought before the Pope, and they were alleged to have confessed again on this occasion, and to have received absolution from him. But the Pope did not confirm this allegation, and was still incredulous. The other Powers of Christendom insisted on a fuller inquiry. The formal sanction of the Papacy was required before the order could be suppressed, and even Clement, pliable as he was, could not proceed on the evidence before him. In the summer, six months later, seventy-two Templars—seventy-two only of the thousands still surviving in France—were found willing to appear before him and give the required answers to the interrogatories. These seventy-two did say that they had abjured Christ, had spit on the cross, had worshipped idols, and the rest of it. They were asked why they had at first denied these things. They said that they had forgotten, but had since remembered. Seventy-two, after all that bribes and tortures and threats could do, were not enough. The Pope was answerable to Christendom. The French bishops themselves were on their trial before the rest of the world ; the sentence could not rest on their word alone. The Pope found himself obliged to appoint an independent commission, when the knights could be heard in their own defence with an appearance of freedom. A cardinal or two, an archbishop, and two or three papal lawyers, were formed into a court which was to sit in Paris. All precautions were alleged to be taken that the Templars should have a fair hearing if they wished it, without fear or prejudice. Every prisoner who would say that he was ready to defend the order was to be brought to Paris to be heard. Notice of the appointment of the commission was sent round to all the courts of Europe.

If Philip, if the bishops, really believed in the Templars' guilt they ought to have welcomed the Pope's action. They had been cruel, but if they could prove their case their rough handling would not be judged severely. They were in no haste, however. The commission was appointed in August, 1308. It did not sit for another year. The Templars were now dying by hundreds. Their death-bed declarations were all protests of innocence. The survivors demanded in vain that these declarations should be made public. When they learned that they were to be heard before representatives of the Pope their hopes revived, and more than a thousand at once gave their names as ready to appear in the defence.

In August, 1309, the court was opened. It sat in the Convent of St. Geneviève. Citations were issued, but no one appeared. The Templars had been brought up to Paris, but they had been told on the way that if they retracted their confessions the Pope intended to burn them as relapsed; and, after the treatment which they had met with, anything seemed possible. They claimed to be heard by counsel. This was refused. The court adjourned till November 22, when some twenty of the knights were brought in and were asked if they were ready with a defence. They said that they were illiterate soldiers; they knew nothing of law pleading. If they might have their liberty with arms and horses they would meet their accusers in the field. That was all that they could do.

It was necessary to begin with the Grand Master. On November 26, De Molay himself was introduced into the court. He was an old man, battered by a life of fighting, and worn by hard treatment in prison. Being asked what he had to say, he complained of the refusal of counsel. He claimed for himself and the order to be heard before a mixed court of lay peers and prelates. To such a judgment he said that they were willing to submit. They protested against a tribunal composed only of churchmen.

Unfortunately for themselves the Templars were a

religious order, and the Church alone could try them. The commission under which the court was constituted was read over. It was there stated that the Grand Master had made a full confession of the order's guilt ; and from his behavior it might have been thought that he was hearing of this extraordinary assertion for the first time. We have the account of the proceedings exactly as they were taken down by the secretary. He crossed himself thrice. "Videbatur se esse valde stupefactum." He seemed entirely stupefied. When he found his voice he said that if the commissioners had not been priests he would have known how to answer them. They were not there, they replied, to accept challenges. He said he was aware of that, but he wished to God that there was the same justice in France as there was among the Turks and Saracens, where a false witness was cut to pieces. No confession was produced to which he had attached his hand, and of other evidence there was none. The King's chancellor read a passage from a chronicle to the effect that Saladin, a hundred and twenty years before, had called the Templars a set of villains. Again De Molay appeared stupefied—as well he might. He claimed privilege, and demanded to be heard by the Pope in person.

The Preceptor of Payens then appeared. He admitted that he had confessed with many of his brethren, but he protested that their confessions were false. They had been handed over to a set of men, some of whom had been expelled from the order for infamous crimes. They had been tortured, and many of them had died on the rack. He for himself had had his hands crushed till the blood ran from his nails. He had been flung into a well and left lying there ; he had been for two years in a dungeon. He could have borne

17

to be killed—to be roasted, to be boiled—anything which would be over in a moderate time, but such prolonged agonies were beyond human strength. If he was treated so again he would deny all that he was then saying, and renew his confession. He was remitted to custody, and the commissioners cautioned the jailer not to deal hardly with him for what he had said. The caution was necessary. Many of the knights were still afraid to speak, or would say nothing except that they had been tortured, and would speak if they were set free. As long as they were kept prisoners they dared not. The commissioners, to encourage them, sent out a warning to the bishops, and again assured the knights of protection. The court, they said, wanted nothing but the truth. The knights might tell it freely; no harm should happen to them.

This gave them courage. Six hundred of them now came forward, one after the other, and told the secrets of their prisons, with the infernal cruelties which they had suffered there. A list was produced of those who had died. One very curious letter was read which had been written by a high official and sent to a party of Templars at Sens. It was to the effect that the Bishop of Orleans was coming to reconcile them. They were advised to make submission, and in that case were promised all kindness; but they were to understand that the Pope had distinctly ordered that those who retracted their confessions should be burnt. The official in question was called in. He said that he did not think that he could have written such a letter; the seal was his, but it might have been written by his clerk.

One prisoner was carried into the court unable to stand. His feet had been held to the fire until they had been destroyed.

The evidence was still utterly inconsistent. Priests came forward, who said they had habitually heard Templars' confessions, yet had heard nothing of the alleged enormities. Others, on the other hand, adhered to the story, telling many curious details—how Templars had told them that they had been required to spit on the cross, how they had been frightened and refused, but had at last consented—" non corde sed ore "—not with their hearts, but with their lips. But the great majority were still resolute in their denials. At last the whole six hundred made a common affirmation that every one of these Articles named in the Pope's bull was a lie— the religion of the Templars was pure and immaculate, and so had always been, and whoever said to the contrary was an infidel and a heretic. This they were ready to maintain in all lawful ways, but they prayed to be released and be heard, if not before a mixed tribunal, then before a general council. Those who had confessed had lied ; but they had lied under torture themselves, or terrified by the tortures which they witnessed. Some might have been bribed, which they said was public and notorious ; the wonder was that any should have dared to tell the truth. As a refinement of cruelty, the bishops had refused the sacraments to the dying.

The commissioners were now at a loss. Individuals might be worked upon by fear and hope to repeat their confessions, but the great body of the order were consistent in their protest. The commissioners said that they could not hear them all. They had asked for counsel ; let them appoint proctors who could speak for them. This seemed fair ; but the unfortunate men were afraid of trusting themselves to proctors. Proctors being few, might be tempted or frightened into betraying them. They still trusted the Pope. They had been invited to speak, and they had been promised protection. The members of the court had some kind of conscience, and it began to seem likely that the case might not end as the King and the bishops required. They could not afford to let it go forth to the world that the Templars were innocent after all and had been brutally and barbarously treated without sufficient cause ; public opinion did not go for much in those days, but they were at the bar of all Europe.

We need not assume that they themselves did not believe in the Templars' guilt ; men have a wonderful power of making themselves believe what they wish to believe. If the Templars had been formidable before the attack on them was begun, they would be doubly formidable if they came out of their trial clean as their own white robes ; it was necessary to stop these pleas of innocence, and the French prelates were equal to the occasion.

While the Pope's commissioners were sitting at St. Geneviève the Archbishop of Sens opened a provincial court of his own in another part of Paris. The list of knights was brought before him who had given their names as intending to retract their confessions. On May 10, 1310, four of the Templars demanded audience of the Papal judges. They said that the knights had been invited by the Pope to defend the order ; they had been told to speak the truth without fear, and had been promised that no harm should happen to them. They now learned that in consequence of what they had said on the very next day a great number were to be put on their trial before the Archbishop of Sens as relapsed heretics. They said truly, that if this was permitted, it would make the inquiry a farce—it would stain irreparably the honor of the Holy See. They entreated the commissioners to interpose and prevent the Archbishop from proceeding.

The commissioners professed to be sorry—they could hardly do less; but they said that the Archbishop was not under their jurisdiction. They themselves represented the Holy See; the bishops had an independent authority; they had no power over the bishops nor the bishops over them. They did promise, however, to think the matter over and see if anything could be done.

The Archbishop did not allow them time for much thinking; he was a sturdy prelate and had the courage of his office. Two days after, on the morning of the 12th, just as the commissioners were going to chapel (they were particular about all these things it seems), word was brought them that fifty-four of the knights who had applied to be heard before them had been tried and sentenced and were to be burned at the stake that very afternoon. This time the commissioners were really disturbed. They were not prepared for such prompt action—their own dignity, the Holy Father's dignity, was compromised. They sent in haste to the Archbishop, to beg him at least to postpone the execution; every Templar who had died hitherto had declared the order innocent, and these would do the same. If witnesses were invited to speak, and were then burned for speaking, they would have to close their court. Already the very report of the Archbishop's intentions had so terrified the knights that some of them had gone out of their minds.

The Archbishop was made of tougher stuff—Fouquier Tinville and the Revolutionary tribunal were not more resolute. To terrify the knights into silence was precisely what he intended. Accordingly that same afternoon, as he had ordered, those fifty-four "poor brothers in Christ," whose real fault had been that they were too faithful to the Father of Christendom, were carried out to the Place St. Antoine, near where the Bastile stood, and were there roasted to death. They bore their fate like men. Every one of them, torn and racked as they had been, declared with his last breath that, so far as he knew, the accusations against the order were ground-less and wilful slanders. Half a dozen more were burned a day or two after to deepen the effect. The Archbishop clearly was not afraid of man or devil. Some say a sensitive conscience is a sign of a weak character. No one can accuse the Archbishop of Sens of having a weak character; he knew what he was doing and what would come of it.

I will read you a declaration made the next day before the Pope's commissioners by Sir Amaric de Villiers, one of the prisoners. He said that he was fifty years old and had been a brother of the order for twenty. The clerk of the court read over the list of crimes with which the order was charged. He turned pale; he struck his breast; he raised his hand to the altar; he dropped on his knees. On peril of his soul, he said, on peril of all the punishments denounced on perjury, praying that if he was not speaking truth the ground might open and he might go down quick into hell, those charges were all false. He allowed that he had confessed on the rack. He had been taken to St. Antoine the evening before. He had seen his fifty-four brethren brought in carts and thrown into the flames. He had been in such fear that he doubted if he himself could endure to be so handled. With such an end before him, he might say if he was brought again before the bishops, and they required it of him, that he had not only denied his Lord, but had murdered him. He implored the judges to keep to themselves what he was then saying. If the Archbishop got hold of it, he would be burned like the rest.

The terror had cut deep. The Pope's commissioners had neither the courage to adopt the Archbishop's methods nor to repudiate and disown them. They sent to him to say that they must suspend their sittings. He answered scornfully that they might do as they pleased. He and his suffragans had met to finish the process against the Templars, and they intended to do it. A few more victims were sacrificed. The rest of the knights, who had offered to speak before the commissioners, were naturally silent. The commissioners could not help them. They withdrew their defence, and the commission was adjourned till the following November.

The tragic story was now winding up. When November came the court sat again, reduced in number and reduced to a form. The duty of it thenceforward was simply to hear such of the order as had been broken into submission, and were willing to repeat the story which had been thrust into their mouths, with such details as imagination or reality could add to it. I do not suppose that the accusations were absolutely without foundation. Very often the witnesses seemed to be relating things which they really remembered. The Templars were a secret society, and secret societies have often forms of initiation which once had a meaning, with an affectation of solemnity and mysticism. I am not a Freemason. Many of you no doubt are. I have heard that the ceremonies of that order, though perfectly innocent, are of a kind which malice or ignorance might misinterpret, if there was an object in bringing the Freemasons into disrepute. You know best if that is so. Somewhere abroad I was myself once admitted into a mysterious brotherhood. I was sworn to secrecy, and therefore I can tell you little about it. I was led through a narrow passage into a vast darkened hall, where some hundred dim, half-seen figures were sitting in silence. I was taken to a table in the middle with a single candle on it. There—but my revelations must end. I could have believed myself before the famous Vehm Gericht. The practices alleged against the Templars as crimes were in fact most of them innocent. They were accused of worshipping a skull; some said it had jewels in its eyes, some that it had none. An accidental question brought out that it was a relic of an Eastern saint, such as any Catholic might treat with reverence. The officers of the order were accused of hearing confessions and giving priestly absolution, and this was a deadly offence. By the rules of the order the lay superiors were directed to hear confessions and inflict penance, but were forbidden to absolve. Confusion might easily have arisen.

The Novices were said to receive licenses to commit an abominable sin, yet there was scarcely a single knight who could be brought to say that he had even heard of such a sin being committed.

The spitting on the cross and the denial of Christ are less easy to explain. Thousands of the knights absolutely denied that such outrages were ever seen or heard of, yet a great many did with considerable consistency describe a singular ceremony of that kind. It has been supposed that the Templars by their long residence in Syria had ceased to be Christians, and had adopted Eastern heresies, that they were Gnostics, Manichees, or I know not what. This is a guess, and I do not think a likely one. They were mere soldiers. They were never a learned order. They left no books behind them, or writings of any kind. The services in the Templars' churches were conducted with peculiar propriety. Every witness declared that the very crosses which they said had been spit upon were treated afterward with the deepest reverence. Nor was there really any attempt at concealment. Those who had been frightened at the forms of initiation were told to go and confess to secular priests in the neighborhood. Several instances of such confessions were produced. The confessors sometimes had treated what they heard as of no consequence. They had satisfied their penitents' consciences, not always in the same way. One said that the spitting on the cross was meant as a trial of constancy. The Saracens if they were taken prisoners would require them to deny Christ or be killed. The officers of the order wanted to see how they would abide the test. Another said it was a trial of obedience. The Novice swore to obey his superiors in all things without exception. The spitting on the cross may have been the severest trial which could be imagined. In no instance at all was it ever suggested that the forms of initiation pointed to any real impiety.

So strange a tale is not likely to have rested upon nothing. I suppose the custom may have varied in different houses. Men are men, and may not have been uniformly wise. But the more one reads the evidence the plainer it becomes that the confessions, and even the terms of them, were arranged beforehand. The witnesses produced after the commission met again told one tale. If they ever varied from it they were brought swiftly back into harmony. Sir John de Pollencourt gave the stereotyped answer. He had spat on the cross. He had done this and that; but we read in the Record : " The commissioners, seeing him pale and terrified, bade him for his soul's welfare speak the truth whatever it might be. He need not fear. They would tell no one what he might say. He hesitated; then, on his oath, he declared that he had spoken falsely. He had not denied Christ. He had not spat on the cross. He had not received license to sin. He had confessed before the bishops in fear of death; and because his fellow-prisoners said that they would be killed unless they admitted what the bishops required."

The commissioners were not as secret as they promised to be. Sir John de Pollencourt was made to know behind the scenes what would happen to him if he was not submissive. Accordingly, four days after, the same witness was brought in again, withdrew his denial and again confessed. It is easy to see what had happened in the interval.

So handled, the rest of the process went on smoothly. Parties of knights who had escaped the torture-chambers of the bishops and thus had not been forced into confession continued to speak out. On one occasion twenty or thirty appeared in a body, and pointed to the red crosses broidered on their clothes. That cross, they said, signified that they would shed their blood for their Redeemer. If, as they were told, their Grand Master had confessed that they had denied Christ, or if any of their brethren had confessed it, they had lied in their throats, to the peril of their own souls. But the mass of the knights had by this time abandoned their cause as hopeless. By the end of nine months a sufficient number of so-called confessions had been repeated before the commissioners to satisfy the Pope's scruples. The commissioners were themselves only too eager to wind up the scandalous inquiry. Not so much as an effort had been made to discover the real truth. The result was a foregone conclusion, and every utterance which could interfere with it had been stifled by cord or fire. The report was sent to Clement. A council of bishops was called together. It was laid before them and accepted as conclusive. The order of the Templars was pronounced to have disgraced itself and was suppressed. The sinning knights were scattered about the world—some went back to the world—some became Benedictines or Cistercians. Some gave their swords and services to secular princes, having had enough of the Church. Some disappeared into their families. Their estates the Pope had insisted must be reserved to the Church; and were nominally given to the Knights Hospitalers. But the King extorted such an enormous fine from them that the Hospitalers gained little by their rivals' overthrow.

The Grand Master's end remains to be told. The confessions which he and three of the head preceptors were alleged to have made are extant, and resemble the rest, but we have seen how he behaved when the confession attributed to himself was read over to him before the commissioners. He had appealed to the Pope, but without effect, and had been left with the three preceptors in prison. When the edict for the suppression was issued, and the other knights were dismissed, De Molay and his companions were sentenced to perpetual confinement. But the world was after all less satisfied of the Templars' guilt than Philip could have wished, and in some way or other it was necessary to convince the public that the Grand Master's confession was genuine.

The bull of suppression was to be read aloud to the people of Paris. It was brought up with special solemnity by a bishop and a cardinal, and De Molay and the others were to be publicly shown upon a stage on the occasion. On March 18, 1314, a platform had been erected in one of the squares, with chairs of state for the cardinal, the Archbishop of Sens, and other distinguished persons. The Grand Master and his comrades were produced and were placed where the world could see them. The cardinal rose to read the sentence. When he came to the list of enormities of which, as the bull alleged, the Templars had been found guilty, and when the Grand Master heard it stated that he had himself admitted the charges to be true, he rose up, and in a loud voice which everyone could hear, he cried out that it was false.

Philip himself was not present, but he was in Paris and not far off. Word was brought him of the Grand Master's contumacy. Not troubling himself with forms of law he ordered that the Grand Master should be instantly burned, and his provincials along with him, unless they saved themselves by submission. Two of them, Sir Hugh von Peyraud and Geoffrey de Gonville, gave in and were sent back to their dungeons. De Molay and the third were carried directly to the island in the Seine, and were burned the same evening in the light of the setting sun.

In his end, like Samson, De Molay pulled down the fabric of the prosecution. There was thenceforward a universal conviction that the Templars had been unjustly dealt with. The popular feeling shaped itself into a tradition (possibly it was a real fact), that as the flames were choking him, the last Grand Master summoned the Pope and the King to meet him before the tribunal of God. Clement died in agony a few weeks after. A little later Philip the Beautiful was flung by a vicious horse, and he too went to his account.

A very few words will tell now how the Templars

fared in the rest of Europe. There was no real belief in their guilt; but their estates had been given to them for a purpose which no longer existed. They were rich, and they had nothing to do. They were an anachronism and a danger. When the Pope agreed to their suppression, there was no motive to resist the Pope's decision ; and they did not attempt to resist it themselves. Nothing is more remarkable in the whole story than the almost universal acquiescence of an armed and disciplined body of men in the Pope's judgment. They had been trained to obedience. The Pope had been their sovereign. The Pope wished that they should cease to exist ; and they fell to pieces without a word, unless it were to protest their innocence of the crimes of which they were accused.

In England Philip's charges had at first been received with resentful incredulity, but neither King, nor peers, nor Church had any motive to maintain the Templars after the Pope had spoken. For form's sake there was an investigation on the lines of the French interrogatories, but there was no torture or cruelty. They knew that they were to go, and that they would be dealt with generously. The process was a curious one. As a body the English Templars stated that the forms of admission to the order were, as far as they knew, uniform. What was done in one house was done in all. If any of the brethren liked to depose to this or that ceremony being observed they would not contradict them, and thus the difficulty was got over. A certain number of knights were ready to give the necessary evidence. Some hundreds of outside persons, chiefly monks or secular priests, deposed to popular rumors, conversations, and such like, names not given ; a certain person heard another person say this and that. What was got at in this way was often not dreadful. A preceptor in Lincolnshire had been heard to maintain that "men died as animals died ; " therefore, it might be inferred that he did not believe in immortality. Templars sometimes had crosses worked into their drawers ; therefore they were in the habit of sitting upon the cross. The English evidence threw light often on the manners of the age, but I cannot go into that. I have tried your patience too long already. I will, therefore, sum up briefly.

When all is said the story is a strange one, and I cannot pretend to leave it clear of doubt. But no lawyer, no sensible man, can accept as conclusive evidence mere answers to interrogatories extorted by torture and the threat of death. A single denial made under such circumstances is worth a thousand assents dragged out by rack and gibbet. If the order had really been as guilty as was pretended, some of the knights at least would have confessed on their deathbeds. Not one such confession was ever produced, while the dying protestations of innocence were all suppressed. The King and the Inquisitors force us into incredulity by their own unscrupulous ferocity. It is likely enough that, like other orders, the Templars had ceremonies, perhaps not very wise, intended to impress the imagination, but that those ceremonies were intentionally un-Christian or diabolical, I conceive to be entirely unproved. They fell partly because they were rich, partly for political reasons, which, for all I know, may have been good and sound ; but the act of accusation I regard as a libel invented to justify the arbitrary destruction of a body which, if not loved, was at least admired for its services to Christendom.

It remains only to emphasize the moral that institutions can only be kept alive while they answer the end for which they were created. Nature will not tolerate them longer, and in one way or another shakes them down. The Templars had come into existence to fight the infidels in Palestine. Palestine was abandoned to the infidels, and the Templars were needed no longer. They were outwardly strong as ever, brave, organized, and in character unblemished, but the purpose of them being gone, they were swept away by a hurricane. So it is with all human organizations. They grow out of man's necessities, and are mortal as men are. Empires, monarchies, aristocracies, guilds, orders, societies, religious creeds, rise in the same way, and in the same way disappear when they stand in the way of other things.

But mankind are mean creatures. When they destroy these creations of theirs they paint them in the blackest colors to excuse their own violence. The black colors in which Philip the Beautiful and his bishops were pleased to paint the Templars will, perhaps, if history cares to trouble itself about the matter, be found to attach rather to the extraordinary men calling themselves successors of the Apostles who racked and roasted them.

You in Scotland found no great reason to love bishops, and the history of the Templars does not increase our affection for them.

THE NORWAY FJORDS

On June 30, 1881, we sailed from Southampton Water
in the steam yacht Severn to spend ten weeks in the
Norway Fjords—Fjords or Friths, for the word is the
same. The Scandinavian children of the sea carried
their favorite names with them. Frith is Fjord;
our Cumberland Scale *Force* would be called Scale
Foss between the North Cape and the Baltic. The
yacht was spacious; over three hundred tons. Cabins,
equipments, engines, captain, steward, crew the best of
their kind. Our party was small; only four in all.
My friend, whose guest I was, and whom I shall call
D——, two ladies, and myself. D—— had furnished
himself with such knowledge as was attainable in London for the scenes which we were to explore. He had
studied Norse. He could speak it : he could understand
and be understood. He was a sportsman, but a sportsman only as subsidiary to more rational occupations.
He was going to Norway to catch salmonidæ ; not, however, to catch them only, but to study the varieties of
that most complicated order of fish. He was going also
to geologize and to botanize, to examine rocks and
river and glaciers and flowers ; while all of us were
meaning to acquaint ourselves as far as we could with
the human specimens still to be found in the crater of
the old volcano from which those shiploads of murdering "Danes" poured out ten centuries ago to change
the face of Europe.

And to see Norway, the real Norway, within moderate compass of time is possible only with such means as a steam yacht provides. There are great lines of road in Norway along the practicable routes, but very few *are* practicable ; nine-tenths of the country, and the most interesting parts, are so walled off by mountains, are so intrenched among the fjords, as to be forever unapproachable by land, while the water highways lead everywhere—magnificent canals, fashioned by the elemental forces, who can say how or when ?

From the west coast there run inland with a general easterly direction ten or twelve main channels of sea, penetrating from fifty to a hundred miles into the very heart of the Northern Peninsula. They are of vast depth, and from half a mile to two miles broad. The mountains rise on both sides sheer from the water's edge ; the lower ranges densely timbered with pine and birch and alder. Above these belts of forest soar ranges of lofty peaks, five or six thousand feet up, the snow lying thick upon them in the midst of summer, glaciers oozing down the gorges, like cataracts arrested in their fall by the Frost Enchanter, motionless, yet with the form of motion. From the snow, from the ice when the glaciers reach a warmer level, melt streams which swell at noon, as the sun grows hot, descend in neverending waterfalls, cascade upon cascade, through the ravines which they have cut for themselves in millions of years. In the evening they dwindle away, and at night fall silent as the frost resumes its power.

From the great central fjords branches strike out right and left, some mere inlets ending after a few miles, some channels which connect one fjord with another. The surface of Norway, as it is shown flat upon a chart, is lined and intersected by these water-

18

ways as the surface of England is by railways. The
scenery, though forever changing, changes like the pattern of a kaleidoscope, the same materials readjusted in
varying combinations; the same great rivers of sea-
water, the same mountain walls, the same ice and snow
on the summits, the same never-ending pines and
birches, with an emerald carpet between the stems
where in summer the universal whortleberry hides the
stones under the most brilliant green. The short fjords
and the large are identical in general features, save that,
lying at right angles to the prevailing winds, the surface
of these lateral waters is usually undisturbed by a single
ripple; the clouds may be racing over the high ridges,
but down below no breath can reach. Hence the light
is undispersed. The eye, instead of meeting anywhere
with white water, sees only rocks, woods, and cataracts
reversed as in a looking-glass. This extreme stillness
and the optical results of it are the cause, I suppose, of
the gloom of Norwegian landscape-painting.

How these fjords were formed is, I believe, as yet un-
determined. Water has furrowed the surface of the
globe into many a singular shape; water, we are told,
cut out the long gorge below Niagara; but water, acting
as we now know it, scarcely scooped out of the hardest
known rock these multitudinous fissures, so uniform in
character, between walls which pierce the higher strata
of the clouds, between cliffs which in some places
rise, as in the Geiranger, perpendicular for a thousand
feet; the fjords themselves of such extraordinary depth,
and deepest always when furthest from the sea. Where
they enter the Atlantic, there is bottom generally in a
hundred fathoms. In the Sogne, a hundred miles inland, you find 700 fathoms. Rivers cutting their way
though rock and soil could never have achieved such

work as this. Ice is a mighty thaumaturgist, and ice
has been busy enough in Norway. The fjords were once
filled with ice up to a certain level; the level to which
it rose can be traced on the sharp angles ground off the
rounded stone, and the scores of the glacier plane on
the polished slabs of gneiss or granite. But at some
hundreds of feet above the present water-line the ice
action ends, and cliffs and crags are scarred and angular
and weather-splintered to where they are lost in the eternal snow. The vast moraines which occasionally block
the valleys tell the same story. The largest that I saw
was between four and five hundred feet high, and we
have to account for chasms which, if we add the depth
of the water to the height of the mountains above it, are
9,000 feet from the bottom to the mountain crest.

The appearance of Norway is precisely what it would
have been if the surface had cracked when cooling into a
thousand fissures, longitudinal and diagonal, if these
fissures had at one time been filled with sea-water, at
another with ice, and the sides above the point to which
the ice could rise had been chipped and torn and weather-
worn by rain and frost through endless ages. Whether
this is, in fact, the explanation of their form, philosophers
will in good time assure themselves ; meantime, this is
what they are outwardly like, which, for present purposes
is all that need be required.

A country so organized can be traversed in no way so
conveniently as by a steam yacht, which carries the four-
and-twenty winds in its boiler. It is not the romance
of yachting ; and the steamer, beside the graceful
schooner with its snowy canvas, seems prosaic and mechanical. The schooner does well in the open water with
free air and sea room ; but let no schooner venture into
the Norway fjords, where slant winds come not by which

you can make a course by a long reach, where there is either a glassy calm or a wind blowing up or down. If you reached the end of the Sogne you might spend a season in beating back to the sea, and, except in some few spots, where you might not be able to go, you cannot so much as anchor on account of the depth of water. Shut in among these mountains, you may drift becalmed in a sailing yacht for weeks together, while to a steamer the course is as easy and sure as to a carriage on a turnpike road. Your yacht is your house; like a wishing carpet, it transports you wherever you please to go, and is here and there and anywhere. You note your position on the chart; you scan it with the sense that the world of Norway is all before you to go where you like; you choose your next anchoring-place; you point it out to the pilot; you know your speed—there is no night in the summer months—you dine; you smoke your evening cigar; you go to your berth; you find yourself at breakfast in your new surroundings.

So then, on that June evening, we steamed out of the Solent. Our speed in smooth water was ten knots; our distance from Udsire Light, for which our course was laid, was 700 miles. It was calm and cloudless, but unusually cold. When night brought the stars we saw the comet high above us, the tail of him pointing straight away from the sun, as if the head was a lens through which the sun's rays lighted the atoms of ether behind it. Sleep, which had grown fitful in the London season, came back to us at once in our berths unscared by the grinding of the screw. We woke fresh and elastic when the decks were washed. The floors of the cabins lifted on hinges, and below were baths into which the sea-water poured till we could float in it. When we came up and looked about us we were running past the North

Foreland. With the wind aft and the water smooth we sped on. I lay all the morning on a sofa in the deck cabin, and smoked and read Xenophon's "Memorabilia." So one day passed, and then another. On the evening of July 2 we passed through a fleet of English trawlers, a few units of the ten thousand feeders of the London stomach, the four million human beings within the bills of mortality whom the world combines to nourish. We were doing two hundred miles a day. The calm continued, and the ladies so far had suffered nothing. There was no motion save the never-resting heave of the ocean swell. Homer had observed that long undulation; Ulysses felt it when coming back from Hades to Circe's island. The thing is the same, though the word "ocean" has changed its meaning. To Homer ocean was a river which ran past the grove of Proserpine. It was not till the ship had left the river mouth for the open sea that she lifted on the wave.*

On the third afternoon the weather changed. The cold of the high latitude drove us into our winter clothes. The wind rose from the northwest, bringing thick rain with it, and a heavy beam sea. The yacht rolled 20° each way. Long steamers, without sails to steady them, always do roll, but our speed was not altered. We passed Udsire Light on the 3d, at seven in the evening, and then groped our way slowly, for, though there was no longer any night, we could see little for fog and mist. At last we picked up a pilot, who brought us safely into the roadstead at Bergen, where we were to begin our acquaintance with Norway. Bergen stands fifteen miles inland, with three fjords leading to it, built on a long

---

* Αὐτὰρ ἐπεὶ ποταμοῖο λίπεν ῥόον Ὠκεανοῖο
Νηῦς, ἀπὸ δ' ἵκετο κῦμα θαλάσσης εὐρυπόροιο.
Odyssey, xii. 1, 2.

tongue of rock between two inlets, and overhung with mountains. There is a great trade there, chiefly in salt fish, I believe—any way the forty thousand inhabitants seemed, from the stir on shore and in the harbor, to have plenty to occupy them. We landed and walked round. There are no handsome houses, but no beggars and no signs of poverty. "You have poor here," I said to a coal merchant, who had come on board for orders, and could speak English. "Poor!" he said; "yes, many; not, of course, such poor as you have in England. Everyone has enough to eat." To our sensations it was extremely cold, cold as an English January. But cold and heat are relative terms; and an English January might seem like summer after Arctic winters. The Bergen people took it to be summer, for we found a public garden where a band played; and there were chairs and tables for coffee out of doors. Trees and shrubs were acclimatized. Lilacs, acacias, and horse-chestnuts were in flower. There were roses in bud, and the gardeners were planting out geraniums. We saw the fish-market; everywhere a curious place, for you see there the fish that are caught, the fishermen who catch them, with their boats and gear, the market woman, and the citizens who come to buy. It is all fish in Bergen. The telegrams on the wall in the Bourse tell you only how fish are going in Holland and Denmark. The talk is of fish. On the rocks outside the town stand huge ricks, looking like bean stacks, but they are of dried cod and ling. The streets and squares smell of fish. A steamer bound for Hull lay close to us in the roadstead, which to leeward might have been winded for a mile. Lads stagger about the streets cased between a pair of halibuts, like the Chelsea paupers between two advertisement boards inviting us to vote for Sir Charles Dilke at an election.

Still, excepting the odors, we liked Bergen well. You never hear the mendicant whine there. Those northern people know how to work and take care of themselves, and loafers can find no living among them. I do not know whether there is so much as a beggar in the whole town. They are quiet, simple, industrious folk, who mind their own business. For politics they care little as yet, not supposing that on this road is any kind of salvation for them, though, perhaps, their time will come. They are Lutherans, universally Lutherans. It is the national religion, and they are entirely satisfied with it. Protestant dissent is never heard of. There is a Catholic church in Bergen for the foreign sailors, but I doubt if the priests have converted a single Norwegian. They are a people already moderately well to do in body and mind, and do not need anything which the priests could give them. The intellectual essentials are well looked after, the schools are good and well attended. The Bergen museum is a model on a small scale of what a local museum ought to be, an epitome of Norway itself past and present. Perhaps there is not another in Europe so excellent of its kind. In the gallery of antiquities there is the Norway of the sea kings, Runic tablets and inscriptions, chain armor, swords and clubs and battle-axes, pots of earthenware, stone knives and hammers of a still earlier age. There are the traces of their marauding expeditions, Greek and Italian statuettes, rings, chains, bracelets, and drinking-cups, one or two of these last especially curious, for glass was rare and precious when they were made or mended. The glass of one has been broken, and has been pieced with silver. These obviously were the spoils of some cruise in the Mediterranean, and there is old church plate among them which also tells its story. By the side of

these are the implements of the Norsemen's other trade—
fishing : specimens of nets, lines, hooks, spears and har-
poons, for whale and walrus, and crossbows, the barbed
arrow having a line attached to it for shooting seals. In
the galleries above is a very complete collection of the
Scandinavian mammalia—wolves, bears, lynxes, foxes,
whales, seals, and sea-horses, every kind of fish, every
bird, land or water, all perfectly well classified, labelled,
and looked after. Superior persons are in charge of it,
who can hold their own with the leading naturalists of
France or England ; and all this is maintained at modest
cost by the Bergen corporation.

The houses are plain, but clean ; no dirt is visible
anywhere, and there is one sure sign of a desire to make
life graceful. The hardiest flowers only will grow out
of doors, but half the windows in the town are filled
with myrtles, geraniums, or carnations. With the people themselves we had little opportunity of acquaintance ; but one evening, the second after our arrival,
we were on deck after dinner between ten and eleven.
The sunshine was still on the hills. Though chilly to
us, the air was warm to Bergen ; the bay was covered
with boats ; family groups of citizens out enjoying
themselves ; music floating on the water and songs
made sweet by distance. Others were anchored fishing.
D—— rowed me out in the yacht's punt to a point
half a mile distant. We brought up at an oar's length
from some young ladies with a youth in charge of
them. Some question asked as an excuse for conversation was politely answered. One of them spoke excellent English ; she was a lively, clever girl, had been
in Ireland, and was quick with repartee, well bred
and refined. Their manners were faultless, but they
fished as if they had been bred to the trade. They had

oilskin aprons to save their dresses, and they pulled
up their fish and handled their knives and baits like
professionals.

Our first taste of Norway, notwithstanding the perfume of salt ling, was very pleasant ; but we had far to
go—as far as Lofoden if we could manage it—and we
might not loiter. We left Bergen on the 6th with a local pilot. Trondhjem or Drontheim was the next point
where we were to expect letters, and two courses led to
it—either by the open sea outside the shoals and islands,
or inland by the network of fjords, longer but infinitely
the most interesting, with the further merit of water perfectly smooth. We started at six in the morning and
flew on rapidly among tortuous channels, now sweep-
ing through a passage scarcely wider than the yacht's
length, now bursting into an archipelago of islets. The
western coast of Norway is low and level—a barren, undulating country, with the sea flowing freely through the
hollows. Here and there are green patches of meadow
with a few trees, where there would be a bonder's or
yeoman's farm. Prettily painted lighthouses with their
red roofs marked our course for us, and a girl or two
would come out upon the balconies to look at us as we
rushed by within a gun-shot. Eider-ducks flashed out
of the water, the father of the family as usual the first to
fly, and leaving wife and children to take care of themselves. Fishing-boats crossed us at intervals, and now
and then a whale spouted. Other signs of life there were
none. Toward midday we entered the Sogne Fjord ;
we turned eastward toward the great mountain ranges ;
and, as in the fairy tale the rock opens to the Enchanted
Prince, and he finds himself amid gardens and palaces,
so, as we ran on seemingly upon an impenetrable wall,
cliff and crag fell apart, and we entered on what might

be described as an infinite extension of Loch Lomond, save only that the mountains were far grander, the slopes more densely wooded, and that, far up, we were looking on the everlasting snow, or the green glitter of the glaciers.

On either side of us as we steamed on we crossed the mouths of other fjords, lateral branches precisely like the parent trunk, penetrating, as we could see upon our chart, for tens of miles. Norse history grew intelligible as we looked at them. Here were the hiding-places where the vikings, wickelings, hole-and-corner pirates, ran in with their spoils ; and here was the explanation of their roving lives. The few spots where a family can sustain itself on the soil are scattered at intervals of leagues. The woods are silent and desolate ; wild animals of any kind we never saw ; hunting there could have been none. The bears have increased since the farming introduced sheep ; but a thousand years ago, save a few reindeer and a few grouse and ptarmigan, there was nothing which would feed either bear or man. Few warm-blooded creatures, furred or feathered, can endure the winter cold. A population cannot live by fish alone, and thus the Norsemen became rovers by necessity, and when summer came they formed in fleets and went south to seek their sustenance. The pine forests were their arsenal ; their vessels were the best and fastest in the world ; the water was their only road ; they were boatmen and seamen by second nature, and the sea-coasts within reach of a summer outing were their natural prey.

We were bound for Trondhjem, but we intended to stop occasionally on the way and see what deserved to be seen. We were looking for an anchoring-place where there was a likelihood of fishing ; and we had seen an inlet on the chart, turning out of the Sogne, which seemed promising. At the upper end two rivers appeared to run into it out of fresh-water lakes close by, conditions likely to yield salmon. It was our first experiment. A chart is flat. Imagination, unenlightened by experience, had pictured the fjord ending in level meadows, manageable streams winding through them, and, beyond, perhaps some Rydal or Grasmere lying tranquil among its hills. The pilot said that he knew the place, but could give us no description of it. Anticipation generally makes mistakes on such occasions, but never were fact and fancy more startlingly at variance. Lord Salisbury advised people to study geography on large maps. Flat charts are more convenient than models of a country in relief, but they are treacherous misleaders. Grand as the Sogne had been, the inlet into which we were now striking was grander still. The forests on the shores were denser, the slopes steeper, the cliffs and peaks soaring up in more stupendous majesty. We ran on thus for eight or ten miles ; then turning round a projecting spur, we found ourselves in a landlocked estuary smooth as a mirror, the mountains on one side of it beautiful in evening sunlight, on the other darkening the water with their green purple shadows ; at the far extremity, which was still five miles from us, a broad white line showed, instead of our " meadow stream," a mighty torrent pouring in a cataract over the face of a precipice into the sea.

At the foot of this fall, not three hundred yards from it (no bottom was to be found at a greater distance) we anchored half an hour later, and looked about us. We were in the heart of a primitive Norwegian valley, buried among mountains so lofty and so unbroken that no road had ever entered, or could enter, it. It was the first of many which we saw afterward of the same type, and one description will serve for all.

We were in a circular basin at the head of the fjord. In front of us was a river as large as the Clyde rushing out of a chasm a thousand feet above us, and plunging down in boiling foam. Above this chasm, and inaccessible, was one of the lakes which we had seen on the chart, and in which we had expected to catch salmon. The mountains round were, as usual, covered with wood. At the foot of the fall, and worked by part of it, was a large saw-mill with its adjoining sheds and buildings. The pines were cut as they were wanted, floated to the mill and made into planks, vessels coming at intervals to take them away. The Norwegians are accused of wasting their forests with these mills. We could see no signs of it. In the first place, the sides of the fjords are so steep that the trees can be got at only in comparatively few places. When they can be got at, there is no excessive destruction; more pines are annually swept away by avalanches than are consumed by all the mills in Norway; and the quantity is so enormous that the amount which men can use is no more likely to exhaust it than the Loch Fyne fishermen are likely to exhaust the herring shoals.

On the other side of the basin where we lay was the domain of the owner of the mill. Though the fjord ended, the great ravine in which it was formed stretched, as we could see, a couple of miles farther, but had been blocked by a moraine. The moraines, being formed of loose soil and stones deposited by ice in the glacial period, are available for cultivation, and are indeed excellent land. There were forty or fifty acres of grass laid up for hay, a few acres of potatoes, a red-roofed sunny farmhouse with large outbuildings, carts and horses moving about, poultry crowing, cattle grazing, a boathouse and platform where a couple of lighters were unloading. Here was the house of a substantial, prosperous farmer. His nearest neighbor must have been twelve miles from him. He, his children, and farm-servants were the sole occupants of the valley. The saw-mill was theirs; the boats were theirs; their own hands supplied everything that was wanted. They were their own carpenters, smiths, masons, and glaziers; they sheared their own sheep, spun and dyed their own wool, wove their own cloth, and cut and sewed their own dresses. It was a true specimen of primitive Norwegian life complete in itself—of peaceful, quiet, self-sufficient, prosperous industry.

The snake that spoiled Paradise had doubtless found its way into Nord Gulen (so our valley was named) as into other places, but a softer, sweeter-looking spot we had none of us ever seen. It was seven in the evening when we anchored; a skiff came off, rowed by a couple of plain stout girls with offers of eggs and milk. Fishing-lines were brought out as soon as the anchor was down. The surface water was fresh, and icy cold as coming out of the near glaciers; but it was salt a few fathoms down, and almost immediately we had a basket of dabs and whiting.

After dinner, at nine o'clock, with the sun still shining, D—— and I went ashore with our trout rods. We climbed the moraine, and a narrow lake lay spread out before us, perfectly still, the sides steep, in many places precipitous, trees growing wherever a root could strike. The lake was three miles long, and seemed to end against the foot of a range of mountains 5,000 feet high, the peaks of which, thickly covered with snow, were flushed with the crimson light of the evening. The surface of the water was spotted with rings where the trout were rising. One of the farmer's boys, who had followed us, offered his boat. It was of native manufacture, and not particularly water-tight, but we stowed ourselves, one in the bow and the other at the stern. The boy had never seen such rods as ours; he looked incredulously at them, and still more at our flies; but he rowed us to the top of the lake, where a river came down out of the snow-mountain, finishing its descent with a leap over a cliff. Here he told us there were trout if we could catch them; and he took us deliberately into the spray of the water-fall, not understanding, till we were nearly wet through, that we had any objection to it. As the evening went on the scene became every minute grander and more glorious. The sunset colors deepened; a crag just over us, 2,000 feet high, stood out clear and sharp against the sky. We stayed for two or three hours, idly throwing our flies and catching a few trout no longer than our hands, thereby confirming our friend's impression of our inefficiency. At midnight we were in the yacht again—midnight, and it was like a night in England at the end of June five minutes after sunset.

This was our first experience of a Norway fjord, and for myself I would have been content to go no further; have studied in detail the exquisite beauty which was round us; have made friends with the owner and his household, and found out what they made of their existence under such conditions. There in epitome I should have been seeing Norway and the Norwegians. It was no Arcadia of piping shepherds. In the summer the young men are away at the mountain farms, high grazing ground underneath the snow-line. The women work with their brothers and husbands, and weave and make the clothes. They dress plainly, but with good taste, with modest embroidery ; a handsome bag hangs at the waist of the housewife. There is reading, too, and scholarship. A boy met us on a pathway, and spoke to us in English. We asked him when he had been in England. He had never been beyond his own valley ; in the long winter evenings he had taught himself with an English grammar. No wonder with such ready adaptabilities the Norwegians make the best of emigrants. The overflow of population which once directed itself in such rude fashion on Normandy and England now finds its way to the United States, and no incomers are more welcome there.

But a yacht is for movement and change. We were to start again at noon the next day. The morning was hot and bright. While the engineer was getting up steam, we rowed to the foot of the great fall. I had my small trout rod with me, and trolled a salmon fly on the chance. There were no salmon there, but we saw brown trout rising ; so I tried the universal favorites— a March brown and a red spinner—and in a moment had a fish that bent the rod double. Another followed, and another, and then I lost a large one. I passed the rod to D——, in whose hands it did still better service. In an hour we had a basket of trout that would have done credit to an English chalk stream. The largest was nearly three pounds weight, admirably grown, and pink ; fattened, I suppose, on the mussels which paved the bottom of the rapids. We were off immediately after, still guided to a new point by the chart, but not in this instance by the chart only. There was a spot which had been discovered the year before by the Duke of ——, of which we had a vague description. We had a log on board which had been kept by the Duke's mate, in which he had recorded many curious experiences ; among the rest an adventure at a certain lake not very far from where we were. The Duke had been successful there, and his lady had been very nearly successful. " We had grief yesterday," the mate wrote, " her Grace losing a twelve-pound salmon which she had caught on her little line, and just as they were going to hook it, it went off, and we were very sorry." The grief went deep, it seemed, for the next day the crew were reported as only " being as well as could be expected after so melancholy an accident." We determined to find the place, and, if possible, avenge her Grace. We crossed the Sogne and went up into the Nord Fjord—of all the fjords the most beautiful ; for on either side there are low terraces of land left by glacier action, and more signs of culture and human habitations. After running for fifty miles, we turned into an inlet corresponding tolerably with the Duke's directions, and in another half-hour we were again in a mountain basin like that which we had left in the morning. The cataracts were in their glory, the day having been warm for a wonder. I counted seventeen all close about us when we anchored, any one of which would have made the fortune of a Scotch hotel, and would have been celebrated by Mr. Murray in pages of passionate eloquence. But Strömen, or " the Streams," as the place was called, was less solitary than Nord Gulen. There was a large farm on one side of us. There was a cluster of houses at the mouth of a river, half a mile from it. Above the village was a lake, and at the head of the lake an establishment of saw-mills. A gun-shot from where we lay, on a rocky knoll, was a white wooden church, the Sunday meeting-place of the neighborhood ; boats coming to it from twenty miles round bringing families in their bright Sunday attire. Roads there were none. To have made a league of road among such rocks and precipices would have cost the State a year's revenue. But the water was the best of approaches, and boats the cheapest of carriages. We called on the chief proprietor to ask for leave to fish in the lake. It was granted with the readiest courtesy; but the Norsemen are proud in their way, and do not like the Englishman's habit of treating all the world as if it belonged to him. The low meadows round his house were bright with flowers; two kinds of wild geranium, an exquisite variety of harebell, sea-pride, pansies, violets, and the great pinguicola. Among the rocks were foxgloves in full splendor, and wild roses just coming into flower. The roses alone of the Norway flora disappointed me; the leaves are large, dark, and handsome; the flower is insignificant, and falls to pieces within an hour of its opening. We were satisfied that we were on the right spot. The church stood on a peninsula, the neck of which immediately adjoined our anchorage. Behind it was the lake which had been the scene of the Duchess's misfortune. We did not repeat our midnight experiment. We waited for a leisurely breakfast. Five of the crew then carried the yacht's cutter through fifty yards of bushes; and we were on the edge of the lake itself, which, like all these inland waters, was glassy, still, deep, and overhung with precipices. The owner had suggested to us that there were bears among them, which we might kill if we pleased, as they had just eaten seven of his sheep. So little intention had we of shooting bears that we had not brought rifle or even gun with us. Our one idea was to catch the Duchess's twelve-pound salmon, or, if not that one, at least another of his kindred.

In a strange lake it is well always to try first with

19

spinning tackle, a bait trolled with a long line from the stern of a boat rowed slowly. It will tell you if there are fish to be caught; it will find out for you where the fish most haunt, if there are any. We had a curious experience of the value of this method on a later occasion, and on one of our failures. We had found a lake joined to an arm of a fjord by a hundred yards only of clear running water. We felt certain of finding salmon there, and if we had begun with flies we might have fished all day and have caught nothing. Instead of this we began to spin. In five minutes we had a run; we watched eagerly to see what we had got. It was a whiting pollock. We went on. We hooked a heavy fish. We assured ourselves that now we had at least a trout. It turned out to be a cod. The sea fish, we found, ran freely into the fresh water, and had chased trout and salmon completely out. At Strömen we were in better luck. We started with phantom minnows on traces of strong single gut, forty yards of line, and forty more in reserve on the reel. Two men rowed us up the shore an oar's length from the rocks. Something soon struck me. The reel flew round, the line spun out. In the wake of the boat there was a white flash, as a fish sprang into the air. Was it the Duchess's salmon? It was very like it, any way; and if we had lost him, it would have been entered down as a salmon. It proved, however, to be no salmon, but a sea trout, and such a sea trout as we had never seen; not a bull trout, not a peel, not a Welsh sewin, or Irish white trout, but a Norwegian, of a kind of its own, different from all of them. This was the first of many which followed, of sizes varying from three pounds to the twelve pounds which the mate had recorded; fine, bold, fighting fish, good to look at, good to catch, and as good to eat when we tried them. Finally, in the shallower water, at the upper end, a fish took me, which from its movements was something else, and proved to be a large char, like what they take in Derwentwater, only four times the weight. Looking carefully at the water we saw more char swimming leisurely near the surface, taking flies. We dropped our spinning tackle, and took our fly rods ; and presently we were pulling in char, the blood royal of the salmonidæ, the elect of all the finned children of the fresh water, as if they had been so many Thames chub.

What need to talk more of fish ? The mate's log had guided us well. We caught enough and to spare, and her Grace's wrongs were avenged sufficiently. We landed for our frugal luncheon—dry biscuits and a whiskey flask —but we sat in a bed of whortleberries, purple with ripe fruit, by a cascade which ran down out of a snow-field. Horace would have invited his dearest friend to share in such a banquet.

The next day was Sunday. The sight of the boats coming from all quarters to church was very pretty. Fifteen hundred people at least must have collected. I attended the service, but could make little of it. I could follow the hymns with a book ; but copies of the Liturgy, though printed, are not provided for general use, and are reserved to the clergy. The faces of the men were extremely interesting. There was little in them to suggest the old freebooter. They were mild and gentle-looking, with fair skins, fair hair, and light eyes, gray or blue. The expression was sensible and collected, but with nothing about it especially adventurous or daring. The women, in fact, were more striking than their husbands. There was a steady strength in their features which implied humor underneath. Two girls, I suppose sisters, reminded me of Mrs. Gaskell. With the Lutheran, Sunday afternoon is a holiday. A yacht in such a place was a curiosity, and a fleet of boats surrounded us. Such as liked came on board and looked about them. They were well bred and showed no foolish surprise. One old dame, indeed, being taken down into the ladies' cabin, did find it too much for her. She dropped down and kissed the carpet. One of our party wondered afterward whether there was any chance of the Norwegians attaining a higher civilization. I asked her to define civilization. Did industry, skill, energy, sufficient food and raiment, sound practical education, and piety which believes without asking questions, constitute civilization; and would luxury, newspapers, and mechanics' institutes mean a higher civilization? The old question must first be answered, What is the real purpose of human life?

At Strömen, too, we could not linger; we stopped a few hours at Daviken on our way north, a considerable place for Norway, on the Nord Fjord. There is a bishop, I believe, belonging to it, but him we did not see. We called at the parsonage and found the pastor's wife and children. The pastor himself came on board afterward—a handsome man of sixty-seven, with a broad, full forehead, large nose, and straight grizzled hair. He spoke English, and would have spoken Latin if we had ourselves been equal to it. He had read much English literature, and was cultivated above the level of our own average country clergy. His parish was thirty miles long on both sides of the fjord. He had several churches, to all of which he attended in turn, with boats in summer, and occasionally, perhaps, with the ice in winter. We did not ask his salary; it was doubtless small, but sufficient. He had a school under him which he said was well attended. The master, who had a State certificate, was allowed £25 a year, on which he was able to maintain himself. We could not afford time to see more of this gentleman, however. We were impatient for Trondhjem ; the engineer wanted coals ; we wanted our letters and newspapers, and the steward wanted a washerwoman. On our way up, too, we had arranged to give a day or two to Romsdal, Rolf the Ganger's country. On an island in Romsdal Fjord the ruins can still be seen of Rolf's Castle. It was there that Rolf, or Rollo as we call him, set out with his comrades to conquer Normandy, and produce the chivalry who fought at Hastings and organized feudal England. This was not to be missed ; and as little, a visit which we had promised to a descendant of one of those Normans, a distinguished Tory member of the House of Commons, and lord of half an English county, who had bought an estate in these parts, with a salmon river, and had built himself a house there.

Romsdal, independent of its antiquarian interest, is geologically the most remarkable place which we saw in Norway. The fjord expands into a wide estuary or inland lake, into which many valleys open and several large streams discharge themselves. Romsdal proper was once evidently itself a continuation of the Great Fjord. The mountains on each side of it are peculiarly magnificent. On the left Romsdal's Horn shoots up into the sky, a huge peak which no one at that time had ever climbed, and will try the mettle of the Alpine Club when they have conquered Switzerland. On the right is a precipitous wall of cliffs and crags as high and bold as the Horn itself. The upper end of the valley which divides them terminates in a narrow fissure, through which a river thunders down that carries the water of the great central ice-field into the valley. From thence it finds its way into the fjord, running through the glen itself, which is seven or eight miles long, two miles wide, and richly cultivated and wooded. From the sea the appearance of the shore is most singular. It is laid out in level grassy terraces, stretching all round the bay, rising in tiers one above the other, so smooth, so even, so nicely scarfed, that the imagination can hardly be persuaded that they are not the work of human engineers. But under water the formation is the same. At one moment you are in twenty fathoms, the next in forty, the next your cable will find no bottom ; and it is as certain as any conclusion on such subjects can be, that long ago, long ages before Rolf, and Knut, and the Vikings, the main fjord was blocked with ice ; that while the ice barrier was still standing, and the valleys behind it were fresh-water lakes, the rivers gradually filled them with a *débris* of stone and soil. Each level terrace was once a lake bottom. The ice broke or melted away at intervals. The water was lowered suddenly forty or fifty feet, and the ground lately covered was left bare as the ice receded.

We found our Englishman. His house is under the Horn at the bend of the valley, where the ancient fjord must have ended. It stands in a green, open meadow, approached through alder and birch woods, the first cataract where the snow-water plunges through the great chasm being in sight of the windows, and half a dozen inimitable salmon pools within a few minutes' walk. The house itself was simple enough, made of pine wood entirely, as the Norway houses always are, and painted white. It contained some half-dozen rooms, furnished in the plainest English style, the summer house of a sportsman who is tired of luxury, and finds the absence of it an agreeable exchange. A man cannot be always catching salmon, even in Norway, and a smattering of science and natural history would be a serviceable equipment in a scene where there are so many curious objects worth attending to. Our friend's tastes, however, did not lie in that direction. His shelves were full of yellow-backed novels — French, English, and German. His table was covered with the everlasting *Saturday Review, Pall Mall Gazette, Times,* and *Standard.* I think he suspected science as a part of modern Liberalism ; for he was a Tory of the Tories, a man with whom the destinies had dealt kindly, in whose eyes therefore all existing arrangements were as they should be, and those who wished to meddle with them were enemies of the human race. He was sad and sorrowful. The world was not moving to his mind, and he spoke as if he was *ultimus Romanorum.* But if an aristocrat, he was an aristocrat of the best type—princely in his thoughts, princely in his habits, princely even in his salmon fishing. The pools in the river being divided by difficult rapids, he had a boat and a boatman for each. The sport was ample but uniform. There was an ice-cellar under the house where we saw half a dozen great salmon lying which had been caught in the morning. One salmon behaves much like another ; and after one has caught four or five, and when one knows that one can catch as many more as one wishes, impatient people might find the occupation monotonous. Happily there was a faint element of uncertainty still left. It was possible to fail even in the Romsdal. We were ourselves launched in boats in different pools at the risk of our lives to try our hands ; we worked diligently for a couple of hours, and I at least moved not so much as a fin. It was more entertaining a great deal to listen to

our host as he declaimed upon the iniquities of our
present radical chief. Politics, like religion, are matters
of faith on which reason says as little as possible. One
passionate belief is an antidote to another. It is impossible to continue to believe enthusiastically in a creed
which a fellow-mortal with as much sense as one's self
denies and execrates, and the collision of opinion produces the prudent scepticism which in most matters is
the least mischievous frame of mind.

Here, too, in these pleasant surroundings we would
gladly have loitered for a day or two ; but the steward
was clamorous over his dirty linen, and it was not to be.
My last impressions of Romsdal fell into the form of a
few doggerel verses, an indulgence on which I rarely
venture, and which for once, therefore, may be pardoned.

ROMSDAL FJORD.

July 11, 1881.

So this, then, was the Rovers' nest,
   And here the chiefs were bred
Who broke the drowsy Saxon's rest
   And scared him in his bed.

The north wind blew, the ship sped fast,
   Loud cheered the Corsair crew,
And wild and free above the mast
   The Raven standard flew.

Sail south, sail south, there lies the land
   Where the yellow corn is growing ;
The spoil is for the warrior's hand,
   The serf may have the sowing.

Let cowards make their parchment laws
　　To guard their treasured hoards ;
The steel shall plead the Rovers' cause,
　　Their title-deeds their swords.

The Raven still o'er Romsdal's peaks
　　Is soaring as of yore,
But Viking's call in cove or creek
　　Calm Romsdal hears no more.

Long ages now beneath the soil
　　The Ganger has been lying,
In Romsdal's bay his quiet toil
　　The fisherman is plying.

The English earl sails idly by,
　　And from his deck would trace,
With curious antiquarian eye,
　　The cradle of his race.

With time and tide we change and change,
　　Yet still the world is young,
Still free the proudest spirits range,
　　The prize is for the strong.

We deem it chief of glorious things
　　In parliaments to shine,
That orators are modern kings
　　And only not divine.

But men will yet be ruled by men,
　　Though talk may have its day,
And other Rolfs will rise again
　　To sweep the rogues away.

Trondhjem, on which our intentions had been so long
fixed, was reached at last. The weather had grown cold
again, cold with cataracts of rain. Let no one go to Nor-

way even in the dog-days without a winter wardrobe.
The sea-water in our baths was at 47° ; we had fires in
the cabin stove, and could not warm ourselves ; we shivered under four blankets in our berths.   The mountains
were buried in clouds, and the landscape was reduced to
a dull gray mist ; but the worst of weathers will serve
for reading letters, laying in coal, and wandering about
a town.

Trondhjem ought to have been interesting.   It was
the capital of the old Norse kings.   There reigned the
Olafs.   It lies half-way up the Norway coast in the very
centre of the kingdom, on a broad landlocked bay.   The
situation was chosen for its strength ; for a deep river
all but surrounds the peninsula on which the town is
built, and on the land side it must have been impregna-
ble.   The country behind it is exceptionally fertile, and
is covered over with thriving farms ; but streets and
shops are wearisome, and even the cathedral did not
tempt us to pay it more than a second visit.   It is a stern
solid piece of building, early Norman in type, with doors,
windows, and arches of zigzag pattern.   It had fallen
out of repair and was now being restored by the State ;
hundreds of workmen were busy chipping and hammer-
ing, and were doing their business so well that the new
work can hardly be distinguished from the old.   But
Catholic Christianity never seems to have got any hearty
hold on Norway.   St. Olaf thrust it upon the people
at the sword's point, but their imaginations remained
heathen till the Reformation gave them a creed which
they could believe.   I could find but few tombs in the
cathedral.   I inquired where the old kings and chiefs
were buried, and no one could tell me.   I found, in fact,
that they had usually come to an end in some sea-battle,
and had found their graves in their own element.   Olaf

Tryggveson went down, the last survivor in the last ship of his fleet, the rays of the sunset flashing on his armor as the waves closed over him. St. Olaf died in the same way. The absence of monumental stones or figures in the great metropolitan church of Norway is strange, sad, and impressive.

The town being exhausted, we drove a few miles out of it to see a foss, one of the grandest in the country. We said "Oh!" to it, as Wolfe Tone did to Grattan. But waterfalls had become too common with us, and, in fact, the excitement about them has always seemed exaggerated to me. I was staying once in a house in the north of New York State when a gentleman came in fresh from Niagara, and poured out his astonishment over the enormous mass of water falling into the caldron below. "Why is it astonishing?" asked a Yankee who was present. "Why shouldn't the water fall? The astonishing thing would be if it didn't fall."

In short, we left the washerwoman in possession of the linen, which we could return and pick up when it was done, and we steamed away to examine the great Trondhjem Fjord; fishing and making bad sketches as the weather would allow. The weather generally allowed us to do very little, and drove us upon our books, which we could have read as well in our rooms at home. I had brought the "Elective Affinities" with me. I had not read it for thirty years. Then it had seemed to me the wisest of all didactic works of fiction. "Unconscious cerebration," as Dr. Carpenter calls it, when I read the book again, had revolutionized my principles of judgment. I could still recognize the moral purpose. There are tendencies in human nature, like the chemical properties of material substances, which will claim possession of you, and even appear to have a moral right

over you. But if you yield you will be destroyed. You
can command yourself, and you must. Very true, very
excellent; and set forth with Goethe's greatest power of
fascination; but I found myself agreeing with the rest
of the world that it was a monstrous book after all. To
put the taste out I tried Seneca, but I scarcely improved
matters. Seneca's fame as a moralist and philosopher
was due, perhaps, in the first instance, to his position
about the Court, and to his enormous wealth. A little
merit passes for a great deal when it is framed in gold,
and once established it would retain its reputation, from
the natural liking of men for virtuous cant. Those lectures to Lucilius on the beauty of poverty from the greatest money-lender and usurer in the Empire! Lucilius is
to practise voluntary hardships, is to live at intervals on
beggars' fare, and sleep on beggars' pallets, that he may
sympathize in the sufferings of mortality and be independent of outward things. If Seneca meant all this,
why did he squeeze five millions of our money out of the
provinces with loans and contracts? He was barren as
the Sahara to me. Not a green spot could I find, not
a single genial honest thought, in all the four volumes with which I had encumbered myself. His finest
periods rang hollow like brass sovereigns. The rain
would not stop, so we agreed to defy the rain and to
fish in spite of it. We had the fjord before us for a
week, and we landed wherever we could hear of lake
or river. For twelve hours together the waterspout
would come down upon us; we staggered about in
thickest woollen, with macintoshes and india-rubber
boots. With flapped oilskin hats we should have been
waterproof, but with one of these I was unprovided;
and, in spite of collars and woollen wrappers, the
water would find its way down my neck till there was

nothing dry left about me but the feet. Clothes grow heavy under such conditions ; we had to take our lightest rods with us, and now and then came to grief. I was fishing alone one day in a broad, rocky stream fringed with alder bushes, dragging my landing-net with me. At an open spot where there was a likely run within reach I had caught a four-pound sea trout. I threw again ; a larger fish rose and carried off my fly. I mounted a "doctor," blue and silver, on the strongest casting line in my book, and on the second cast a salmon came. The river in the middle was running like a mill-sluice. I could not follow along the bank on account of the trees ; my only hope was to hold on and drag the monster into the slack water under the shore. My poor little rod did its best, but its best was not enough ; the salmon forced his way into the waves, round went the reel, off flew the line to the last inch, and then came the inevitable catastrophe. A white streak flashed wildly into the air, the rod straightened out, the line came home, and my salmon and my bright doctor sped away together to the sea.

We were none the worse for our wettings. Each evening we came home dripping and draggled. A degree or two more of cold would have turned the rain into snow. Yet it signified nothing. We brought back our basketfuls of trout, and the Norwegian trout are the best in the world. We anchored one evening in a chasm with the mountain walls rising in precipices on both sides. The next morning as I was laying in my berth I heard a conversation between the steward and the captain. The captain asked the orders for the day ; the steward answered (he was the wit of the ship), "Orders are to stretch an awning over the fjord that his lordship may fish."

But the weather so far beat us that we were obliged to abandon Lofoden. We were now at the end of July, and it was not likely to mend, so we determined to turn about and spend the rest of our time in the large fjords of South Norway. Trondhjem had been our farthest point; we could not coal there after all, so we had to make for Christiansund on the way. I was not sorry for it, for Christiansund is a curious little bustling place, and worth seeing. It is the headquarters of the North Sea fishing trade near the open ocean, and the harbor is formed by three or four islands divided by extremely narrow channels, with a deep roomy basin in the middle of them. One of our crew was ill, and had to be taken for two or three days to the hospital. The arrangements seemed excellent, as every public department is in Norway. The town was pretty. The Norwegians dress plainly; but they like bright colors for their houses, and the red-tiled roofs and blue and yellow painted fronts looked pleasant after our clouds of mist.

The climate from the proximity of the ocean is said to be mild for its latitude. The snow, we were told, lay up to the lower windows through the winter, but that went for nothing. There were stocks and columbines in the gardens; there were ripe gooseberries and red currants and pink thorn and laburnum in flower. The harbor was full of fishing smacks, like Brixham trawlers, only rather more old-fashioned. Gay steam ferry-boats rushed about from island to island; large ships were loading; well-dressed strangers were in the streets and shops; an English yacht had come like ourselves to take in coal, and was moored side by side with us. There are fewer people in the world than we imagine, and we fall on old acquaintances when we least expect them. The once beautiful —— was on board, whom I had known forty-five years before. She had married a distinguished engineer, who was out for his holiday.

We stayed at Christiansund or in the neighborhood till our sick man was recovered, and then followed (under better auspices as regarded weather) ten days of scenery hunting which need not be described. We went to Sondal, Lærdal, Nordal, and I don't know how many " dals," all famous places in their way, but with a uniformity of variety which becomes tedious in a story. One only noticeable feature I observed about the sheds and poorer houses in these out-of-the-way districts. They lay turf sods over the roofs, which become thick masses of vegetation ; and on a single cottage roof you may see half a dozen trees growing ten or fifteen feet high. For lakes and mountains, however beautiful, the appetite becomes soon satiated. They please, but they cease to excite ; and there is something artificial in the modern enthusiasm for landscapes. Velasquez or Rubens could appreciate a fine effect of scenery as well as Turner or Stanfield ; but with them it was a framework, subordinate to some human interest in the centre of the picture. I suppose it is because man in these democratic days has for a time ceased to touch the imagination that our poets and artists are driven back upon rocks and rivers and trees and skies ; but the eclipse can only be temporary, and I confess, for myself, that, sublime as the fjords were, the saw-mills and farmhouses and fishing-boats, and the patient, industrious people wresting a wholesome living out of that stern environment, affected me very much more nearly. I cannot except even the Geiranger, as tremendous a piece of natural architecture as exists in the globe. The fjord in the Geiranger is a quarter of a mile wide and 600 fathoms deep. The walls of it are in most places not

figuratively, but literally, precipices, and the patch of
sky above your head seems to narrow as you look up.
I hope I was duly impressed with the wonder of this;
but even here there was something which impressed me
more, and that was the singular haymaking which was
going on. The Norwegians depend for their existence
on their sheep and cattle. Every particle of grass available for hay is secured; and grass, peculiarly nutritious,
often grows on the high ridges 2,000 feet up. This
they save as they can, and they have original ways of
doing it. In the Geiranger it is tied tightly in bundles
and flung over the cliffs to be gathered up in boats below. But science, too, is making its way in this northern wilderness. The farmhouses, for shelter's sake, are
always at the bottom of valleys, and are generally near
the sea. At one of our anchorages, shut in as usual
among the mountains, we observed one evening from
the deck what looked like a troop of green goats skipping
and bounding down the cliffs. We discovered through
a binocular that they were bundles of hay. The clever
bönder had carried up a wire, like a telegraph wire,
from his courtyard to a projecting point of mountain; on
this ran iron rings as travellers which brought the grass
directly to his door.

Twice only in our wanderings we had fallen in with our
tourist countrymen: once at Lærdal, where a high road
comes down to a pier, and is met there by a corresponding steamer; the second time coming down from the
Geiranger, when we passed a boat with two ladies and
a gentleman, English evidently, the gentleman touching
his hat to the Yacht Club flag as we went by. Strange
and pleasant the short glimpse of English faces in that
wild chasm! But we were plunged into the very middle of our countrymen at the last spot in which we went

in search of the picturesque—a spot worth a few words
as by far the most regularly beautiful of all the places
which we visited. At the head of one of the long inlets which runs south, I think, out of the Hardanger
Fjord (but our rapid movements were confusing) stands
Odde, once a holy place in Scandinavian mythological
history. There is another Odde in Iceland, also sacred
—I suppose Odin had something to do with it. The
Odde Fjord is itself twenty miles long, and combines
the softest and grandest aspects of Norwegian scenery.
The shores are exceptionally well cultivated, richer than
any which we had seen. Every half mile some pretty
farmhouse was shining red through clumps of trees, the
many cattle-sheds speaking for the wealth of the owner.
Above, through the rifts of higher ranges you catch a
sight of the Central Icefield glacier streaming over
among the broken chasms and melting into waterfalls.
At Odde itself there is an extensive tract of fertile soil
on the slope of a vast moraine, which stretches completely across the broad valley. On the sea at the land-
ing-place is a large church and two considerable hotels,
which were thronged with visitors. A broad road ex-
cellently engineered leads down to it, and we found a
staff of English - speaking guides whose services we
did not require. We had seen much of the ice action
elsewhere, but the performances of it at Odde were
more wonderful even than at Romsdal. The moraine is
perhaps four hundred and fifty feet high ; the road
winds up the side of it among enormous granite bowl-
ders, many of them weighing thousands of tons, which
the ice has tossed about like pebble-stones. On reaching the crest you see a lake a quarter of a mile off ; but
before you come to it you cross some level fields, very
rich to look at, and with patches of white-heart cherry-

20

trees scattered about, the fruit, when we came there at
the end of August, being actually ripe and extremely
good. These fields were the old lake bottom; but the
river has cut a dike for itself through the top of the
moraine, and the lake has gone down some twenty feet,
leaving them dry.

The weather (penitent, perhaps, for having so long
persecuted us) was in a better humor. Our days at
Odde were warm and without a cloud, and we spent
them chiefly by the lake, which was soft as Windermere.
We had come into a land of fruit; not cherries only,
but wild raspberries and strawberries were offered us
in leaves by girls on the road.   The road itself followed
the lake margin, among softly rounded and wooded
hills, the great mountains out of sight behind them,
save only in one spot where, through a gorge, you looked
straight up to the eternal snow-field, from which a vast
glacier descended almost into the lake itself, the ice imitating precisely the form of falling water, crushing its
way among the rocks, parting in two where it met a projecting crag, and uniting again behind it, seeming even
to heave and toss in angry waves of foam.

From this glacier the lake was chiefly fed, and was
blue, like skimmed milk, in consequence.   We walked
along it for several miles.   Fishing seemed hopeless in
water of such a texture.   As we turned a corner two
carriages dashed by us with some young men and dogs
and guns—cockneys out for their holiday.   "Any sport,
sir?" one of them shouted to me, seeing a rod in my
hand, in the cheerful familiar tone which assumed that
sport must be the first and only object which one could
have in such a place.   They passed on to the hotel, and
the presence of so many of our own countrymen was
inclining us to cut short our own stay.   Some of the

party, however, wished to inspect the glacier. We were
ourselves assured that there were salmon in the lake,
which, in spite of the color, could be caught there. It
was the last opportunity which we should have, as after
Odde our next move was to be Christiania. So we agreed
to take one more day there and make the most of it.
We got two native boats, and started to seek adventures.
Alas! we had the loveliest views ; but the blue waters of
Odde, however fair to look upon, proved as ill to fish in
as at the first sight of them we were assured they must be.
Our phantom minnows could not be seen three inches
off, and the stories told us we concluded to be fables invented for the tourists. I, for my own part, had gone
to the farthest extremity of the lake, where it ended in
a valley like Borrodale. I was being rowed listlessly
back, having laid aside my tackle, and wishing that I
could talk to my old boatman, who looked as if all the
stories of the Edda were inside him, when my eye was
suddenly caught by a cascade coming down out of a
ravine into the lake which had not been bred in the
glaciers, and was as limpid as the Itchen itself. At the
mouth of this it was just possible that there might be a
char or something with fins that could see to rise. It
was my duty to do what I could for the yacht's cuisine.
I put together my little trout rod for a last attempt, and
made my boatman row me over to it. The clear water
was not mixing with the blue, but pushing its way
through the milky masses, which were eddying and
rolling as if they were oil. In a moment I had caught
a sea trout. Immediately after I caught a second, and
soon a basketful. They had been attracted by the purer
liquid, and were gathered there in a shoal. They were
lying with their noses up the stream at the farthest
point to which they could go. I got two or three, and

those the largest, by throwing my fly against the rocks exactly at the fall. D—— came afterward and caught more and bigger fish than I did ; and our sport, which indeed we had taken as it came without specially seeking for it, was brought to a good end. The end of August was come, and with it the period of our stay in the fjords. We had still to see Christiania, and had no time to lose. But of all the bits of pure natural loveliness which we had fallen in with, Odde and its blue lake, and glacier, and cherry orchards, and wild strawberries has left the fairest impression ; perhaps, however, only because it was the last, for we were going home ; and they say that when a man dies, the last image which he has seen is photographed on his retina.

But now away. The smoke pours through the funnel. The engine is snorting like an impatient horse. The quick rattle of the cable says that the anchor is off the ground. We were off and had done with fjords. The inner passages would serve no longer ; we had to make for the open sea once more to round the foot of the peninsula. It is at no time the softest of voyages. The North Sea is not the home of calm sunsets and light-breathing zephyrs, and it gave us a taste of its quality, which, after our long sojourn in smooth water, was rather startling. If the wind and sea are ever wilder than we found them in those latitudes, I have no desire to be present at the exhibition. We fought the storm for twenty-four hours, and were then driven for refuge into a roadstead at the southern extremity of Norway, near Mandal. The neighborhood was interesting, if we had known it, for at Mandal Mary Stuart's Earl of Bothwell was imprisoned when he escaped from the Orkneys to Denmark. The dungeon where he was confined is still to be seen, and as the Earl was an exceptional

villain, the authentic evidence of eyesight that he had
spent an uncomfortable time in his exile would not
have been unwelcome. But we discovered what we had
lost when it was too late to profit by our information.
We amused ourselves by wandering on shore and observing the effect of the change of latitude on vegetation. We found the holly thriving, of which in the
north we had not seen a trace, and the hazel bushes
had ripe nuts on them. There was still a high sea
the next day ; but we made thirty miles along the coast
to Arendal, an advanced thriving town of modern aspect,
built in a sheltered harbor, with broad quays, fine buildings, and a gay parade. It was almost dark when we
entered ; and the brilliant lights and moving crowds and
carriages formed a singular contrast to the unfinished
scenes of unregenerate nature which we had just left.
The Norse nature, too, hard and rugged as it may be,
cannot resist the effect of its occupations. Aristotle observes that busy sea-towns are always democratic. Norway generally, though Republican, is intensely Conserva-
tive. The landowners, who elect most of the representatives, walk in the ways of their fathers, and have
the strongest objection to new ideas. Arendal, I was
told, sends to Parliament an eloquent young Radical, the
admired of all the newspapers. There is, I believe,*
no present likelihood that he will bring about a revolution. But there is no knowing when the king is an
absentee. We spent one night at Arendal. In the
morning the storm had left us, and before sunset we
were at anchor at Christiania. It was Sunday. The
weather was warm, the water smooth, the woody islands
which surround and shelter the anchorage were glowing

---

* Written in 1881. The movement for separation from Sweden
has advanced rapidly in the last ten years.

in gold and crimson. Christiania, a city of domes and
steeples, lay before us with its fleets of steamers and
crowded shipping. Hundreds of tiny yachts and pleas-
ure-boats were glancing round us. There is no sour
Sabbatarianism in Norway. One of the islands is a kind
of Cremorne. When night fell the music of the city
band came fitfully across the water ; blue lights blazed
and rockets flashed into the sky with their flights of
crimson stars. It was a scene which we had not expected in these northern regions ; but life can have its
enjoyments even above the sixtieth parallel.

There is much to be seen in Christiania. There is a
Parliament house and a royal palace, and picture galleries and botanical gardens, and a museum of antiquities,
and shops where articles of native workmanship can be
bought by Englishmen at three times their value, and
ancient swords and battle-axes, and drinking-horns and
rings and necklaces, genuine, at present, for all I know
to the contrary, but capable of imitation, and likely in
these days of progress to be speedily imitated. If the
Holy Coat of Trèves has been multiplied by ten, why
should there not be ten swords of Olaf Tryggveson ?
But all these things are written of in the handbook of
Mr. Murray, where the curious can read of them. One
real wonder we saw and saw again at Christiania, and
could not satisfy ourselves with seeing ; and with an account of this I shall end. It was a viking's ship ; an
authentic vessel in which, while Norway was still heathen, before St. Olaf drilled his people into Christianity
with sword and gallows, a Norse chief and his crew had
travelled these same waters, and in which, when he died,
he had been laid to rest. It had been closed in with peat,
which had preserved the timbers. It had been recovered
almost entire—the vessel itself, the oars, the boats, the

remnants of the cordage, even down to the copper caldron in which he and his men had cooked their dinners; the names, the age, the character of them all buried in the soil, but the proof surviving that they had been the contemporaries and countrymen of the " Danes " who drove the English Alfred into the marshes of Somersetshire.

Our yacht's company were as eager to see this extraordinary relic as ourselves. We went in a body, and never tired of going. It had been found fifty miles away, had been brought to Christiania, and had been given in charge to the University. A solid weather-proof shed had been built for it, where we could study its structure at our leisure.

The first thing that struck us all was the beauty of the model, as little resembling the old drawings of Norse or Saxon ships as the figures which do duty there as men resemble human beings. White, of Cowes, could not build a vessel with finer lines, or offering less resistance to the water. She was eighty feet long, and seventeen and a half feet beam. She may have drawn three feet, scarcely more, when her whole complement was on board. She was pierced for thirty-two oars, and you could see the marks on the side of the rowlocks where the oars had worn the timber. She had a single mast, stepped in the solid trunk of a tree which had been laid along the keel. The stump of it was still in the socket. Her knee timbers were strong; but her planks were unexpectedly slight, scarcely more than half an inch thick. They had been formed by careful splitting; there was no sign of the action of a saw, and the ends of them had been trimmed off by the axe. They had been set on and fastened with iron nails, and the seams had been carefully calked. Deck she had none—a level floor a couple of feet below the gunwale ran from stem to stern. The shields of the crew formed a bulwark, and it was easy to see where they had been fixed. Evidently, therefore, she had been a war-ship; built for fighting, not for carrying cargoes. But there was no shelter, and could have been none; no covered forecastle, no stern cabin. She stood right open fore and aft to wind and waves; and though she would have been buoyant in a sea-way, and in the heaviest gale would have shipped little water, even Norsemen could not have been made of such impenetrable stuff that they would have faced the elements with no better protection in any distant expedition. That those who sailed in her were to some extent careful of themselves is accidentally certain. Among the stores was a plank with crossbars nailed upon it, meant evidently for landing on a beach. One of our men, who was quick at inferences, exclaimed at once: "These fellows must have worn shoes and stockings. If they had been barelegged they would have jumped overboard and would not have wanted a landing-plank."

I conclude, therefore, that she was not the kind of vessel of which the summer squadrons were composed that came down our English Channel, but that she was intended either for the fjords only, or for the narrow waters between Norway and Sweden and Denmark at the mouth of the Baltic. Her rig must have been precisely what we had been lately seeing on the Sogne or Hardanger; a single large sail on a square yard fit for running before the wind, or with the wind slightly on the quarter, but useless at any closer point. The rudder hung over the side a few feet from the stern, a heavy oar with a broad blade and a short handle, shaped so exactly like the rudders of the Roman vessels on

Trajan's Column, that the Norsemen, it is likely, had seen the pattern somewhere and copied it.

Such is this strange remnant of the old days which has suddenly started into life. So vivid is the impression which it creates, that it is almost as if some Sweyn or Harold in his proper person had come back among us from the grave. If we were actually to see such a man we should be less conscious perhaps of our personal superiority than we are apt to imagine. A law of compensation follows us through our intellectual and mechanical progress. The race collectively knows and can execute immeasurably greater things than the Norsemen. Individually they may have been as ready and intelligent as ourselves. The shipwright certainly who laid the lines of the Viking's galley would have something to teach as well as to learn in the yard of a modern yacht-builder.

But enough now of Norway. Our time was out; our tour was over; we seated ourselves once more on our wishing carpet, and desired to be at Cowes; we were transported thither with the care and almost the speed with which the genius of the lamp transported the palace of Aladdin, and we felt that we had one superiority at least which the Viking would have envied us.

NORWAY ONCE MORE

WHEN I published two years ago a sketch of a summer holiday in the Norway fjords I supposed that I had seen my last of Norse mountains and lakes, and bönder farms, and that this little record would be all which would remain to me of a time which was so delightful in the enjoyment. The poor Severn, which in 1881 was our floating home, now lies among the krakens at the bottom of the North Sea, or ground to pieces by the teeth of the rocks which one treacherous July morning seized and devoured her. Faithfully the poor yacht had done her duty bearing us from lake to lake and wonder to wonder, like Prince Ahmed's enchanted carpet. She had been cut off in her youth, before her engines had rusted or screw-shaft cracked. She had ended in honor, and had not been left to rot away ingloriously or subside into tug or tender.

Dead, however, as was the Severn's body, the soul or idea of her was not dead, but in another year had revived again, and gathered a second body about it, more beautiful than the first. In spite of Destiny, her owner persevered in his resolution to penetrate again those virgin inlets, which are yet unhaunted by tourists; to fish again in those waters where the trout are still *feræ naturæ*, unreared in breeding ponds, and unwatched by gamekeepers. He invited me to be once more his companion, and here, in consequence, is a second record of our wanderings, set idly down for my own pleasure. In one sense the whole experience was new, for in 1881 winter stayed to spend the summer in Norway, and when it did not rain it snowed. In 1884, for half July at least, we were treated to sky and mountain which were dazzling in their brilliancy, and to the tropical temperature of which we had read in guide-books, hitherto with most imperfect belief. But besides, I have actual novelties (three at least) which deserve to be each in some way related—one an incident instructive to English visitors in those parts, one a freak of nature in a landscape, the third a small idyllic figure of Norwegian life. If I can do justice to these, or even to either of them, I flatter myself that I shall not be reproached with being tedious. They will come in their places, and I will note each as I arrive at it.

We were going to amuse ourselves—to fish, perhaps, in the first instance, but not entirely to fish. We had no river of our own. The best salmon streams were all let, and we had to depend on the hospitality of the native proprietors. And of the brown trout, which are so large and so abundant in the inland waters, there are none in those which communicate with the fjords, for they are eaten up by their large relations from the sea, which annually spend the autumn there. We meant to loiter at our pleasure among the large estuaries while the woods were still green and the midnight sun was still shining on the snow-peaks ; to anchor where we could find bottom, which in those long water-filled crevasses is usually out of cable reach ; in the way of fishing, to take what might offer itself, and be as happy with a little as with much. Our party was small—our host, myself, and my son A., who had just done with the University, and had his first acquaintance to make with the Salmonidæ.

We steamed out of Harwich in the first gray of morning on June 27. The engines waking into life, and the rattling of the anchor chains, disturbed our dreams; but we sank to sleep again under the even pulsation of the screw. When we came on deck we were far out in the North Sea, the water shining like oil, the engines going a hundred to the minute, our head pointing as on our first expedition to Udsire Light, 500 miles N.N.E. of us, and the yacht rushing steadily on at an accurate nine knots. Yacht life is active idleness—we have nothing to do and we do it. Vessels come in sight and pass out of it. We examine them with our binoculars, ascertain what they are and whither they are bound. We note the water, and judge the depth of it by the color. We have the chart before us; we take our observations, and prick down our position upon it with a precision which can be measured by yards. We lie on sofas and read novels; I read a translation in MS., which our entertainer himself was just completing, of a Norse novel, a story of an old rough sea-captain who in an ill day for himself fell among the Methodists, had his tough heart nearly broken by them, and recovered only his wits and his native strength of soul when his life was leaving his body. When we tire of our studies we overhaul our fishing tackle, knot casting lines, and splice new traces. Our host himself is an experienced fisherman. His skill in this department is inherited. He tells us a story of his great-grandfather, who, when he could walk no longer, for gout and rheumatism, fished from the back of a steady old cart-horse, and had the mane and tail of his charger shaved off to prevent his flies from catching in them.

At midday we see a smack ahead of us making signals. She lowers a boat. We stop our engines and the boat comes alongside, with three as choice specimens of English sea ruffians as eye had ever rested on.

They had mackerel to dispose of. They wanted to exchange their mackerel for schnapps. They would not
take money. It was to be *spirits* or no trade. They
looked already so soaked with spirits that a gallon of
alcohol might have been distilled out of the blood of
either of them. They had a boy with them with a
bright, innocent, laughing face. Poor little fellow, flung
by the fates into such companionship! They got no
schnapps from us, and we got no mackerel. They
rowed back, and probably, before the day was out, fell
in with less scrupulous passers-by.

Our yacht is proud of her punctuality. We know
our speed and we know our distance each within a deci-
mal fraction. We had sent word that we should reach
Bergen at 3 o'clock on Sunday afternoon. At the
mouth of the fjord which leads up to the great empo-
rium of the fish trade we were five minutes before our
time, but the error was accounted for by three hours of a
favorable tide. As we passed in we saw the glassy swell
combing over the rock where the Severn lies buried.
On that fatal morning it so happened that the sea was
absolutely still; the treacherous surface was unbroken
even by a line of foam, and she had rushed blindly upon
her fate. We do as the wise men bid us do, waste no
time in mourning over the unalterable past. We were
not wrecked this time. In a few minutes we were flying up the low, deep, narrow channels between the islands which fringe the western side of the Scandinavian
peninsula. The smallest boats traverse these natural
roads without danger from wind or wave; the largest,
when the entrance is once passed, fear nothing from
rock or shoal, the few dangerous spots being faithfully
marked by perches. Instead of fog and mist and rain,
with which Norway had last welcomed us, we saw it now

under the softest, bluest, calmest summer sky. Snow was
still visible on the high interior ranges, but in patches
which were fast dissolving, the green farmsteads and
woods and red-roofed houses gleaming as if we were in
a land of eternal sunshine. In two hours we were at
Bergen, the City of Hills. Twice I had been there before. I had studied its markets and its museums, and
I thought I knew what it was like. But Bergen itself I
had never seen till now. The roof of cloud which had
lain half down the mountain had now lifted off. As it
was Sunday the shipyards were silent. The harbor
was dotted over with boats, with smart young ladies
in bright dresses and with colored parasols. Steam
launches rushed to and fro. The merchants' villas
shone white among the elms and limes. Brigs and
schooners were resting at their anchors. Even the huge
and hideous Hull steamers suggested life and prosperous energy. " Have you many rich people here? " I asked
of a citizen who came on board. " Not rich," he said,
" but plenty who can have everything they wish for."
In Norway too they have at last caught the plague of
politics. Parties run high, and Bergen is for progress
and Radicalism ; but Radicals there, as the same gentleman explained to me, would be called Conservatives in
England ; they want ministers responsible to the Storth-
ing, economy in the government, and stricter adher-
ence to the lines of the Constitution—that is all. We
landed and heard the Lutheran evening service at the
Cathedral, which has been lately repaired—the wave of
church restoration having spread even to Norway.

We gave one clear day to Bergen, and on July 2, with
pilot on board, we lifted anchor and sped away through
the inland channels up north to the Sogne Fjord. We
had no clear route laid out for us. Our object, as before,

was to find quiet nooks or corners where we could stay
as long as we pleased, with the yacht for quarters, go
ashore, fish, botanize, geologize, and make acquaintance
with the natives and their ways. The Sogne runs up
into the heart of the Giant Mountains—the home of the
Trolls and Jotuns ; the shores on either side rising sheer
out of the narrow channel ; the great glaciers, showing
between the rents of the crags, four thousand feet above
us, pouring out their torrents of melted ice, and in such
sultry weather as we were then experiencing tinting the
lakes with blue. Our Bergen friends had marked out a
few places which they thought might answer for us, and
we tried them one after the other. We saw scenery of
infinite variety—now among precipices so vast that the
yacht seemed dwarfed into a cock-boat ; now in sunny
bays with softer outlines, where the moraines, left by
the ice, were covered with thriving homesteads, pretty
villages with white church and manse and rounded pine
woods. There, for the most part, are the homes of the
Norway peasantry. Eleven-twelfths of the whole surface
of the country is rock or glacier or forest, uncultivated,
uninhabitable by living creature, brute or human. But
the Norwegian makes the most of the stinted gifts which
nature has allowed him. Wherever there is a rood of
soil which will feed cattle or grow an oat-crop, there his
hand is busy. If he cannot live there, he carries over
his sheep and cows in his boats to feed. On the ancient lake-bottoms, formed when the fjords were filled
with ice, and left dry when the water fell, there are tracts
of land which would be called rich and beautiful in any
country in the world. In such spots, and in such weather,
we might well be tempted to linger. Tourists make long
journeys to see Windermere or Loch Katrine. We had
Windermere and Loch Katrine ten times magnified at

every turn of the winding Sogne—we could choose as
we pleased between desolate grandeur and the gentler
homes of industry and human life.

Any one of these places might have suited us had we
been obliged to stay there, but we had free choice to go
anywhere, and we wanted all the various charms combined. We wanted a good harbor. We wanted trout
or salmon for ourselves, and sea-fish for the crew, fresh
meat being hard to come by. At one place we were
promised a sheep, if the bears had not eaten it. I believe
in that instance we did get the sheep, being a lean,
scraggy thing which the bears had despised ; but we
had many mouths to feed, and the larder could not be
left to chance. The flowers everywhere were most
beautiful ; the wild roses, which in 1881 had been checked
by the cold, were still short-lived, but the fullest, reddest,
and most abundant that I had ever seen. The long
daylight intensifies the colors. The meadows were
enamelled with harebells. On the moist rocks on the
lake sides grew gigantic saxifrages, pure white, eighteen
inches high. On a single stem I counted three hundred
blossoms, and they were so hardy that one plant lived
in full flower for a fortnight in a glass on our cabin table.
There were curious aspects of human life too. One night,
July 2—St. John's Day by the old reckoning—as we lay
at anchor in a gorge, which from the land must have been
inaccessible, we saw a large fire blazing, and figures leap-
ing through the flame. It was the relic of a custom, once
wide as the Northern hemisphere, on the festival of the
summer solstice, old as the Israelitish prophet who saw
the children passed through the fire to Moloch. I
observed the same thing forty-three years ago in the
market-place at Killarney. Thousands of years it has
survived, down to these late times of ours, in which, like

much besides, it will now end—dissolved in the revolutionary acids of scientific civilization.

These things had their interest, but we were still dissatisfied, and we flew from spot to spot in a way to make
the pilot think us maniacs. "Tout va bien," said the
Paris Terrorist in 1793 ; "mais le pain manque." All
was well with us, but fish were wanting ; and when we
had wasted a week of our month in following the directions of our acquaintance at Bergen, we decided to lose
no more time in exploring, and to make for quarters of
which we had ourselves had experience on our first
visit. I shall mention no names, for one of these places
is a secret of our own, and we do not wish them to become tourist-haunted. No road goes near them, nor ever
can, for they are protected on the land side by mountains
steeper and vaster than the walls of Rasselas's enchanted
valley. But yacht visitors might reach them, nay, have
actually reached, not the one I speak of, but another,
leaving an unpleasant taste behind them. I will not ex-
tend their opportunities of making Englishmen unpop-
ular.

Well, then, to decide was to execute. A few hours
later we found ourselves anchored in a landlocked bay
which I will call for convenience's sake Bruysdal. There
are fifty Bruysdals in Norway, and this is *not* one of them.
That is all which I need say. It forms the head of a
deep inlet, well stocked with dabs and haddock, and
whiting, and wolf-fish and other monsters. The landscape is at once grand and gentle ; mighty snow-capped
mountains cleft into gorges so deep and dark that the
sun, save in the height of summer, can never look into
them, while on the immediate shores rich meadow land
and grassy undulating hills stretch along the fjord for
miles ; and from the estate of a prosperous yeoman who

21

rules paternally over his mountain valley, a river runs in near our anchorage, which, after leaving a lake half a mile from the sea, winds down with an ever-flowing stream, through heathery pine-clad slopes and grassy levels covered with wild roses and bilberries. The cuckoos were calling in the woods as we came up; widgeon and wild duck were teaching their young broods to take care of themselves; oyster catchers flew to and fro—they have no fear of men in a place where no one cares to hurt them. Boats with timber were passing down the river to a saw-mill opposite the mouth. The lake out of which it flows is two miles long, and ends in a solitary glen, closed in by precipices at the head and on either side. There was beauty here, and grandeur, with food of all kinds, from mutton to bilberries, now ripe and as large as outdoor grapes. Above all, we knew by past experience that sea-trout swarmed in the lake, and trout in the river. The owner's acquaintance we had made before, and the old man, learning from the pilot who we were, came on board at once with his son and the schoolmaster to pay his respects. He himself was hale and stout, age perhaps about sixty; with dark hair which as yet had no gray streaks in it; in manner very much that of a gentleman doing the honors of his country and his dominions with rough dignity. His lake, his river, all that he had, he gave us free use of. The fish had not come up in any number yet, but perhaps there might be some. He accepted a glass of wine, being temperate, but not severely abstemious. The younger ones touched nothing of that kind—*To-tallers* they called themselves. They were two fine-looking men, but without the father's geniality, and with a slight tinge of self-righteousness. The interest of the moment was a bear which they had just killed among them, hav-

ing caught him committing murder among the sheep.
As the flocks increase the bears multiply along with
them, and the shooting one is an event to be made much
of.   This particular offender's head came home with us,
swinging in the rigging, and looked so savage, grinning
there, as much to reduce the pleasure of the crew in
going ashore among the bilberries.

At Bruysdal all our desires were at last fulfilled. The
steward could get his milk and mutton.   The sea-fish
swarmed.   The spot itself combined the best beauties
of the Norwegian landscapes—wild nature and thriving
human history.   In the lake, as our entertainer had
said, there were not many fish, but there were enough.
The water was as clear as the air.   A tropical sun shone
fiercely on its windless surface, conditions neither of
them especially favorable for salmon fishing ; but, rowing along the shores, on the edge " between the deep
and the shallow," with our phantom minnows, we caught
what satisfied, without surfeiting, the appetite for destruction ; salmon-peel, sewin, sea-trout, or whatever we
pleased to call them, from three to nine pounds weight,
gallant fellows that would make the reel spin and scream.
And then the luncheon, never to be forgotten, on biscuits soaked in the ice-cold stream, the purple bilberries,
the modest allowance from the whiskey flask, and the
pipe to follow, in the heather under the shade of a pine-
tree or a juniper, surrounded by ferns and flowers of
exquisite variety.   I should have no good opinion of
any man who, in such a scene, had anything left to wish
for.

One day there was another bear-hunt.   Three sheep
had been killed in the night again, in the glen at the
head of the lake.   The bönder's people turned out, and
the cries of the beaters among the crags, and the cow-

horns echoing from cliff to cliff, brought back memories
of old days, on the middle lake at Killarney; when the
Herberts reigned at Mucross, and the bay of the blood-
hounds was heard on the hills, and the driven deer
would take the water, and meet his end from a rifle
bullet, and the huntsman would wind his death-note on
the bugle. Beautiful! all that was, and one cannot think
of it without regret that it is gone. But it was artificial,
not natural. Our Norway bear-hunt was nature and
necessity, the genuine chase of a marauding and dangerous animal. This time unfortunately it was not successful. The brown villains had stolen off through a pass in
the mountains, and escaped the penalties of their sins.

Settled down as we were in Bruysdal we did not hurry
ourselves, and took our pleasure deliberately. One
evening after dinner our host and A. went to the lake ;
I stayed behind, and was rowed about by one of the
crew with a fly-rod in the mouth of the river. The soft
midnight gloaming, the silence broken only by the late
call of the cuckoo in the woods, made me careless about
the trout, and, after catching four or five, I preferred to
talk to my companion. As a seaman he had been all
over the world. He had been up the great rivers in the
tropics, had seen pythons and alligators there, and was
rather disappointed to find no alligators in the fjords. Alligators, I explained to him, would find a difficulty in getting a living there. In the winter they would be frozen
into logs, and would be found dead when they thawed
again, and on the whole they preferred a warm climate.
As the thermometer had been standing at 80° that day
in our deck cabin, and was 70° at that moment though
it was midnight, my account was clearly unsatisfactory,
but he dropped the subject, and from alligators travelled
to human beings. He admired his own countrymen,

but could not absolutely approve of them. He had seen
savages little if at all superior to apes, but nowhere had
he fallen in with *men* of any description who made such
brutes of themselves as Englishmen and Scotchmen
when the drink was in them. He himself had drunk
water only for fifteen years, and intended to keep to it.
I could not but admit that it might be so. Those precious beauties whom we had just seen in the North Sea
were illustrations not to be gainsaid.

One difficulty was to know when to go to bed. The
sun might set, but the glow lasted till it rose again ; and
the cool night air was so delicious and so invigorating that
to sleep was a waste of our opportunities. That evening
when I went to my cabin, I stood looking out through
the port-hole on the pink flushed hills and water, the
full moon just rising behind a hollow between the high
mountains and pouring a stream of gold upon the fjord.
Now would be the time, I thought, if any Nixie would
rise out of the water and sing a song to me of the times
long ago. It would have been a rash experiment once.
The knight who listened to the Nixie's song forgot
country, and home, and wife, and child, plunged wildly
into the waters, and was borne away in the white arms
of the seducing spirit, never to be seen on earth again.
But the knight was young—and I, with the blood creep-
ing slowly in my old veins, felt that for my part I could
listen safely, and should like for once to hear such a
thing. Alas ! as I stood at the window there came no
Nixie, but the pale figure floated before me of ——, first
as she was in her beauty five-and-forty years ago, then
dissolving into the still fair, but broken and aged, woman
as I had last seen her, fading away out of a life which
had blighted the promise of the morning. Her widowed
daughter sleeps beside her, having lost first her young

husband and then the mother whom she worshipped.
The Nixies are silent. The Trolls work unseen among
the copper veins in the mountain chasms, and leave un-
vexed the children of men. Valhalla is a dream, and
Balder has become a solar myth ; but ghosts still haunt
old eyes which have seen so many human creatures flit
across the stage, play their parts, sad or joyful, and vanish as they came.

We stayed a whole week at Bruysdal. There was
another spot which we knew of, as wild, as inaccessible,
and as fertile, when we tried it last, in the desired sea-
trout ; and besides sea-trout there were char—not miserable little things like those that are caught in Derwentwater and Crummock, but solid two and three
pounders that would fight for their lives like gentlemen.

Across the mountain to Elversdale (that, again, is not
the right name) an eagle might fly in half an hour, but
he would fly over sheets of glacier and peak and ridges
six thousand feet high. In fact, for human feet there
was no road from Bruysdal thither, and the way round
by water was nearly a hundred miles. But what were
a hundred miles to the fiery dragon in the yacht's engines ? All he asks for is a ton or two of coal, and he
thinks as little of taking you a hundred miles as you
think yourself of an afternoon walk. We had the ship's
washing, too, to pick up on the way, and, besides the
washing, the letters and newspapers which had been ac-
cumulating for a fortnight, something to amuse us in
the few hours which would be required for our trans-
portation. After a week or two's absence from London
one finds one's self strangely indifferent to what seems so
important when one is in the middle of it. Speeches in
Parliament remind one of the scuffling of kites and
crows which Milton talks of. On this occasion, however,

we had all of us a certain curiosity to hear what had become of the Franchise Bill, especially as our host is a sound hereditary Liberal, sounder and stancher a great deal than I am, and had duly paired on the Government side before he sailed. We bore the news, when it reached us, with extraordinary equanimity. Our appetite for luncheon was not affected. The crew did not mutiny, though three-fourths of them must have been among the two millions expectant of votes. For my own particular, I was conscious of pleasure greater than I had ever expected to receive from any political incident in the remainder of my life. In the first place, it is always agreeable to see men behave courageously. The Peers had refused to walk this time through Coventry with halters about their necks. In the next, if they persevered, it might, one way or another, bring another sham to an end. The House of Lords had seemed to be something, and they were becoming a *nothing*. The English Sovereign, too, is in a position not altogether befitting a human being with an immortal soul. No man or woman ought to be forced to say this or that, to profess to approve of what he or she detests, in obedience to majorities in the House of Commons. Some day, perhaps, an English Sovereign will be found to say : "If you want an ornamental marionette at the top of you, to dance at your bidding, you must find someone else. I, for one, decline to figure any longer in that character. I will be a reality, or I will not be at all." In constitutional countries those who hold high offices do tend to drift into a similar marionette condition. A dean and chapter who receive a mandate to choose A. B. as their bishop, who invite divine assistance to help them to elect a fit person, and then duly appoint the said A. B., they too are not to be envied. Sovereigns and high

persons of all kinds in such situations are idols set up
in high places, with the form of dignity and without the
power ; and if we must have idols they should be wood
or stone, or gutta-percha, as more flexible, not human
creatures, with blood running in the veins of them.   I
had been very sorry to see the English peers, ostensibly
the flower of the whole nation, lapsing gradually into a
similar gilded degradation, the lay lords sinking to the
level of the spiritual, and by the wise to be mentioned
only with a smile.   They had at last stood fast, though,
alas, it was only for a time.   They had recovered the
respect of all honest men in doing so, and seemed on
the way to become honest men themselves again in one
shape or another, and not despised humbugs.

I have high honor for the Peers; I think them an
excellent institution, political and social, but one must
draw a line somewhere, and I draw one at dukes.   From
their cradle upward all persons, things, circumstances,
combine to hide from dukes that they are mortal, subject to limitations like the rest of us.   A duke, at least
an English duke, though he may be called a peer, yet is
a peer only by courtesy.   He has no social equal.   He
is at the summit of the world, and has no dignity beyond
his own to which he can aspire.   He grows up in possession of everything which the rest of mankind are striv-
ing after.   In his own immediate surroundings, on his
vast estates, among his multitudinous dependants, he has
only to will to be obeyed.   When he goes out among his
fellow-creatures, they bow before so great a presence
with instinctive deference.   In him offences are venial
which would be fatal to an ordinary man.   The earth, so
far as he is able to know anything of it, is a place where
others have to struggle, but where he has only to desire.
To do without what at any moment he happens to wish

for, which moralists consider so important a part of
education, is a form of discipline denied to a duke from
his cradle, and if the moralists are right he is so much
the worse for the want of it.

I think we could do without dukes. That is the only
reform which I wish for in the Upper House. At any
rate, they are over-large figures for a quiet Norwegian
valley. " There came three Dukes a-riding." * Several
Dukes have looked in at Elversdale of late years in their
floating palaces. They have gone for sport there, as in
fact we were doing ourselves, and it is hard to say that
they had not as good a right as we had. But the Norse
proprietors, at least some of them, are Republicans, and
are not altogether pleased to see these lordly English
looking in upon their quiet homes. The shores of the
fjord, the rivers, the lakes, are their property. They are
liberal and hospitable ; the land they live in is their
own ; but they are courteous and gracious, and have
been willing hitherto to allow their visitors all fair
opportunities of entertaining themselves. They are
aware, however (it cannot be a secret to them), that if
a Norwegian, or any stranger, American, French, or
German, travelling without introduction in Scotland,
were to ask for a day's sporting in a preserved forest
or salmon river, he would not only be refused, but
would be so refused as to make him feel that his request was an impertinence. The Lord of the soil in
Norway perhaps may occasionally ask himself why he
should be expected to be more liberal. His salmon and
trout are an important part of his winter provision. He
nets them, salts and stores them for the long nights and
short days, when the lakes are frozen, and the valleys
are full of snow, and there is no food for man or beast,

* Neither of them was the good duke alluded to at page 287.

save what is laid up in summer. Why should he give
it away?

There are two rivers in Elversdale and two sets of
lakes, the respective valleys meeting at the head of the
fjord, where on a vast and prettily wooded moraine there
stands, as usual, a white church, the steeple of which
shows far up along the glens, the scattered peasants
gathering thither in their boats on Sundays. Two great
owners divide the domain, one of them having the best
fishing. It was in one of his lakes close to the fjord that
in 1881 we filled our baskets, and now hoped to fill them
again. For this lake, at what we considered an unusually high price, we got leave ; but we soon found
that it had been given us in irony. The sultry weather
had melted the edges of the great glacier which we
could see from our deck. The ice-water, pouring down
in a cataract, tinted the limpid water into a color like
soap-suds, and not a fish would take. Round and round
the lake we rowed, with wearisome repetition ; nothing
came to our minnows. In the boats we sat, tormented,
ourselves, by flies such as are seen nowhere but in Norway. There is one as big as a drone, and rather like
one, but with a green head, and a pair of nippers in it
that under a magnifying-glass are a wonder to look at.
This, I suppose, is the wretch described by "Three in
Norway," who speak of a fly that takes a piece out of
you, and flies to the next rock to eat it. We were tortured, but caught nothing save a few tiny char, which
ventured out upon the shallows when the monsters were
lying torpid. We soon saw how it was. Where we
were there was nothing to be done, but two miles up the
valley, above the hay meadows and potato fields, was
another lake into which no glacier water ran, splendidly
rich in char and trout. There flies might torment, but

there was at least sport—legitimate, ample, and subject to no disappointment. Thither we applied for leave to go, and (it was perhaps the first time that such a thing ever happened to any Englishman in that country) we met with a flat refusal. The owner was tired of being called upon to provide sport for strangers of whom he knew nothing. He gave no reasons ; when we pressed for one he answered quietly that the fish were his, and that he preferred to keep them for himself. In our first impatience we anathematized him to ourselves as a brute, but we reflected that he was doing only what every one of us at home in possession of a similar treasure would do as a matter of course. England is more advanced than Norway, but English principles and habits are making way there ; that is all. This is the first of my three novelties.

By the proprietor of the other glen and the other lakes we were entertained more graciously. He remembered us. He and his family had visited the drowned yacht. His boys had been fed with sugar-plums, his daughters had been presented with books and colored prints, which still hung about his farm-house. His waters were not the best ; but the scenery about them was at any rate most beautiful, and river, lakes, boats, all that he had, was placed at our disposal. Three lovely days we spent there—rocks and mountains, trees and cataracts, the belts of forest, and the high peaks above them soaring up into the eternal blue. These were our surroundings, changing their appearance every hour as the shadows shifted with the moving sun. The rare trout rose at the fly, the rarer salmon-trout ran at the phantoms at distant intervals. In the hot midday we would land and seek shade from nut bush or alder. The ice-cold rivulets trickled down out of the

far-off snow. The cuckoos called in the woods. The
wild roses clustered round us, crimson buds and pale
pink flowers shining against the luxuriant green of the
leaves. The wild campanulas hung their delicate heads
along the shores, fairest and daintiest of all the wild
flowers of nature, like pieces of the azure heaven itself
shaped into those cups and bells. The bilberry clustered among the rocks, hanging out its purple fruit to
us to gather as we sat. All this was perfectly delightful, and it was only the brutal part of our souls that remained a little discontented because we had not fish
enough, and sighed for the yet more perfect Eden from
which we were excluded.

Sunday came, and it was very pretty to see, on the
evening before and in the early morning, the boats
streaming up the fjord and down from the inland lakes.
One boat passed the yacht, rowed by ten stalwart young
women, who handled their oars like Saltash fishwives.
With a population so scattered, a single priest has two
or more churches to attend to at considerable distances,
pastors being appointed according to the numbers of
the flock, and not the area they occupy. Thus at Elversdale there was a regular service only on alternate
Sundays, and this Sunday it was not Elversdale's turn.
But there was a Samling—a gathering for catechising
and prayer—at our bönder's house, where the good man
himself, or some itinerant minister, officiated. Several
hundreds must have collected, the children being in the
largest proportion. The Norse people are quiet, old-
fashioned Lutherans, who never read a newspaper, and
have never heard of a doubt about the truth of what
their fathers believed. When the meeting was over,
many of them who were curious to see an English yacht
and its occupants came on board. The owner welcomed

the elders at the gangway, talked to them in their own
tongue, and showed them over the ship. A—— had
handfuls of sugar-plums for the little ones. They were
plain-featured for the most part, with fair hair and blue
eyes — the men in strong homespun broadcloth, the
women in black serge, with a bright sash about the
waist, and a shawl over the shoulders with bits of modest
embroidery at the corners. They were perfectly well-
behaved, rational, simple, unself-conscious, a healthy
race in mind and body whom it was pleasant to see. I
could well understand what the Americans mean when
they say that, of all the colonists who migrate to them,
the Norse are the best—and many go. Norway is as
full as it can hold, and the young swarms who in old
days roved out in their pirate-ships over France and
England and Ireland now pass peaceably to the Far West.

Our time was slipping away, we had but a few days
left. Instead of exploring new regions we agreed to go
back once more to Bruysdal, and its trout, and its bears.
We knew that there we should be welcome again. And
at Elversdale, too, we were leaving friends. Even the
stern old fellow who had been so sulky might have
opened his arms if we had stayed a little longer. But
we did not put him to the test. The evening before we
sailed our landlord came to take leave, bringing his wife
with him, a sturdy little woman with a lady's manners
under a rough costume. He was presented with a few
pounds of best Scotch oatmeal, a tin of coffee for his old
mother, and a few other delicacies in true Homeric style.
He in turn came next morning at daybreak, as the anchor was coming up, with a fresh-run salmon, which he
had just taken out of his trammels. We parted with
warm hopes expressed that we might one day meet
again ; and the next quiet Englishman who goes thither

will find all the waters open to him as freely as they used to be.

Yacht life gives ample leisure. I had employed part of mine in making sketches. One laughs at one's extraordinary performances a day or two after one has completed them. Yet the attempt is worth making. It teaches one to admire less grudgingly the work of real artists who have conquered the difficulties. Books are less trying to vanity, for one is producing nothing of one's own, and submitting only to be interested or amused, if the author can succeed in either. One's appetite is generally good on these occasions, and one can devour anything ; but in the pure primitive element of sea, and mountains, and unprogressive peasantry I had become somehow fastidious. I tried a dozen novels one after the other without success ; at last, perhaps the morning we left Elversdale, I found on the library shelves "Le Père Goriot." I had read a certain quantity of Balzac at other times, in deference to the high opinion entertained of him. N——, a fellow of Oriel and once member for Oxford, I remembered insisting to me that there was more knowledge of human nature in Balzac than in Shakespeare. I had myself observed in the famous novelist a knowledge of a certain kind of human nature which Shakespeare let alone—a nature in which healthy vigor had been corrupted into a caricature by highly seasoned artificial civilization. Hothouse plants, in which the flowers had lost their grace of form and natural beauty, and had gained instead a poison-loaded and perfumed luxuriance, did not exist in Shakespeare's time, and if they had they would probably not have interested him. However, I had not read "Le Père Goriot," and as I had been assured that it was the finest of Balzac's works, I sat down to it and deliber-

ately read it through. My first impulse after it was
over was to plunge into the sea to wash myself. As we
were going ten knots, there were objections to this
method of ablution, but I felt that I had been in abominable company. The book seemed to be the very worst
ever written by a clever man. But it, and N——'s ref-
erence to Shakespeare, led me into a train of reflections.
Le Père Goriot, like King Lear, has two daughters.
Like Lear, he strips himself of his own fortune to provide for them in a distinguished manner. He is left to
poverty and misery, while his daughters live in splendor.
Why is Lear so grand? Why is Le Père Goriot detestable? In the first place, all the company in Balzac are
bad. Le Père Goriot is so wrapped up in his delightful
children that their very vices charm him, and their
scented boudoirs seem a kind of Paradise. Lear, in the
first scence of the play, acts and talks like an idiot, but
still an idiot with a moral soul in him. Take Lear's own
noble nature from him, take Kent away, and Edgar, and
the fool, and Cordelia—and the actors in the play, it
must be admitted, are abominable specimens of humanity—yet even so, leaving the story as it might have been
if Marlowe had written it instead of Shakespeare, Goneril and Regan would still have been terrible, while the
Paris dames of fashion are merely loathsome. What is
the explanation of the difference? Partly, I suppose, it
arises from the comparative intellectual stature of the
two sets of women. Strong natures and weak may be
equally wicked. The strong are interesting, because
they have daring and force. You fear them as you fear
panthers and tigers. You hate, but you admire. M.
Balzac's heroines have no intellectual nature at all.
They are female swine out of Circe's sty; as selfish, as
unscrupulous as any daughter of Adam could conven-

iently be, but soft, and corrupt, and cowardly, and sen-
sual ; so base and low that it would be a compliment to
call them devils. I object to being brought into the society of people in a book whom I would shut my eyes
rather than see in real life. Goneril and Regan would
be worth looking at in a cage in the Zoological Gardens.
One would have no curiosity to stare at a couple of
dames caught out of Coventry Street or the Quadrant.
From Shakespeare to Balzac, from the 16th century to
the 19th, we have been progressing to considerable purpose. If the state of literature remains as it has hitherto been, the measure of our moral condition, Europe
has been going ahead with a vengeance. I put out the
taste of "Le Père Goriot" with "Persuasion." Afterward I found a book really worth reading, with the un-
inviting title of "Adventures in Sport and War," the
author of it a young Marquis de Compiègne, a ruined
representative of the old French noblesse, who appears
first as a penniless adventurer seeking his fortune in
America as a bird-stuffer, and tempted by an advertisement into the swamps of Florida in search of specimens,
a beggarly experience, yet told with *naïveté* and simplicity, truth and honor surviving by the side of absolute helplessness. Afterward we find our Marquis in
France again, fighting as a private in the war with Germany, and taken prisoner at Sedan ; and again in the
campaign against the Commune, at the taking of Paris,
and the burning of the Tuileries—a tragic picture,
drawn, too, with the entire unconsciousness of the condition to which Balzac, Madame Sand, and the rest of
the fraternity had dragged down the French nation.

But by this time we are back in Bruysdal, and I come
now to the second of my three incidents in which the
reader was to be interested—a specimen of what Norway

can do when put upon its mettle in the way of landscape effect. The weather had changed. When we
left, the temperature in our deck cabin was 80°. The
mercury in our barometer stood at 30 and 3-10ths.
When we returned the pressure had relaxed to 29, while
the temperature had fallen nearly forty degrees. Our
light flannels had gone back to the drawers, and the
thickest woollens would hardly keep out the cold. The
rain was falling as in a universal shower-bath, lashing
into bubbles the surface of the fjord. The cataracts
were roaring down ; the river was in a flood, the shore
and the trees dimly visible through the descending torrent. Here, if ever, was a fishing day for those who
were not afraid of being dissolved like sugar. Our host
challenged us to venture, and we were ashamed to hesitate. In huge boots and waterproof and oilskin hats
(may the wretch who made my mackintosh for me in
London be sent to the unpleasant place and punished
appropriately) we were rowed up into the lake, sent out
our spinners, and were soon in desperate battle each
with our respective monster, half-blinded by wind and
rain. On days like this the largest fish roam the waters
like hungry pike. We had two hours of it. Flesh and
blood could stand no more. We made one circuit of
the lake ; neither we nor the boatmen could face a second, and we went home with our spoils. Enough said
about that. Now for my landscape. On one side of
Bruysdal the mountains rise from the water in a series
of precipices to the snow-line, and are broken into deep
wooded gorges. Down these the cataracts were raging ;
very fine in their way, but with nothing uncommon about
them. The other side of the valley is formed quite dif-
ferently. A long, broad plateau of smooth, unbroken
rock ascends at a low gradient for miles, reaching event-

22

ually an equal altitude, and losing itself among the
clouds.   At the hollow where the lake lies, this plateau
is as if broken sharply off, ending in an overhanging
precipice perhaps a mile long, and from three hundred
to four hundred feet high; higher it may be, for the
scale of everything is gigantic, and the eye often under-
rates what it sees.   Over the whole wide upper area the
rain had been falling for hours with the fury of a tropical
thunder-shower.   There being no hollows or inequali-
ties to collect the water, and neither grass nor forest
to absorb the flood, it ran straight down over the
smooth slopes in an even, shallow stream.   On reaching the cliffs it fell over and scattered into spray, and
there it seemed to hang extended over a mile of perpendicular rock, like a delicately transparent lace veil
undulating in the eddies of the wind.   It was a sight
to be seen once and never to be forgotten.   Water is
a strange Proteus—now transparent as air, now a mirror, now rippled and the color of the sky.   It falls in
foam in the torrent.   It is level as quicksilver, or it
is broken into waves of infinite variety.   It is ice, it
is snow, it is rain, it is fog and cloud, to say nothing of
the shapes it takes in organic substances.   But never
did I see it play so singular a part as when floating to
and fro in airy drapery, with the black wet rock showing
like a ghost behind it.   The whole valley was dim with
the falling rain, the far mountains invisible in mist, the
near rocks and trees drenched and dripping.   Some
artist of the Grosvenor Gallery might make a picture of
the place as a part of Hades, and people it with moist
spirits.

In honor of our endurance and our success, and to
put us in heart again for the next day, we had a bottle
of champagne at dinner, I in silence drinking to myself

the health of the House of Lords in general as well as
that of our entertainer. And now I have only to relate the disgrace which befell myself when the next
day came, to end what I have to say about our fishing. I had a precious phantom minnow, a large one,
which had come victorious out of that day's conflicts.
Before putting it on again my eye was caught by the
frayed look of the gut trace. It seemed strong when
I tried it; but perhaps I wished to save myself trouble,
and treated it as Don Quixote treated his helmet the
second time. Well, we started in our boat again, a
hundred yards below the point where the river leaves
the lake. We were rowing up the strong stream, I care-
lessly letting out my line, and in that place expecting
nothing, when there came a crash; the slack line was
entangled round the reel, which could not run, the rod
bent double from the combined weight of some sea-
trout huger than usual and the rapid water. Alas! in a
moment the rod had straightened again, and sea-trout,
phantom, and my own reputation as a fisherman were
gone together. I could not get over it, and the sport
had lost its charm. We caught several fish afterward,
and my son got one nearly ten pounds weight. I was
glad for him, but for myself the spirit had gone out of
me. In the afternoon, the river being in high order,
we put our lighter rods together to try the pools with
salmon flies. D—— caught a salmon-peel of four pounds
weight. I had another smaller one; afterward scram-
bling along some steep, slippery rocks I reached a prom-
ising-looking run, and, letting my fly go down over it, I
rose a true salmon and a big one. I drew back and
changed my fly. A salmon, under such conditions, will
almost always come again if you wait a minute or two
and throw him a new temptation. I was looking to be

consoled for my morning's misfortune, when at the
moment a native boat dashed over the spot loaded with
timber. My salmon vanished into space and I saw him
no more. I ought to have been disgusted. I discovered
myself reflecting instead, that after all the salmon was
better off as he was, and I no worse—a state of mind
unpermitted to a fisherman, and implying that my connection with the trade, now more than fifty years old,
may be coming to an end. Alas, that all things do come
to an end! Life itself runs to an end. Our Norway
holiday was running to an end, though the prettiest part
of it was still to come. We had to look in at Bergen
again on our way home to pick up letters, etc. Bergen
was nearly two hundred miles from us, and to break the
distance we were to anchor somewhere about half-way.
Our last day at Bruysdal was a Sunday again. We were
popular there, and on Sunday evening we had a small
fleet about us, with boys and girls and music. An ingenious lad had fitted a screw propeller of his own
making to his boat, which he worked with a crank. With
this, and the Norwegian flag flying, he careered round
and round the yacht at a most respectable pace, the lads
and lasses following in their Sunday dresses, like the
nymphs and Tritons after Neptune's car. A boat came
on board us with two men in her whom we did not
know. They had a sick relation at home and wanted
medicine. We gave them what we had. They inno-
cently asked how much they were to pay, bringing out
their pocket-books, and were perplexed when D——
laughed and told them "*nothing*." They doubted, perhaps, the efficacy of the remedies. Anyhow they were
gratified. The Bruysdal community fired a gun when
we steamed away next day, and saluted us with their
flag from the school-house; there too we shall find a

welcome if we ever return : meanwhile we were gone, for the present to see it no more.

In the evening we turned into a spot which our pilot knew of as a quiet anchorage, which I will call Orlestrund. We were by this time far away from the mountains. We found ourselves in a soft landlocked bay, with green meadows and low softly wooded hills ; the air was sweet with the scent of the new-mown hay ; there were half a dozen farm-houses, which seemed to share between them the richly cultivated and smiling soil. A church stood conspicuous near the shore ; on one side of it was what seemed to be a school ; on the other, among high trees, we saw the roof and chimneys of the pastor's house, a respectable and even superior-looking residence. Work for the day was over when we let fall our anchor. It was about eight o'clock, a lovely summer evening, with three hours of subdued daylight remaining. The boys and young men, dismissed from the fields, were scatter- ed about the bay in boats catching haddock and whiting. Looking round the pretty scene we saw a group outside the gate of the manse, which was evidently the pastor and his family, himself an elderly gentleman, his wife, and six young ones, descending from a girl of perhaps sixteen to little ones just able to take care of themselves. They were examining the yacht, and it was easy to see what happened. The old couple, with the three young- est children, turned in to their gate and disappeared. The others, the eldest girl and two brothers, had got leave to go out in the boat and look at us, for they flew along the shore to their boat-house, and presently came out on the fjord. Not wishing to seem too curious they lingered awhile with their lines and caught four or five haddock. They then gradually drew nearer, the girl rowing, her two brothers in the stern. D—— beckoned

to them to come closer, and then, in Norse, invited
them on board. They were roughly dressed, not
better perhaps than the children of the peasantry, but
their looks were refined, their manner modest and
simple, free alike from shyness and forwardness. The
daughter spoke for the rest. She was tall for her years,
with large eyes, a slight but strong figure, and features
almost handsome. D—— took her round the ship.
She moved gracefully, answered questions and asked
them with as much ease as if she had been among
friends and relations. She kept her young brothers in
order by a word, and in short behaved with a composure
which would have been surprising in any girl of such
an age when thrown suddenly among strangers. She
asked if we had ladies on board, and seemed disappointed, but not the least disturbed, when we told her
that there were only ourselves. Presently she began to
speak English, with a fair accent too, better than most
French or Germans ever arrive at. We asked her if she
had been in England. She had never been away from
Orlestrund. She had taught herself English, she said
quite simply, "from book." D—— accuses her of having asked him if he could speak Norse, after he had
been talking in that language to her for ten minutes.
I insisted, with no knowledge of the language myself,
but merely drawing my inference from the nature of
things, that a creature of such fine behavior could not
have put it as question, but must have observed, "And
you too speak Norse !" We asked her name. She was
called Theresa. Theresa certainly, but I could not
catch the surname with entire clearness. She wished
to bring her father to see us. We would gladly have
seen both the father and the mother who in such a spot
had contrived to rear so singular a product. She gath-

ered up her two boys, sprang into her skiff, seized the oars, and shot away over the water. We saw her land and vanish into the shrubbery. In a few minutes she appeared again, but only with a little sister this time. She came to tell us that her father could not leave his house at so late an hour. He was sorry he could not use the opportunity of making our acquaintance. He desired to know who we were. D—— wrote his name and gave it to her. She went down the gangway again, and joined her sister, who had hid herself in her shawl in timid modesty.

They glided off into the gloaming, and we saw them no more. Very pretty, I thought this Norse girl, so innocent, so self-possessed, who seemed in that lonely spot, surrounded only by peasants, to have educated herself into a character so graceful. If our modern schools, with competition and examinations, and the rights of woman, and progress of civilization, and the rest of it, turn out women as good and as intelligent as this young lassie, they will do better than I, for cne, expect of them. Peace be with her, and a happy, useful life at the side of some fit companion ! In the wide garden of the world, with its hotbed luxuriance and feverish exotics, there will be one nook at any rate where nature combined with genuine art will bloom into real beauty.

So ends my brief journal—ends with Theresa, for I can add nothing which will not be poor and trivial after so fair a figure—and, indeed, there is nothing more to say. The next morning we hastened on to Bergen. The afternoon which followed we were out again on the North Sea, which we found this time in angry humor. But the engines made their revolutions accurately. The log gave the speed which was expected, and we made the passage to Harwich again in the exact period which had been predetermined. We were late, indeed, by twelve minutes, after allowing for the difference of longitude, and these minutes lost required to be accounted for. But we recollected that we had stopped precisely that number of minutes on the Dogger Bank to take soundings, and the mystery was perfectly explained. It reminded me of a learned Professor of Oxford, who was engaged on sacred chronology. He told us one night in Common Room that he had the dates of every event complete from the Creation till the present day. He had been so minutely successful that his calculations were right to twelve hours. These hours had puzzled him till he recollected that when the sun was arrested by Joshua it had stood still for a whole day, exactly the period which he wanted, and the apparent error had only verified his accuracy.